HAITI IN CARIBBEAN CONTEXT

HAITI IN CARIBBEAN CONTEXT

Ethnicity, Economy and Revolt

David Nicholls

St. Martin's Press   New York

ISBN 0–312–35659–5

Library of Congress Cataloging in Publication Data
Nicholls, David.
Haiti in Caribbean context.
Bibliography: p.
Includes index.
1. Haiti—History—1804–   2. Haiti–Race
relations. 3. Haiti—Economic conditions. I. Title.
F1924.N53   1985   972.94   84–18392
ISBN 0–312–35659–5

For Aileen

Contents

Preface

This volume is the product of some seventeen years' research on Haiti and its place in the Caribbean. In an earlier book I considered the relationship between ideas of race, colour and national independence in Haiti. Here I examine, in historical perspective, connections between ethnic structures and the economy, showing how the phenomena of political domination and revolt are to be understood in the light of these connections. Although I have used some material which has previously been published, this has been thoroughly remoulded to remove repetition, to update and to produce what I believe to be a coherent publication.

I am indebted to many friends for their advice and comments at various stages of the work. Particularly I should mention Carl Spitz, Malcolm Cross, David Geggus, Albert Valdman, Robin Cohen, François Hoffmann, David Lowenthal, Greg Chamberlain, Roger Désir, Roger Gaillard, Leslie Griffiths. I am grateful to Levantine families in the Caribbean for their help including Joseph Sabga from Trinidad; Linda Younis, Olga Hanna, the Ghisays and Azans in Jamaica; Jean Haché, Hugo Guiliani Cury with other members of the Cury and Khouri families in the Dominican Republic; the Handal family in Haiti. My work on the Levantines has been facilitated by grants from the British Academy and from Emile Elias and Joseph Sabga; I wish to thank them for this help. I have enjoyed the generous hospitality of Michael and Cheryl Dash, Jim and Dora Harkins, Brinsley and Joan Samaroo, Nizam Mohammed, Keith Laurence, Carl Spitz, Jean-Claude de Castro and the Boyer, Désir and Gaillard families.

Littlemore, Oxford   DAVID NICHOLLS

Acknowledgments

I am grateful to editors and publishers for permission to include material, early drafts of which appeared in periodicals or books, as follows:

Chapter 1 in Colin Clarke, ed., *Caribbean Social Relations*, Centre for Latin-American Studies, Liverpool University, 1978

Chapter 2 in *Journal of Interamerican Studies and World Affairs*, 20:4 (1978)

Chapters 3 and 4 in *Race*, 13:2 (1971) and 12:4 (1971)

Chapter 5 as a monograph, published by Centre for Developing-Area Studies, McGill University, Montreal, 1974

Chapter 8 in *Ethnic and Racial Studies*, 4:4 (1981)

Chapter 9 in M. Cross and A. Marks, *Peasants, Plantations and Rural Communities in the Caribbean*, Department of Sociology, University of Surrey, and Department of Caribbean Studies, KITLV, Leiden, 1979.

I am indebted to Cambridge University Press for permission to reproduce the map, which shows departmental boundaries as they were for most of the period covered by this book.

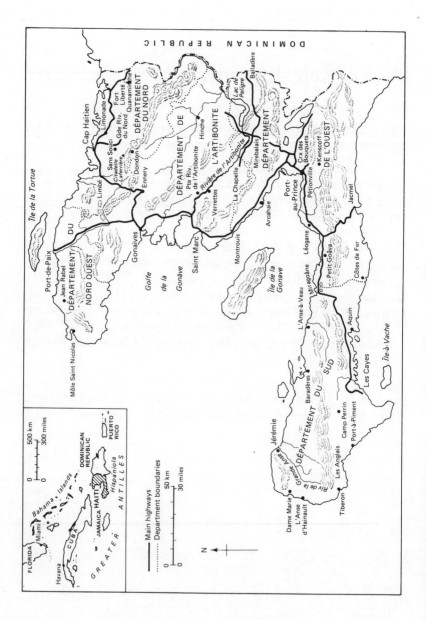

Part I
Introduction

Introduction

If the black power movement of the late sixties, which culminated in the mutiny and state of emergency in Trinidad, was baptism by fire for an independent anglophone Caribbean, the recent United States invasion of Grenada completed the initiation rites. From the safe but stuffy repression of the colonial era the islands have found themselves propelled into the real world of Latin American politics, where assassination, military coup and US occupation are on the agenda. Haiti passed through a similar stage almost two hundred years ago, though the process of decolonisation was somewhat more traumatic.

Haiti does not fit easily into the categories which historians and social scientists employ. Although it is often included in 'Latin America', it is generally ignored by Institutes of Latin American Studies owing to its peculiar linguistic, cultural and ethnic features. Haiti must clearly be included in 'the Caribbean' yet it is frequently overlooked, particularly, as we shall see, in writings about the region published in English. In fact, much of the research and writing on Haiti has come from anthropologists (and political scientists) whose previous work had been on Africa. This has been for the obvious reason that a good deal of Haiti's culture has African roots, as is also true with much of the anglophone Caribbean. Haiti may indeed be the most African of the Antilles but it is not part of Africa; even rural life has aspects which are typically 'creole'. I believe that much of the experience of Haiti from the time of the revolution to the present is indeed of relevance to the rest of the Caribbean region. In the course of this volume a comparative element will never be far from the surface.

HAITI AND THE COMMONWEALTH CARIBBEAN

Living in Trinidad and teaching in the University of the West Indies from the mid 1960s, I soon became aware that – with one

3

noteworthy exception[1] – none of my colleagues teaching in the
field of Caribbean studies claimed to know anything about Haiti,
a country they regarded as lying almost wholly outside their
proper concerns. Historians, of course, made respectful mention
of Toussaint Louverture and the slave revolt, referring to C. L.
R. James's classic *Black Jacobins*, but for the rest Haiti might not
have existed. For generations of West Indian historians the
Public Record Office in London (with occasional day trips to
Rhodes House in Oxford) was the source of all useful knowledge
about the Caribbean past. Economists, sociologists and political
scientists paid even less attention to the black republic. This
attitude among academics was reflected in the general population. I remember once returning from Haiti to my home in
Trinidad and telling a student where I had been. 'I don't know
much about the small islands,' was his reply. He was surprised
to learn that at least twice as many people in the Caribbean
speak *Kréyol* as speak English. These assumptions about the
Caribbean were graphically illustrated in a route map which
used to be issued by British West Indian Airways (the Trinidad
national carrier). The map shows the Commonwealth and colonial Caribbean and Puerto Rico, together with the countries of
Africa, and mainland America (many of which the airline does
not serve) in hard colours; but Cuba and Hispaniola are in
dotted blue lines as though under the sea!

A change has taken place. Excellent work has been done on
Haiti by the head of the French department of the UWI in
Jamaica.[2] The Institute of Social and Economic Research (centred in Jamaica) has produced a couple of volumes which relate
to Haiti,[3] and Leslie Manigat, a Haitian political scientist, was
for some years director of the Institute of International Relations in Trinidad. Professor Edward Brathwaite has written a
(somewhat eccentric) introduction to the paperback edition of
Herskovits's *Life in a Haitian Valley*, and in a recent article he
pointed to the significance of Haiti for the rest of the Caribbean.[4]
It is somewhat surprising therefore to glance at his own textbook
on Caribbean history directed to English-speaking school children of the region. Like other such textbooks, written by respectable historians, including Douglas Hall, Dominica receives as
much attention as the Dominican Republic and more space is
devoted to small islands like Antigua and St Vincent than to
Haiti. Dr Eric Williams wrote that West Indian history, as

written by earlier generations of imperial historians, 'can be viewed as a conspiracy to block the emergence of a Caribbean identity'.[5] Recent historians from the anglophone Caribbean have done little to rectify the situation and indeed are responsible for reinforcing colonial patterns of thought among the younger generation.

Historians are not the only West Indian group to be guilty of this cultural myopia. In a book explicitly claiming to deal with 'the English- and Dutch-speaking Caribbean and Haiti', the Kittitian theologian Kortright Davis is able to write of the 1938 demonstrations in the British colonies as the 'first full-blooded and riotous protest' by the 'masses against the social and economic oppression in the region'.[6] What then happened in Saint-Domingue in the years following 1791? Apart from a few desultory remarks on voodoo, evidently taken from G. E. Simpson, there is hardly a word about Haiti in the whole book; nothing is said of the work of Gérard Bissainthe, J.-C. Bajeux, J. Parisot, Claude Souffrant or Laënec Hurbon.[7]

Again, the Jamaican economist George Beckford states, in his introduction to a collection of essays, 'The use of the term "Caribbean Economy" as the title of this volume is deliberate. It implies that all the economic units within the region share certain basic characteristics'.[8] Yet all the contributors assume that the term 'Caribbean' can properly be used to denote merely those territories (containing 15 or so per cent of the West Indian population) which happen to speak English and which enjoyed the benefits of British colonial rule. In lecture courses, conferences and books on the Caribbean by English-speaking West Indians, an explicit recognition of the existence and importance of Cuba, Haiti and the Dominican Republic will frequently be made at the beginning and this will be regarded as a substitute for having taken them seriously. The fact that Haitians, Dominicans and Cubans are in their own way equally myopic, is no excuse.

It is, then, an assumption of the present volume that Haiti is part of the Caribbean and, indeed, that much of her early post-colonial experience is of relevance to the more recently independent countries of the region. Those who know the Caribbean will find that much of what is said about Haiti applies also to the anglophone islands. The complex relationship between ethnicity and economy in Haiti for example finds analogies elsewhere in the region. I have called colour the badge of class; but it is not the constitutive element of class. There is a small group of rich blacks in Jamaica or Barbados as there is in Haiti; there are also some light-skinned families who are quite poor. It is therefore misleading to speak of 'a *rigid* colour stratification of whites at the top, the mixed in the middle and the black at the bottom'.[9] While there is indeed a *general* stratification of the kind referred to, the language used by this Kittitian author is reminiscent of the *noiriste* mythology propagated by François Duvalier and his associates, which involves a reduction of class struggles in the Caribbean to purely ethnic factors.[10]

THE CARIBBEAN AND WORLD POLITICS

Ever since Columbus set foot in the Antilles, European and later North American powers have been deeply involved in the affairs of the region. The recent US invasion of Grenada is but the latest in a series of such interventions. I shall return to this particular incident in the conclusion to this volume. Three of the chapters deal explicitly with the international dimension. Much of Chapter 5 is concerned with Haitian ideas about the proper role of foreign capital and the foreign ownership of land. In the early years the country was diplomatically isolated and under a continual threat of military intervention. It was necessary to play off one great power against another. Some, though not I think all, of the actions of early heads of state which at first sight appear to be encouraging an unacceptable degree of foreign intervention in the affairs of the country, are to be understood in this perspective. As they saw the situation their only hope was to balance the British against the French and the USA against both. There was no unaligned block of 'third world' nations with which Haiti could identify. Even today, the leaders of any small nation desiring to maintain some degree of independence and self respect will need to be aware of this kind of manoeuvre.[11]

The twentieth century saw an increasing tendency for the USA to intervene in the affairs of Caribbean nations. This culminated in the military invasion and occupation of Cuba, Puerto Rico, the Dominican Republic, Haiti, Nicaragua and other countries of the region. The basic reason for these actions was the desire of the USA to gain strategic control of the Caribbean, to minimise European influence and to make these countries safe for US investment.[12] Military operations were often justified in terms of high moral duty which lay upon the shoulders of the USA to improve the conditions of life in Caribbean countries; the rhetoric even convinced some of its authors. One dogma, which has taken a remarkably long time to die, was that the supposed absence of a middle class was a principal cause of the problems of these small Caribbean countries. This was explicitly stated by US officials in Haiti during the occupation, and a policy was adopted which would create such a class. It was from precisely this class that François Duvalier came. Again, it was thought that the military forces in these countries needed retraining and professionalising. Steps were taken to this end, which eventually produced such leaders as Anastasio Somoza and Rafael Trujillo.

The USA still plays the major role in determining developments in the Caribbean. Direct unilateral intervention is generally avoided and military action has usually been taken under the umbrella of the Organisation of American States, as in the 1965 invasion of the Dominican Republic, or – in the case of Grenada – in collaboration with other states of the region. On other occasions covert intervention has taken place by sponsoring exile armies, as is happening today in Nicaragua. The power of the USA is, however, immensely enhanced by the tendency among radicals to exaggerate the influence of the CIA, and by a general belief that ultimately Washington's permission is necessary for any change. The author of a recent paper was criticised by the Washington-based editor of the volume in which it was to appear for failing to state that, in Haiti and the Dominican Republic, no government unacceptable to the United States could survive. The author declined to modify his text on the grounds first that it was not true, and secondly that its continual assertion helps to make it true.

European countries, particularly France, Britain and the USSR, take an active interest in Caribbean developments, owing to considerable investments they have in the region, and especially in the case of the latter to a desire to maintain a strategic foothold in the western hemisphere. In recent years Canada, through its banks and insurance companies, has come to play an important role in the affairs of Haiti and the countries of the

Commonwealth Caribbean. Venezuela and Mexico also appear to have Caribbean ambitions. Falling oil prices and acute balance of payments problems, particularly for the latter, have, however, diverted the attention of these governments from regional aspirations.

ETHNICITY

The first chapter, on 'Caste, Class and Colour', serves as an introduction to the social structure of Haiti as it has developed since colonial times. It draws attention to the complex relationship between social distinctions based on the three factors of status, economic function and physical appearance. It is this subtle relationship which has enabled politicians and publicists to employ an ethnic rhetoric (usually of colour or race) in order to fight battles which – on closer inspection – are more concerned with a clash of economic, regional or even personal interests and loyalties. This applies equally to those who seek to change the situation and those who endeavour to maintain the status quo. In the revolts of the last century (some of which are discussed in Chapter 9), in the protests of middle class black Haitians of the 1930s (considered in Chapter 3), and in the Trinidadian black power movement in the late 1960s (the subject of Chapter 4), issues of race and colour seem to loom large. Yet a careful analysis of the true aims of these movements would suggest that ethnic factors are symbols representing more complex realities. It is similarly so when we consider the phenomenon of political domination in Haiti and in the rest of the Caribbean. In Chapter 11 we see how linguistic and religious divisions join other ethnic factors in being manipulated by contending parties in their efforts to seize or to retain political power.

Elsewhere I have suggested that Haitian interpretations of the past are characterised by the elaboration of rival 'legends' which are closely related to colour.[13] Chapters 2 and 3 deal with very specific manifestations of ethnicity in Haitian history. The first describes how a legendary view of President Salomon has become a part of *noiriste* ideology in Haiti. I examine claims made by some writers about Salomon and conclude that the available evidence does not generally support the picture of the black president which is often painted.

The following chapter points to the way in which ideas about race in Haiti changed as a result of the so-called ethnological movement in the early decades of the present century. Prior to this, Haitian writers of all traditions and tendencies had unanimously maintained the equality and essential sameness of the human races. The movement, associated with the names of J. C. Dorsainvil, Jean Price Mars, Arthur Holly and later with the writers of the *Griots* group of black intellectuals, asserted that the races are different and that the black race has culturally and socially significant characteristics which distinguish it from other human groups. Some of the more extreme writers in this *négritude* tradition asserted a physical determinism, according to which biology determines psychology, which in turn determines the social structure and dynamics of a human group; these factors prescribe the kind of political system appropriate to that group. It is interesting to compare the way some followers of the French nineteenth-century writer Gobineau employed his racial theories to justify a change in French colonial policies with respect to subject races. It was argued, by such men as Saussure,[14] that attempts to 'assimilate' non-European colonial peoples were misconceived owing to these fundamental differences. Duvalier, and some of those associated with him in the 1930s, used these racial theories to justify a kind of authoritarian populism as particularly suitable to people of African descent.

Négritude ideas seem to have been rather more prominent among francophone blacks than among anglophones. The movement was, at least in part, a reaction against the determination of French administrators to impose upon their colonial subjects and upon others who came under their influence a pattern of European – particularly French – culture. In the development of *négritude* theories, the Haitians were soon followed by black students in Paris, led by Léopold Senghor, Léon Damas and Aimé Césaire.[15] Nevertheless, that extraordinary West Indian figure Edward Wilmot Blyden, born in 1832 on the Danish island of St Thomas, must be recognised as having anticipated some of the principal themes of *négritude*.[16] At a time when most black writers were insisting that the races are all the same, he had asserted the existence of a distinct 'African personality'. These ideas were to some extent taken up by Marcus Garvey,[17] but it was not until the black power movement of the 1960s that *négritude* ideas found widespread and significant echoes among the blacks of the anglophone Caribbean.

RACE AND RELIGION

One of the features of Caribbean social and political life which strikes the observer from a secularised Europe, is the central role played by religion. The importance of religious symbolism and rhetoric and also of churches and other religious institutions is therefore liable to be underestimated or misunderstood. In Haiti the Roman Catholic church has had a major influence in the history of the country and until quite recently it was unequivocally identified with the interests of the mulatto elite. With the rise of the ethnological movement the church hierarchy was faced for the first time by a challenge to the christian religion from articulate sections of the population. *Noiristes* of the nineteenth century had indeed been critical of the institutional church, but did not attack the christian faith or defend the voodoo religion as did some intellectuals of the 1930s. The 'anti-superstition' campaign of 1941–2 was, as I have argued elsewhere, part of a desperate attempt by the mulatto elite to retain hegemony in the cultural sphere. Though it had to back down, the Roman Catholic church remained identified with the interests of the elite, opposing Estimé, supporting Magloire and backing Duvalier's principal rival in the elections of 1957. Protestant churches, which have been less identified with the mulatto elite (with the exception of the Methodists of Jérémie), have played a somewhat different role. The Episcopal (Anglican) church, particularly in the capital, has been strongly promoted by the black middle class, many of whom were among the principal supporters of François Duvalier. Bishop C. Alfred Voegeli was indeed instrumental in convincing the US embassy of the acceptablity of Duvalier during the election campaign of 1957.

In the anglophone Caribbean too, the 'established' churches, Anglican or Roman Catholic, tended to speak for the elites and defend the colonial regime. In Trinidad each church was identified with rival white elites: the English and French creoles. Hindu and muslim leaders, while less identified with elite groups in Trinidad, have normally used their influence in a conservative direction. In Jamaica, Barbados and most of the smaller islands, the Anglican hierarchy was part of the ruling class and the voice of the church was frequently raised in support of stability and the status quo. Even as late as 1970, in response to a 'Public Order Bill', proposed by the Trinidad government, the Diocesan Council of the Anglican church quoted the tag *salus populi suprema lex* in order to give some kind of legitimacy to the bill. As I pointed out in a statement to the Anglican congregations in Tunapuna and in Kelly Village:

> *salus* means . . . much more than 'safety' of the people. Roman and medieval political theorists used the term to mean 'welfare' or 'well-being'; and it is certainly relevant to consider whether the Public Order Bill contributes to the well-being of the people. One is forced to conclude that the word *salus* was either wilfully or ignorantly mistranslated to give some kind of bogus justification for the Bill.

The statement by the Council bears the inimitable stamp of the chancellor of the diocese, Henry Hudson-Phillips, who happened to be the father of the government minister chiefly responsible for the Bill.

While it would be true to say that the influence of religion in the Caribbean, including folk religions like voodoo, pokomania and rastafarianism, has generally been conservative, this has by no means always been so. Christian and other religious beliefs and practices have on occasions supplied the vision and the impulse for social change; religion may be utopian as well as ideological. Baptist and other protestant missionaries inspired many slaves and ex-slaves with a love of freedom, and were accordingly denounced by the planters. The importance of voodoo in the Haitian slave rebellion is a much contested issue. The voodoo religion was in fact one of the means by which African beliefs and practices were perpetuated in the new world, and it does seem likely that religious symbolism provided inspiration for the blacks and the practice of the cult brought them together. Péralte and Batraville, the two leaders of the *cacos* revolt against the US occupation of Haiti in 1918–19, derived inspiration from their religion.[18]

The protest movements of the late 1930s in the anglophone Caribbean had deep religious roots, as Ken Post has recently shown. The Garveyite movement had important religious facets and was in certain respects indebted to the earlier Bedward crusade. I remember the Grenadian, Tubal Uriah 'Buzz' Butler, popular hero of the Trinidad revolts of 1937–8, speaking at a meeting of students and staff at the University of the West Indies in the early 1970s. At what appeared to be the end of his discourse he said, to the embarrassment of some of his audience, 'We are now going to pray'. Looking around he declared, 'There are some of you not closing your eyes'. It was faintly amusing to witness rows of radical students and marxist lecturers with eyes firmly closed, listening to Butler embarking upon the second half of his oration in the form of a prayer. His political meetings of earlier times had often included hymns and prayers. More recently, Michael Manley and his supporters in Jamaica skilfully employed a number of religious images, particularly from the Old Testament, to add legitimacy to his radical policies.

ECONOMY

Haitian independence was proclaimed in 1804 as a symbol of black 'rehabilitation' (a term used by Hannibal Price). Yet Haitians soon recognised that if this affirmation of ethnic independence was to be permanent and effective it must be built on a solid economic base. How did Haitians confront this problem of the conditions necessary for a true independence? This is the subject of the long Chapter 5. Those familiar with the anglophone Caribbean in the period following the independence of the major British colonies of the region will recognise many similar arguments and propositions. Such issues as the proper role of foreign capital in economic development, or the part which should be played by the state in protecting local industry, controlling foreign companies and sponsoring commercial enterprises, are hotly debated among West Indians of the Commonwealth Caribbean today. The further issue of the right of foreigners to own land, which very much concerned Haitians of the nineteenth century, seems to be of less interest to West Indians of the contemporary Commonwealth Caribbean. Yet the tourist industry as at present organised would face major changes if this right were seriously to be called in question.

A word must be said about Cuba at this point. It is clearly the case that steps taken by Fidel Castro's government in the 1960s freed Cuba from the kind of economic dependence which is characteristic of most of the Caribbean. The power of foreign capital was decisively broken, with ownership and control of the major industries being taken over by the state. Nevertheless, owing to military threat and economic pressure from the USA, Cuba was pushed into a growing dependence on the Soviet Union, who welcomed this opportunity for intervention in the hemisphere. Today Russian influence on the foreign policy of Cuba is paramount.[19] In particular, Cuba's earlier role as a revolutionary vanguard in the Caribbean has been tempered to fit in with the global policies of the Soviet Union.

While there is today among educated West Indians a general rejection of unrestricted capitalism and a healthy suspicion of foreign-owned or multinational companies, this is often accompanied by a somewhat uncritical approach to the role of the state and an assumption that state ownership or control will be the answer to all problems. For some time the Cuban model replaced the Puerto Rican model which had been popular among West Indian nationalists of the 1950s and 1960s. Many Haitian and other West Indian radicals have been prepared to ignore the growing bureaucratisation, inefficiency and lack of individual liberty which has become a feature of Cuban life. Undoubtedly the unremitting hostility of the USA has been partially responsible for these developments, as Cuba has been pushed into ever greater dependence on the Soviet Union. The tragic involvement of the USA in backing dictatorial and oppressive governments in Central America, and their undisguised attempt to overthrow the Sandinista government is likely to push Nicaragua along the same road that Cuba has taken.

In the Caribbean, as elsewhere, there is a danger that people will spend all their energies getting the state to do things which they can perfectly well do for themselves as individuals or in groups. One need only look at the situation in Guyana to see how state ownership may not only be inefficient but is also liable to centralise power and encourage corruption. It is a great mistake to see nationalisation as necessarily a move towards socialism.[20] Furthermore, increasing the wealth and patronage of the state makes the struggle for political power more desperate than it would otherwise be, and reduces the likelihood of any group giving it up, having once tasted its fruits. Suggestions that a Haitian government should take over the marketing of coffee, for example, are misconceived. Though the present system is by no means one of perfect competition, state ownership would simply open the way to further financial corruption at the

expense of the peasant producer and lead to widespread unemployment among that much-maligned group of middlemen (and
women) known by the somewhat unfortunate term *spéculateurs*.

This leads to a consideration of the role which might be played
by local entrepreneurs. Any comprehensive discussion of entre-
preneurship would require consideration of co-operative ven-
tures and in Chapter 7 I point to some of the relevant literature.
Chapters on Haitian women and on the arab minorities of the
region, look at two very different entrepreneurial elements in the
population. Chapter 6, like that which follows it, is little more
than an introduction to the literature on the subject, while
Chapter 8 on the arabs is a preliminary essay on a subject with
which I hope to deal in a forthcoming book.

For some marxists this question of entrepreneurial minorities
will no doubt raise the spectre of a 'national bourgeoisie' and the
controversies surrounding its role in 'third world' countries.
Those less encumbered with nineteenth-century cultural bag-
gage should be more willing to acknowledge the importance and
value of entrepreneurial groups. Part of the problem is, of course,
that these groups often pursue a course of action which takes no
account of the interests of their fellow citizens and shows scant
concern for the country in which they live. Most of their profits
are invested abroad. The reason for this is often that they feel
insecure, and in the case of ethnic entrepreneurial minorities –
particularly in Haiti but also to some degree in Trinidad – they
are not accepted as part of the nation by the majority ethnic
groups. They have, in turn, little loyalty to their adopted homeland, which many of them regard as a mere temporary lodging.
In Chapter 8 I have suggested that the situation of the arab
groups is strikingly different in the Dominican Republic, where
there has been more willingness to accept them, and a consequently greater involvement in and commitment to national life.
Nor is it the case that the political role they play is always a
conservative one; some of the most progressive political figures
in the Dominican Republic are of Levantine or part Levantine
origin. The same is true in parts of Central America.

For centuries the Caribbean was a region of immigration and
the arabs were the last major ethnic group to arrive. The late
nineteenth century saw the beginning of an intra-Caribbean
migration, with large numbers of workers being recruited for the
building of the Panama Canal and some railway systems. Also

the rapid development of the sugar industry in the Spanish-speaking islands and the later growth of the oil industry in Venezuela and Trinidad led to further population movements. Haitians joined West Indians from the British colonies in these migrations.

The USA, like other countries of the hemisphere, has long been the recipient of migrants from less-developed southern European and Asian countries. The movement has continued with new waves of migration from poorer countries of Latin America and the Caribbean. The second half of the century has also witnessed large-scale migration to the countries of Western Europe. Rapid expansion in the economies of these metropolitan centres led to demands for cheap labour. The arrival of millions of workers, ethnically distinguishable from the local proletariat, has had important consequences. The so-called 'guest workers' in West Germany, Switzerland and other European countries, coming from Turkey, Greece, Italy and Portugal, have had few political rights and occupy an inferior position which is legally defined. When industrial recession sets in they can be deported with relative ease to their home countries. Lately, however, action by various civil rights groups in Western Germany has done something to improve the situation.

With respect to Puerto Ricans in the USA and West Indians in Britain, France and Holland, these countries were hoist with their own imperial petard: for years they had been telling their colonial subjects to think of themselves as citizens of a great empire and that the metropolis is their home. The legal situation in these countries sometimes made it difficult to deny full rights to migrants, but more recent nationality legislation in Britain has attempted to remedy the situation and reduce the status of immigrants and their families to that of second-class citizens. Nevertheless, despite recession, these ethnic minorities play an important role in the social relations of North Atlantic countries. Whole industries and public services depend on their relatively cheap labour but, although the jobs they do have often been rejected by the native population, their presence is used by unscrupulous politicians to suggest a common interest on the part of workers and bosses in the face of the ethnic minorities. Some groups of white workers have responded eagerly to these suggestions, seeing themselves as a 'colour aristocracy'.

Haitians have been involved in both the intra-Caribbean and

in the later migratory movements to metropolitan countries; Chapter 10 gives an indication of the extent of this migration and looks at some of the effects.

DOMINATION AND REVOLT

The fourth section of the book deals with the structures of political domination in Haiti and some movements of revolt against them. It is central to the argument that these phenomena can be understood only in the light of the economic and ethnic forces discussed in earlier chapters. A good deal has been written in recent years both about the slave revolt of the late eighteenth century in Saint-Domingue and also about the *cacos* resistance to the US occupation of Haiti in the twentieth century.[21] In Chapter 9, I consider some of the lesser-known movements of revolt which occurred in the intervening years. I have tried to show the complex relationship between class and colour divisions as they manifested themselves in these three insurrections.

It is also legitimate to regard the migration of hundreds of thousands of Haitians in recent decades as a movement of protest – against economic misery and political oppression. The subject is a large one, and whole books have been written on single aspects of the migration. Chapter 10 can then be little more than an introduction to Haitian migration with an indication of some recent writing on the subject. Within the limits of one chapter it is not possible to deal with all facets of the migration. A satisfactory consideration of this population movement must consider, in the context of a world economy, both its causes and its effects, and not only the effects on Haiti but also on the countries to which the migrants go. Factors of economy and ethnicity are central to all these aspects of the phenomenon.

Political domination is the other side of the same coin, for it is precisely against the structures of government and the social order which they protect that these protests and revolts are directed. A full treatment of the instruments of domination would of course include an account of the army and of para-military forces in Haiti, together with an analysis of the system of public administration. In Chapter 12 these matters are briefly referred to, in an attempt to describe and account for the transition from the regime of François Duvalier to that of his son.

The peaceful transfer of power is ascribed largely to the fact that some key groups in the country gave general support to the regime of François Duvalier, who had systematically undermined the power of potential centres of opposition. Yet the part played by beliefs, habits and assumptions together with the institutions which propagate or preserve these systems of ideas, practices and symbols, should not be underestimated. Chapter 11 is concerned with two components of the Haitian cultural heritage, religion and language. The relation between christianity and voodoo on the one hand, and between French and *Kréyol* on the other, is discussed. I suggest that the peculiar cultural dualism in religion and language is a remote consequence of the colonial system and that, since independence, those in power have attempted to use these dualisms to maintain and strengthen the hegemony of a small elite which has in recent years incorporated elements of the middle class.

There is a widespread but mistaken belief among radical intellectuals that the masses in the Caribbean are a revolutionary force whose natural inclination to revolt is held down by force of arms or by a sinister conspiracy of school teachers, clergy and newspaper proprietors. While it is of course true that some changes will be welcomed by the majority of the population and that enthusiasm may be generated on occasions, there is a limit to the present sacrifices they are willing to endure for the sake of future benefits. The fact that ordinary people in Jamaica could elect a government headed by Mr Seaga and that 90 per cent or so of the voters in his own constituency support him is greeted with a kind of incredulity, which leads two writers to describe his victory in 1980 as an 'electoral *coup d'état*'.[22] The fall of Mr Manley is ascribed to the fact that he did not go far enough, fast enough.

Undoubtedly a similar reaction to the tragic events in Grenada will be evinced. The New Jewel Movement appears to have enjoyed considerable popular support for its modest programme of reforms, yet it was criticised by Fitzroy Ambursley as a 'revolutionary petty bourgeois workers' party'. The 'petty bourgeois' nature of the government is established partly on the grounds that Maurice Bishop's father was 'a local merchant'.[23] Why the masses did not embrace such benefactors of the human race as Mr and Mrs Coard for delivering the country from 'bonapartism' will surely be a mystery to this author, and the evident welcome given by large numbers of Grenadians to the US troops who invaded their country will be a matter of astonishment. I have suggested in Chapter 12 that a failure to appreciate the conservatism of rural Haitians and their well-founded suspicion of reformers has continually led foreign observers as well as Haitian exiles to underestimate the durability of Duvalierism. Analogous situations are to be found in other parts of the Caribbean and beyond.

Part II
Ethnicity

1 Caste, Class and Colour in Haiti

In 1968, some 20 000 feet above the Caribbean Sea, I found myself sitting next to a fairly well-known Haitian exile. I mentioned to him that I had recently seen the venerable Dr Jean Price Mars, who appeared remarkably vigorous for his 90-odd years. The exiled Haitian was particularly concerned about the physical health of Price Mars, and expressed surprise that I had not heard that he had been 'beaten up by the *tontons macoutes*'. I was somewhat sceptical about the story, not least because of my doubts about the ability of the *macoutes* to beat up a man of over ninety without killing him. A subsequent visit to Haiti confirmed that the story was untrue. It was Price Mars's *Open Letter to Dr René Piquion* on the colour question in Haiti and the hostile review it had received in the press from the minister of the interior,[1] together with the unconnected search by police for a criminal who was thought to be hiding near Price Mars's, Pétionville home, which had led to the story.

How is it that this open letter could have been thought to have been the occasion of a physical assault on 'the father of *négritude*' by a government which was publicly committed to this very ideology? Price Mars wrote his pamphlet in reply to René Piquion's *Manuel de Négritude*, where the author ascribed Price Mars's failure to be elected president of the republic in 1930 to his unwillingness to enunciate and exploit to his own profit the colour question, which remained, according to Piquion, the fundamental social problem of Haiti. In his vigorous and ill-humoured reply Price Mars denied that the social problem could be reduced to the question of colour, insisting that class conflict in the history of independent Haiti has always been a more complicated matter than one of colour. The problems of Haiti derived from the opposition between a mass of poor exploited peasants and workers on the one hand, and a small selfish elite

21

on the other; each of these classes was composed of both blacks and mulattoes. He appealed to the guerrilla leader Louis Jean-Jacques Acaau, who in 1843 posed the social problem in terms of the poor of all colours against the rich of all colours, and who was the first to proclaim the well-known proverb *nèg rich sé mulat, mulat pov sé nèg* (a rich negro is regarded as mulatto, a poor mulatto is regarded as a negro).[2]

In challenging Piquion, however, Price Mars was implicitly challenging the traditional *noiriste* thesis, which had been put forward in one of its most radical forms by François Duvalier and Lorimer Denis in their essay on 'The Class Problem in the History of Haiti', first published in 1946. It was this fact that led the minister of the interior to denounce Price Mars as 'this stupid old man'. Duvalier and Denis saw the history of Haiti as a struggle between a mulatto elite and the black masses, insisting that colour prejudice on the part of the mulattoes had been at the basis of the social problem since colonial times. Although they recognised the existence of free blacks and mulatto slaves in colonial Saint-Domingue, these cases did not significantly challenge the association between colour and caste. Furthermore, it was practically impossible for a black to own a mulatto slave owing to the sense of superiority which the lighter skinned people felt.

Price Mars was therefore challenging the *noiriste* position that the colour and class issues were one – that poor mulattoes and rich blacks were insignificant and could safely be ignored in a consideration of the social problem. As one black group had put it in 1946: 'We can wrangle endlessly about historical materialism and other such things but the colour question will still remain for a long time at the basis of the Haitian social problem'.[3]

At this stage it is necessary to say something about the class, caste and colour situation in colonial Saint-Domingue and to examine what has happened in Haiti since that era. We shall return to the ideological conflicts of more recent times towards the end of the chapter.

COLONIAL SAINT-DOMINGUE

There were in the colony three 'castes', or legally and customarily defined status groups, into one of which a person was born and out of which it was difficult or impossible to move. At the top of the power structure was the white caste, numbering about 40 000; at the bottom were roughly 450 000 slaves and in the middle were the free coloured people or *affranchis*, numbering around 28 000. Also we should mention the *marrons*, or maroons as they were called in the British colonies; these were slaves who had escaped from the plantations and lived in the hills as outlaws. Finally there were a number of foreign white residents. My reason for putting the word 'caste' in inverted commas is that the divisions were not quite as inflexible as they are in a fully fledged caste system. It was possible for slaves, through manumission, to become *affranchis*; it was even possible for *affranchis* to pass for white.

With respect to colour, there were the whites, coinciding with the first caste. There were the blacks, the vast majority of whom were slaves (though there was a small group of free blacks). Thirdly there were the coloured people of all shades from near-white to near-black, known as *sacatra, griffe, marabou, mulâtre, quateron* and so on, depending upon how many 'parts' white and how many 'parts' black they were.[4] Members of this middle category were frequently called *mulâtre* or *jaune* or *gens de couleur*, whatever their shade. Not all the *affranchis* were mulatto, then, and not all the slaves were black. In fact it has been maintained by Jean Fouchard that there were more free blacks than free mulattoes in colonial Saint-Domingue. This he does by including in the category of *affranchis* those maroons who had moved into the towns and who were able to work and live as *de facto* free coloureds.[5]

It is possible to distinguish a number of occupational classes in colonial Saint-Domingue. First there were the colonial administrators who were all whites, many of them – including the governor-general – being army officers. Then there were the large landowners and merchants, almost all of whom were white, though a few wealthy mulatto *affranchis* might properly be included among them. Then the lawyers, doctors and other professionals were again mostly white. The *petite bourgeoisie*, including small landowners, traders, craftsmen, and soldiers was composed of all colours. Manual labour and domestic work were performed by the slaves.

The social situation in the colony was thus a complicated one, with divisions based upon three factors – caste, colour and class – largely (though not completely) reinforcing each other. The most important colour division was between white and non-white and the most important caste division was between slave and free. The *affranchis* thus found themselves having certain economic interests and legal rights in common with the whites but, suffering various forms of social disability and discrimination due to their colour, they also had common interests with the slaves. The role which the *affranchis* played during the revolutionary years, from 1789 to 1803, was due to this ambivalence. Their eventual acceptance of the leadership of Dessalines in 1803, in alliance with the former slaves, led to the end of the colonial system.

In 1793 slavery was abolished in Saint-Domingue and civil rights were accorded to all men irrespective of colour. Thus from a legal point of view the caste system came to an end. Nevertheless the division between *anciens libres* (former *affranchis*) and *nouveaux libres* (liberated slaves) remained a significant one, largely coinciding with the class division between those who owned property and those who did not. Colour prejudice also remained. Dessalines tried to abolish these divisions. He offered the hand of his daughter to the mulatto leader Alexandre Pétion and the 1805 Constitution proclaimed that 'all Haitians whatever their shade shall be called black'. Nevertheless throughout the nineteenth century the colour question played a crucial role in political and social developments, continually raising its head to divide Haitians into hostile parties whose leaders would frequently prefer inviting foreign intervention in the affairs of the country to allowing their opponents to gain power.[6]

CASTE AND COLOUR IN THE NINETEENTH CENTURY

During the post-independence period, politics was dominated by two rival elites. One was black, landowning and rural-based, with its strength in the North and in the regions around Jérémie and Les Cayes in the South. The other was light-skinned, commercial and landowning, with its strength in the capital and in the cities of the South. The great mass of the people was for the most part politically dormant, intervening only occasionally under the leadership of some aspirant to political power by invading the capital and overturning the government.[7] Both the rival elites were generally unscrupulous and paid little attention to the interests of the masses. Some of the black elite had closer contact with the masses, but even when they emerged from a poor peasant family – usually via promotion in the army – they soon adopted the way of life of the elite. Black and mulatto leaders were equally orientated towards Europe in cultural matters and were publicly hostile towards African customs, particularly towards the voodoo religion. This fact is frequently ignored by black ideologists in the present day, who like to portray the black leaders – Dessalines, Soulouque, Salomon and his National Party – as the fathers of *négritude*, who looked towards Africa rather than towards Europe for inspiration. Actually it is difficult to find the slightest trace of this view being held by writers of the National Party, who were as much concerned as were their Liberal Party rivals to follow European ways.[8]

Dessalines, during his short period in power, not only attempted to deal with the colour problem but also announced his intention of changing the property system, so that land ownership would not be restricted to the predominantly mulatto *anciens libres*, but would be shared by the *nouveaux libres* – the former slaves. In a famous speech he declared:

> The sons of the colonists (by which he meant the mulattoes) have taken advantage of my poor blacks. Be on your guard, negroes and mulattoes, we have all fought against the whites; the properties which we have conquered by the spilling of our blood belong to us all; I intend that they be divided with equity.[9]

It is a gross misrepresentation of the situation to say, as James Leyburn did, that it was Dessalines who set the Haitians on the road to the caste system.[10] He inherited the remains of such a system and he did his best to break it. Leyburn himself states that Dessalines was 'tactless' enough to attack inherited privilege and colour distinctions. Insofar as we can talk intelligibly about a caste system in post-colonial Haiti, the emperor was its adversary. He certainly brought the question of social injustice into the open, and was a spokesman of the disinherited. It is always the lot of the oppressed to be accused of having initiated group antagonism, thereby disturbing the peace and good community relations which had previously existed! Dessalines was assassinated in October 1806 by a conspiracy which included blacks and mulattoes, and Haiti split into two states. We cannot here spend time on a detailed discussion of nineteenth-century Haiti, but there are a number of events which have had a lasting effect upon the social structure of the country which it is important to mention.

In the first place Christophe, the black leader of the North, announced his intention of distributing state land to the people; almost immediately afterwards Pétion adopted a similar policy in the South and West; he began to make grants of land to his officers, the size of holding depending upon rank. Most of the land went to the mulattoes who dominated the high ranks in the republican army, though many smaller plots were given to the blacks. Thus Pétion laid the basis of a land-owning peasantry. Christophe delayed putting his policy into effect for some years but towards the end of his reign began to distribute land, much of which went to members of the black elite. From this time onwards Haiti has been unique among the larger islands of the Caribbean in its land tenure system. Today more than four-fifths of the working population claim to be self-employed or are working on land owned by members of their own family. The situation is therefore quite different from that in the neighbouring Dominican Republic, in Puerto Rico or in Cuba. In these countries large plantations predominate and the rural areas are peopled largely by a landless proletariat.

Religion has played an important role in reinforcing caste and colour divisions in Haiti. Since the *Concordat* of 1860, concluded between President Fabre Nicolas Geffrard and the Vatican, the Roman Catholic church has been a powerful force in the country. Most of the best schools have been run by the church, which has generally adopted a francophile position and has helped to legitimate the claims of the elite. During the second part of the nineteenth century the role of the church was contested by *noiriste* groups, especially under Presidents Salnave (1867–9) and Salomon (1879–88), whose cabinets were dominated by freemasons. During the United States occupation of Haiti (1915–34) the ethnological movement challenged the power of the church and called for a more sympathetic understanding of Haiti's African heritage, particularly the voodoo religion. As part of his effort to secure the hegemony of the mulatto elite, however, President Elie Lescot (1941–6) lent his support to the so-called 'anti-superstition campaign' waged by the Roman Catholic church against the voodoo cult. Although the campaign was terminated in 1942, an intermittent and bitter controversy raged between *noiristes* like François Duvalier and Lorimer Denis on the one hand and catholic apologists like Père Foisset and Bishop Paul Robert, on the other. It is in this context that the *Kulturcampf* waged by Duvalier from 1959 to 1965 must be understood.[11]

Another important factor influencing social relations in Haiti has been the army. In colonial Saint-Domingue the governor-general was invariably a military officer. A tradition of militarism persisted into the period of independence and for its first hundred years of self-government Haiti had a military head of state. The army was, however, an important channel through which a non-elite black Haitian might have some say in the running of the country, at the local level and even at the national level. This is one of the reasons why militarism was continually under attack by writers from the mulatto elite. The US occupation tried to put an end to 'the man on horseback' but the 1946 revolution and the rise of Paul Magloire heralded the revival of an old tradition. It was only the energetic activity of Duvalier, with the help of his *tontons macoutes*, which has in recent years removed the army from its role of arbiter in the political arena.

While the term 'caste' can plausibly be used to describe the three-fold status system in the slave-owning colony of Saint-Domingue, there has been considerable controversy about the applicability of the term to social relations in Haiti since independence. Among Haitian writers in the nineteenth century there was a disagreement about whether there were in the country deep status divisions based on ascription rather than on achievement. Most of the ideologists of the mulatto elite insisted that in Haiti all men were equal and that individual merit was the only factor which determined the status of a citizen. On the question of caste, the mulatto historian Alexis Beaubrun Ardouin denounced his fellow historian Thomas Madiou (also a mulatto, but one who was less committed to the mulatto elite viewpoint). The latter had written of 'the rivalry between the two castes black and mulatto which formed the Haitian nation'. Ardouin insisted that there was no such rivalry, that castes had ceased to exist with independence, and that although it was permissible to speak of classes in Haiti, these did not constitute groups with distinct interests. Furthermore the terms 'black' and 'mulatto' were merely convenient ways of describing the physical appearance of citizens and had no additional significance.[12]

CASTE AND CLASS IN THE TWENTIETH CENTURY

The term 'caste' has been particularly popular among foreign writers on Haiti. In 1837 Jonathan Brown referred to the mulattoes as a 'caste', and Victor Schoelcher stated in 1843 that there were in Haiti 'two distinct castes'.[13] In 1846 Lepelletier de Saint Rémy also noted the existence of two 'castes' in Haiti.[14] Twentieth-century anthropologists have followed this course. The most celebrated attempt to describe Haiti in terms of a caste system is to be found in the writings of James Leyburn and his colleague John Lobb.[15] Setting aside the criticism made by O. C. Cox about the legitimacy of using the term 'caste' about any situation other than that found in hinduism,[16] we may still ask whether the account of Haiti given by Leyburn and Lobb, as a country composed of two quite distinct status groups based on ascribed characteristics rather than on achievement, and separated by an impassable gulf, is true to the facts.

These American social scientists were impressed by the existence of a small, rich, cultivated, light-skinned, educated, literate, French-speaking, Catholic elite in Haiti and tended to assume that the rest of the population could for practical purposes conveniently be lumped together and called 'the masses'. Of the existence of such an exclusive elite from independence to the present day there can be no doubt. Nor can it be denied that there is a deep gulf separating this elite from the rest of the population, though, as we shall see, this has lessened in recent years. Yet the division between elite and non-elite is not sufficiently clear nor rigid to justify the use of the term 'caste' and furthermore there are further significant divisions among the population which need to be noted.

Since the early days of independence, a small black elite has existed in Haiti, particularly in the North and centring on Cap Haïtien. This group goes back to the old free blacks of colonial days who were a group distinct from the mulatto *affranchis*. During the split between Christophe and Pétion a number of these blacks, including Manigat, David Troy and Télémaque, supported the latter. More important today than this black elite is a black middle class. Its importance as an urban phenomenon has increased greatly since the period of the US occupation. The Forbes Commission of 1930 stated that this group was beginning to be regarded by the traditional elite as a threat to its position.[17] It was in fact the policy of the US administration during the 1920s to encourage the development of such a middle class, under the strange impression that such a class would provide a basis for liberalism, democracy and what has later come to be called 'modernisation'. Even as early as the 1880s forward-looking elements among the elite were arguing in favour of the development of such an urban middle class on the grounds that it would facilitate social mobility and thus help to prevent revolution.[18]

There was in the last century also a small urban working class; during the 1940s, particularly in the capital, it became a considerable political force. Under Daniel Fignolé it was active in the 1946 elections and, despite harrassment during the regimes of Estimé and more particularly Magloire, it emerged as a major factor in the confused period leading up to the election of François Duvalier in September 1957. During the early years of the Duvalier government the trade union movement continued to grow and constituted one of the few genuinely independent forces in the Haiti of the early sixties. From 1963, however, the only unions which continued to exist were firmly under government control. The development in the last twenty years of light manufacturing industries and assembly plants in and around the capital has led to an increase in the urban working class. In recent years there has been a cautious re-emergence of independent unionism and occasional strikes have been organised to improve conditions of work.[19]

In considering the class structure of the rural population it is necessary to recognise some significant distinctions. In the first place there are the *gros habitants*, owning large estates and employing wage labour. Some of these owners are absentee landlords who also engage in commerce in the capital or other coastal cities. This class of employers amounts to about 2 per cent of the rural population. At the other end of the scale there is a rapidly growing class of landless (or effectively landless) wage-earners, amounting to perhaps 10 per cent of the rural population. In addition, there is a rural sub-proletariat of perhaps 35 per cent who contribute unpaid labour on small estates owned by members of their own family. There is a large class of *habitants* – constituting over 50 per cent of the rural population – who own their own properties, which they work with assistance from their families and from occasional wage-labour. Their properties vary greatly in size, and large numbers of them also farm land on the system of *de moitié* (when they give half the produce to the land owner). There is also a distinct group who manage estates on behalf of Haitian owners or foreign companies and the various middle men, or *spéculateurs*, who buy from the peasant and sell to the export houses. It must be emphasised that percentages in all cases are approximations, owing to the inaccuracy of census figures and the way in which one class merges into another.

Of particular political significance is a group of *habitants* who are richer than the average, who employ occasional wage-labour, and make small loans to their neighbours for the purchase of seed or fertilizer and thus build up a system of patronage. As I have tried to show elsewhere, many of the rank and file as well as the leadership of the *piquets* and *cacos* in the last century came from this class, as did Charlemagne Péralte, who led the guerrilla resistance to the US occupation in 1918–19.[20] François Duvalier recognised the key role this class play and recruited many of them as local leaders of the *tontons macoutes*. To suggest with Jean Casimir that this rural middle class has played no significant role in Haitian politics is seriously to misrepresent the situation.[21] It is interesting to note that it was precisely this group, rather than the rural proletariat, who played a vital role in Castro's army in the Sierra Maestra.[22]

I began with a discussion of castes and have slipped into a consideration of classes. My excuse is that Haiti during and since the time of the US occupation can be said to have passed through a period of transition from a situation in which social position was based largely on status to one where it is based on contract, to employ a distinction made by Sir Henry Maine. Questions of status are still important, particularly when considering the attitudes and actions of the mulatto elite in their private and social life. But even here some slight modification of the exclusive system noted by Leyburn has occurred. Writing in 1959, Maurice de Young tells of how he was discussing the nature of the elite with 'an individual of unquestioned upper-class status':

the author asked him to define the qualifications necessary for membership which permitted him to determine who were the other members of his class group. He replied that this was very simple in many cases, and he cited twenty or so families, but then he began to doubt one of his own citations. As the question was pursued it became very evident to him that it was not simple at all and finally he said, 'You know there didn't used to be so great a problem twenty years ago but since then so many families have moved in from the provinces that it is difficult to know in many cases'.[23]

THE COLOUR QUESTION

Although economic and social class based upon achievement, particularly upon wealth, is perhaps the most significant category for understanding the social and political structure of Haiti today, there are still to be found status distinctions based upon family and colour. Controversy continues among Haitians as to the importance of these ascriptive distinctions today. Before considering the contemporary situation, though, it is worth sketching briefly the role that colour has played in Haitian history. I have already outlined the close relationship between colour and caste in colonial days; although colour was not the constitutive element of caste (except in the case of the whites) it was generally a reliable badge of caste. From the nineteenth century to the present day a light skin has been an indication of relative prosperity, though as I have insisted there has always been a small black elite. Also there have been poor mulattoes, and the number of these increased during the US occupation, when black Haitian women had children by white American troops. In the past there has undoubtedly been, on the part of the majority of mulattoes, a deep-seated fear of and prejudice against the blacks. Likewise on the part of blacks there has been a resentment of and hostility towards the mulattoes, owing to their pretensions and exclusive attitudes.

There is hardly an important political or social issue into which the colour question has not at some point entered. The war of the South between Toussaint and Rigaud and the struggle between Christophe and Pétion, though they were not primarily matters of colour, did raise the colour question. Each side denounced the other as being animated by colour prejudice.

President Boyer (1818–43) was attacked as 'the oppressor of the black class', while his successor, Charles Hérard (1843–4) told Lord Aberdeen that the blacks in Haiti wished 'entirely to eliminate' their light-skinned neighbours. President Pierrot (1845–6) even found it necessary to introduce a 'race relations act', which stated that 'any person whatever who indulges in idle talk about colour likely to spread dissention among Haitians and to provoke citizens one against another will be arrested, put in prison and delivered to the courts'.[24]

The clash between Liberals and Nationals later in the century had a strong colour component, with President Salomon (1879–88) being widely denounced as *le mangeur des mulâtres*. Colour also played a part in the struggles which led up to the US invasion of 1915. During the nineteen years of occupation the colour question was largely superceded by the nationalist endeavour to rid the country of US troops and by a common resentment on the part of most Haitians of all shades against the racial prejudice of the occupying forces. However, in the early thirties, towards the end of the occupation, young black intellectuals began to relate the ideas of Price Mars and J. C. Dorsainvil on *négritude* to the *noiriste* ideology of the previous century. François Duvalier was among their number.[25]

The regime of Sténio Vincent, (1930–41) managed to maintain something of an equilibrium between black and mulatto, but the government of Elie Lescot (1941–6) excluded blacks from almost all positions of importance and profit. In January 1946 a revolt in the capital removed Lescot from power, and in the ensuing election campaign colour once more emerged as the arbiter of events. Even the marxists were divided into three groups, the mulatto-dominated Parti Socialiste Populaire, the predominantly black Parti Communiste d'Haïti and the young activists of all colours connected to the journal *La Ruche*.[26] Dumarsais Estimé, a moderate *noiriste*, was elected in August 1946 but was removed from office by the same military triumvirate which has secured the overthrow of Lescot. The new president, Paul Magloire (1950–6) was a member of this junta. Although black he was denounced by his opponents as a puppet of the mulatto elite. In the extended election campaign which followed the overthrow of Magloire, colour again played an important role, though not so explicitly as it had in 1946. The victory of Duvalier marked a return of the black middle class, with its *noiriste* ideology, in alliance with a number of socialist politicians and writers.[27]

THE DUVALIER REGIME

The fourteen years of François Duvalier's presidency saw certain changes in the social and political structure of the country. In the first place the increasingly powerful black middle class strengthened its position as a result of political patronage. As Peter Worsley has pointed out with respect to many 'third world' countries, 'wealth derives from political power, it does not create it'.[28] This group not only dominates the civil service and the army, but has also entered the professions and the field of private business, frequently in collaboration with foreign entrepreneurs. The old mulatto elite lost much of its direct political influence and assumed a low profile, but this class still owns most of the wealth of the country, dominating the national sector of Haitian commerce. This elite remained fairly exclusive in its private and leisure activities and no dramatic change has occurred at this level. Only in the second half of his period in office did Duvalier come to terms with a large section of the commercial elite. In the early years most members of this class were implacably opposed to the government, and Duvalier looked to the small but affluent Levantine community for financial support. For the first time, they were incorporated into the political life of Haiti, with two cabinet ministers and the mayor of Port-au-Prince coming from their ranks.

No Haitian government in living memory has done anything substantial for the peasants, and the Duvalier regime was no exception. The most that the peasant hopes for is to be left alone. Duvalier, who well understood the mentality and expectations of rural Haitians, generally avoided alienating the masses, by his policy of non-interference. He also kept in touch with what was happening in the remotest parts of the republic and relied to a considerable extent upon that middle class of independent *habitants* referred to above. He would call some local *houngan* (voodoo priest) or other notable figure from the countryside and, ordering all secretaries and bodyguards from the room, talk with him for an hour or more, gleaning information on what was happening in the region. Here and there avaricious *macoute* leaders overstepped the wavy but real boundary between permitted self-indulgence and excessive corruption, but such men were often removed by the government and blame for their activities did not seem to have been attached by the populace to the president himself.

It is important in this connection to mention one positive achievement of François Duvalier. Perhaps for the first time since the *cacos* guerrilla resistance to the US marines, the rural Haitian *feels* that he belongs to the nation. Populist rhetoric on the one hand and the countrywide organisation of the *tontons macoutes* on the other, have nourished this feeling. I was in Haiti when 'Papa Doc' died, and there was a genuine feeling of loss on the part of many ordinary Haitians, which – considering how little had been done for them in his fourteen years of government – is a tribute to the propaganda of the regime. Nevertheless journalists, novelists and correspondents from abroad, as well as Haitian exiles, continually underestimated – sometimes to their cost – the degree of popular support (or at least benevolent neutrality) enjoyed by Duvalier.

CONCLUSION

In the version of this paper given in 1975, I asked how far the colour question is still a live issue in the country, and concluded that, despite the assurances of many Haitian exiles, 'My impression is that there are still deep-seated prejudices, manifesting themselves in habitual behaviour, which have not seriously been modified as a result of the Duvalierist experience'.[29] Events over the last eight years give no reason for modifying this view of things. As I show in a later chapter, the mulatto elite has strengthened its political ties with the regime of Jean-Claude Duvalier.

Class distinctions and colour differences remain important in understanding the political structure and dynamics of Haiti today. While it would probably be misleading to use the term 'caste' in referring to the position of the elite, nevertheless distinctions based on status play a significant role, particularly in social and domestic life. Politically this status factor is of less importance than it once was, becoming important only when reinforced by economic or other considerations. One thing which keeps the colour question alive is the extraordinary interest that Haitians take in their past. The judgement that a man makes about the relative merits of Pétion and Christophe, or of Boyer Bazelais and Salomon, is largely determined by his present-day political allegiances. There are of course exceptions to this, but in general the supporters of François Duvalier subscribed to a view of the past according to which the heroes were black and the mulattoes were oppressors of the masses. Adversaries of Duvalier frequently took the opposite view. These competing 'legends' of the Haitian past are thus closely connected to the colour question. The reasons for the almost morbid interests which Haitians take in their past are complicated and cannot be explored here. Often, of course, the colour factor is subconscious. I remember a mulatto marxist writer telling me that a black friend of his once pointed out that all his books had been about mulattoes. 'But that never occurred to me', remarked the marxist. 'Precisely', replied his black critic.

2 The Wisdom of Salomon: Myth or Reality?

'History is written by the winners,' wrote Orwell[1]; he went on to suggest that a totalitarian government 'claims to control the past as well as the future'. Yet such a concern with controlling the past is not a distinguishing feature of totalitarianism. Many examples of an ideological or legendary version of the past receiving government sanction can be found in non-totalitarian countries. Professor Hugh Thomas's concern that British history should be taught in a more patriotic mode is by no means unique. While few governments or political parties can afford completely to ignore the past, it is undoubtedly true that in some countries a 'correct' interpretation of the past is of more pressing concern to contemporary politicians than is the case in others. Since the early days of independence Haitians have shown an absorbing interest in their past – not a dead 'historical' past, but a living ideological past.[2] The position which a Haitian takes with respect to past controversies has been closely connected to his political commitments in the present, and rival parties have elaborated competing legends which function as legitimations of their current policies and interests.

Elsewhere[3] I have discussed the development of a mulatto legend of the Haitian past, which grew up during the regimes of Alexandre Pétion (1806–18) and Jean-Pierre Boyer (1818–43) and which received detailed elaboration in the period from 1847 to 1867. In these years mulatto ideologists, including Beaubrun Ardouin, Joseph Saint-Rémy, Emile Nau and Beauvais Lespinasse, presented a picture of the Haitian past in which the heroes were Ogé, Chavannes and Rigaud, rather than Toussaint; Pétion and Boyer rather than Dessalines and Christophe. It was, I suggested, a legend calculated to establish and reinforce the mulatto hegemony in Haiti. A 'correct' view of Dessalines was particularly important in the mulatto legend. The black leader

36

was undoubtedly one of the heroes of Haitian independence – and the mulattoes were as nationalistic as the next man – but he was also seen as a barbarous tyrant whose oppressive rule was deservedly ended by his assassination.

With the fall of Boyer in 1843, black discontent manifested itself in a number of ways. One aspect of the black revival was an attempt to rehabilitate Dessalines. A leading spokesman of this movement was Louis Etienne Lysius Felicité Salomon *jeune*. In a memorial service for the emperor in 1845 at the cathedral in Les Cayes, Salomon declared that Ogé and Chavannes, the mulatto rebels against the French colonial administration, 'misconceived their mission, betrayed their mandate', by claiming rights for the relatively small number of *affranchis* only, and ignoring the plight of the slaves. Toussaint was the 'new Spartacus', who emerged to right these wrongs. But it was Dessalines who completed the work:

> Honour, homage and glory to Dessalines. Before him, as after him, no one has done more for the sons of Africa. In making Haiti a free sovereign and independent state, he assured to black and coloured men of all countries a piece of land where they could preserve all the dignity of their being.

Dessalines' slaughter of the remaining French planters, he concluded, was 'an action grand and terrible, no doubt, but necessary: it consolidated the revolution'.[4]

Salomon was, then, instrumental in establishing a revised view of the Haitian past and of Dessalines in particular – a 'black legend', as we may call it, which was later to receive elaboration in the writings of Louis Joseph Janvier, Alcius Charmant, Antoine Michel and, in the modern period, Arthur Holly, Lorimer Denis, François Duvalier and Leslie Manigat. In the later versions of the black legend Salomon himself appears as one of the principal characters, and it is the purpose of this chapter to examine some of the claims made on behalf of Salomon by a number of present-day *noiriste* writers.

SALOMON AND THE BLACK LEGEND

Salomon *jeune* was born in Les Cayes on 30 June 1815, of a black landowning family. In the crisis of 1843 his father established himself as leader of the southern blacks and was generally known as *'vengeur des noirs'*.[5] With members of his family Salomon *jeune* led a rising of peasant irregulars, known as *piquets*, in 1843–4. This movement demanded, among other things, an end to mulatto domination of the country. Salomon became minister of finance under Soulouque (1847–59) but went into exile soon after Geffrard (1859–67) came to power. Two of his brothers and other relatives were put to death by this regime. He lived for some time in exile in Jamaica but in 1865 was expelled. Under Salnave (1867–9) Salomon represented his country as a diplomat in Europe, unsuccessfully attempting to persuade the British and French governments to observe a strict neutrality in the civil war which was afflicting the country. He returned to Haiti under Domingue (1874–6) but, because of hostile demonstrations against him, was obliged to take refuge in the British consulate and once more left for Jamaica. He returned to his homeland for a short while under Boisrond Canal (1876–9). During this period Salomon *jeune* had become something of a symbol of black interests and in 1879, with the electoral victory of the predominantly black National Party, he was made president of the republic. His regime lasted until 1888, when it was overthrown by a northern rising; he died a few months later in France.

The principal claims made on Salomon's behalf by present-day *noiriste* writers are that he was a proletarian class leader who regrouped the blacks into a viable political force; also that he was a fervent nationalist and a prophet of *négritude*. The most clearly legendary writing on Salomon in recent years comes from Max Antoine, a member of the *griots* group and for many years a minister under François Duvalier. *Salomon jeune: martyr volontaire de sa classe* is introduced by Duvalier himself, who points out the importance of a correct understanding of the past. The present, he insists, 'can be built only if we bind it to the great spiritual forces of the national and ethnic past'.[6] Ulrich Saint-Louis, a duvalierist of long standing, has spoken of François Duvalier as a synthesis of dessalinism and salomonism, and 'Papa Doc' himself frequently referred to Salomon in his political speeches, seeing himself as continuing the work of his black predecessor. Duvalier wrote in 1946, 'The great Salomon, by his energy and his clear sight, regrouped the black forces in order to secure a rational organisation of the class.'[7]

Duvalier used his influence in 1957 to ensure that the presidential election of that year should be held on 22 September, the anniversary of the day when Salomon allowed the Port-au-Prince mob to burn and pillage the houses and business premises of the mulatto elite.[8] This date later became *le jour de la souveraineté nationale*.

Leslie Manigat and Ulrich Saint-Louis make further claims on behalf of Salomon and the National Party. The former suggests that the Nationals were characterised by their 'proud jealousy of national independence' and that they 'desired to work for a blossoming of a new black civilisation by valuing the African foundation of our national culture'.[9] This latter claim is echoed by Saint-Louis, when he writes: 'The National Party advocated the reconnecting of Haiti to a black civilisation, in other words, the return of Haiti to Africa'.[10]

A RETURN TO AFRICA?

A careful reading of Salomon's writings and of National Party propaganda gives not the slightest support to the claim that these men were orientated towards Africa in their cultural ideas and in their vision for the Haitian future. There is in fact no sense in which they can be said to have advocated a 'return to Africa'. With their Liberal Party rivals, the Nationals accepted the fact that, biologically speaking, Haitians belong to the black or African race, but this had for them no cultural implications.[11] They saw civilisation in the nineteenth century as European civilisation. Some of them, to be sure, pointed to the fact that the origin of modern civilisation was in Africa, but they did not use this as an argument for the development in Haiti of a specifically African civilisation. Léon Laroche, a Liberal Party ideologue, denounced Salomon as 'the official protector' of the voodoo religion, but this was a familiar charge in Haitian politics and not to be taken as evidence that Salomon was in any way involved in the cult or approved of it. His government was indeed anti-clerical and dominated by freemasons, but there is no evidence that he had any sympathy for voodoo. As we have already seen, Laroche also accused the National Party of wishing to ensure the isolation of Haiti in a black civilisation, but this again must be viewed as an attempt to slander his political opponents.[12] The truth is quite the opposite. In 1867 Demesvar Delorme, one of the National leaders, wrote to Salomon: 'We have the hope and the sincere intention of building on the ruins which we displace, a regular and new order of things, on the model of the civilisations which exist in Europe'.[13] In his address to the electorate in Haiti, written from Paris, Delorme referred to the forests of central Africa as places where 'indolent people, reclining in ignorance, sleep, protected by the deserts'.[14] His own novels were set in Europe and give little indication of any interest in Africa, nor indeed in Haiti.[15]

Louis Joseph Janvier, one of the spokesmen of the extreme wing of the National Party, known as 'ultranationals', insisted that the Haitian youths of his day were familiar with the latest literary and scientific trends in Europe. Haitian literature was, he maintained, but a daughter of the French; he further claimed that French was the ordinary language of Haiti, which was as untrue then as it is now.[16] Janvier denied the very existence of voodoo in the Haiti of his day, and in later years declared that Haitians should copy the British and French rather than the Africans in their legal and political practice.[17] With respect to the voodoo religion the Nationals were no less hostile than were their political opponents. The National Party journal *L'Oeil* declared that: 'it is important to obstruct the progress of the voodoo cult, whose adepts practise it in a way which is thoughtless and harmful to all people trying to shake off (as ours are) the heavy burden of their origin in order to walk in the path of progress'.[18] *Noiristes* later in the century maintained this attack upon voodoo. J. F. Thalès Manigat assailed those who practised the rites of 'this abominable sect which our ancestors introduced into the country'.[19] It was not until the years just prior to the US invasion of 1915 that sympathy for voodoo became a badge of *noirisme*.

There is thus no evidence to suggest that Salomon and his National Party colleagues were in favour of Haiti moving in the direction of African culture. They did not see in Africa a model of civilisation which Haitians should follow. Salomon's government was in fact resolutely francophile in its foreign policy, as we shall see, and this orientation was partly inspired by a belief that Haiti was a country which had a predominantly French culture. The fact that the president's wife was French constituted a further tie with the former metropolitan power. Salomon voiced these sentiments in a conversation with the French minister in Port-au-Prince: 'Our origin, our language, our instincts incline us towards you; it is France – honest, loyal and generous – whom we prefer to all the other nations.'[20]

In a 'Proclamation' on Independence Day of 1882, Salomon urged his fellow countrymen to prove 'by a prompt and intelligent assimilation' that civilisation is not the exclusive possession of one race. Salomon's policy of encouraging French teachers to work in Haiti, which is recognised by Manigat,[21] was hardly calculated to facilitate the development of a black civilisation based upon Haiti's African roots!

NATIONAL INDEPENDENCE

If there is no truth in the claim that Salomon and the Nationals were the prophets of a return to Africa, can it properly be said that they were outstanding defenders of national independence? This is a more difficult question to settle. There is little to suggest that during his period as minister of finance, under Soulouque, Salomon manifested an unusual degree of concern for national independence. He established certain government monopolies, but this was principally in order to raise public funds. Soulouque's regime was generally favourable to foreign, and particularly to British, interests and Salomon himself was described by the British vice-consul in 1859 as 'a very quiet and inoffensive person'.[22] It is true that Soulouque was determined to reconquer the eastern part of the island which had seceded in 1844; this was due mainly to his not unjustified fears that some foreign power might establish itself in the Dominican Republic and from this base threaten Haiti's independence. His policy on this matter was by no means as unreasonable as has often been suggested.[23] While Haitian ambassador in Paris and London, representing the government of Salnave, Salomon did make efforts to secure the neutral status of Haiti. He warned the old European powers against the rising power of the United States, whose ambition it was to absorb the whole American continent.[24] The government of Salnave, however, was firmly committed to forwarding US interests in the Caribbean. The claims that Salomon and the National party were fierce defenders of Haitian independence must, however, be tested principally in the period of Salomon's presidency, from 1879 to 1888.

Since the days of its independence Haiti had found itself diplomatically isolated in a world of white nations, and particularly vulnerable to foreign intervention in its affairs. Britain, France, the USA and later Germany, had significant interests in the country during the nineteenth century: economic, commercial and strategic. Haitian leaders became aware at an early stage that independence could be maintained only by playing off one power against another and much Haitian foreign policy must be seen as a consequence of this realisation. On the other hand, however, political divisions among Haitians which were closely connected to colour distinctions have frequently been so deep that successive leaders have been willing to seek foreign support and thereby invite foreign intervention rather than allowing their rivals to gain power.[25] It is difficult to decide which of these two intentions plays the major role in the policy of the various Haitian governments, as it is frequently possible to explain their involvement with foreign governments in terms of either intention. President Boyer's alleged willingness to accept French protection is regarded by *noiriste* writers as a cynical attempt to strengthen the mulatto hegemony by betraying Haitian independence,[26] while Salomon's requests for similar protection are explained as the consequence of a proper desire to counterbalance the growing menace of British intervention, thereby preserving effective independence. This is not the place to discuss Boyer's policy, but what is to be said of Salomon?

The British government was certainly opposed to Salomon, partly because of his francophile policies and also because of his unwillingness to settle the Maunder claims. These are complicated claims for compensation by the Maunder family, for damage done to their property in the isle of La Tortue and for wrongful arrest. The Maunders, some of whom possessed British nationality, had suffered under Salnave, had been compensated by Nissage (1870–4) but dispossessed under Domingue. Boisrond Canal had agreed to compensate the family, but the matter was not finally settled when Salomon acceded to power.[27] Salomon's government told the Americans that the British were likely to seize the isle of La Tortue, which was probably not the case. It also rightly claimed that the British were implicated in the invasion of Miragoâne, when a number of Salomon's Liberal Party opponents landed in the south of Haiti in March 1883. The British had indeed allowed the invading group to leave Jamaica and had assisted them in various ways.[28]

Salomon turned for support to France and the USA. In a private talk to the US minister in Port-au-Prince in May 1883, Salomon stated that he wished to put his country 'in such relations, positive and practical, with the Government of the United States of America that the protection of such Government would be assured us'.[29] The US reply was unfavourable and Salomon approached the French. Burdel, French minister in Haiti, reported his confidential discussions with the president on the question: 'After a pause of some moments, during which he seemed absorbed in a melancholy meditation, he resumed with determination: "Would the government of the French Republic accept the protectorate of the Republic of Haiti?" '[30]

Salomon's minister Callisthène Fouchard had already written to the Haitian ambassador in Paris urging him to support these efforts to secure a French protectorate, pointing out that in order to resist British plots it was necessary to have an alliance with France, 'toward whom everything leads us' or to arrange a *marriage de raison* with the United States.[31] The French response to these overtures was not encouraging[32] and Salomon went back to the Americans with an offer of the Môle Saint Nicolas or the isle of La Tortue in exchange for protecting Haiti and providing financial, military and diplomatic assistance.[33] Again this offer was rejected. Throughout the ensuing two years it was Salomon's principal foreign policy aim to secure the protection of one of these two powers. Was this merely to resist British intervention and thereby to protect the true independence of Haiti, or was there more to it? Everything about the situation suggests that one of the purposes of such protection was to strengthen his own position against his Liberal opponents. In a letter to General François Manigat, the president put the position clearly: 'With the support of France we have no need to fear any other power which threatens us or any enterprise of what remains of the Liberal faction. What an advantage for us to know that at the least movement by exiles a French warship will oppose their attempt.'[34]

It appears that Salomon's government was thus prepared to sacrifice – or to risk the sacrifice of – Haitian independence partly in order to prevent his opponents from gaining power, and that resistance to the British threat was not the only reason for these frantic but fruitless efforts for foreign protection.

All this is not, however, to say that Salomon was any worse than his opponents in this matter, for many of them were busily

approaching the British minister in Port-au-Prince with requests
for a similar protection. These were principally 'light coloured
Haitians, who belong to the best educated class of Natives . . .
The Haitians,' his report went on, 'who wish for a protectorate
are principally the owners of property and the traders'. Such a
move would, the diplomat continued, be opposed by the
majority of blacks, 'who have been taught by their leaders to
regard white people as their bitter enemies'.[35] It is sad to think
that these very leaders were in the process of attempting to sell
national independence to the French or the Americans.

THE NATIONAL BANK AND THE AGRARIAN LAWS

With respect to the question of whether Salomon was an outstanding defender of national independence there are two further
considerations. In the first place, the founding of the *Banque
Nationale* in 1880–1 with French capital led to increased foreign
intervention in the life of the country. In Salomon's defence it
might be argued that his intention was to undermine the small
foreign lending agencies which had sprung up in Haiti, by
founding a strong central bank over which the government
might at least have some control. Whatever his intentions,
however, the long-term consequences were disastrous. The
take-over of the *Banque* by US interests in 1911 was a decisive
step towards the occupation of the country by US marines in
July 1915.[36] The prognostications of Salomon's leading Liberal
opponents were realised. 'Salomon, the apostle of evil', wrote
Boyer Bazelais, 'in decreeing the Bank, has delivered our country to the whites'.[37] Edmond Paul, as we shall see, likened the
bank to a Trojan horse which would introduce into the country
foreigners bent on annexation.[38]

The second way in which Salomon's government might be
said to have risked national independence is on the question of
the agrarian law of 1883. The first constitution of independent
Haiti had stipulated in 1805 that no 'white' should be allowed to
own landed property in the country. This provision (with slight
modification) remained in force until the Constitution of 1918,
which was, in the words of Warren Harding, jammed down the
throats of the Haitians 'at the point of bayonets borne by United
States marines'.[39] The prohibition was a continual matter of

contention in Haiti throughout the nineteenth century.[40] On the one side it was argued that the provision was necessary in order to maintain national independence, on the other, that the law should be changed so that much-needed foreign capital would be attracted to the country. Positions taken on this issue cut across party and colour lines. While many National Party spokesmen, particularly the ultranationals Janvier and Pinckombe, were fierce defenders of the prohibition, Salomon himself and Delorme were noticeably non-committal. Before his election to the presidency, the former told his political friends that the time was not ripe for a change in the law and he denounced those who campaigned for such a change.[41] The black leader knew that the mass of the people would oppose such a reform. Yet, as president, Salomon made it clear in private that he favoured a change. He told François Manigat that although it was impossible to repeal the law, it could be modified. 'Public opinion,' he stated, 'proclaims itself against larger concessions'.[42] The British minister in Port-au-Prince reported to London: 'President Salomon assured me that he was fully aware of the pernicious effect of Art 6 of the Constitution, and that he intended to change it as soon as he was able to overcome the prejudice of the Haitians to Foreigners holding land'.[43] In reply to the French minister's question on the same subject, Salomon admitted that it would be difficult to change the constitution, 'but that which cannot be attacked head-on, may be secretly undermined'.[44]

The question arises whether these comments made to diplomats were merely sweet words designed to foster good relations, or whether they represent a genuine reflection of the president's ideas and intentions. One might be tempted to incline towards the former view, if the legislature had not been in the process of passing – on the initiation of the cabinet – a law which had precisely the effect of undermining the prohibition. The agrarian law of 1883 not only provided for a distribution of state land to those who would grow crops for export, but it also contained the less celebrated but equally significant Article 5, which reads: 'The factories founded for processing the said products, the limited companies . . . will enjoy, as moral persons, the privileges of nationality'.[45] The law which had been prepared by François Manigat, minister of agriculture, was criticised in the senate. One senator, Stewart, raise the issue of the foreign ownership of land, which would be facilitated by Article 5.

Another senator, Riboul, explicitly defended it on these grounds. The senate committee which recommended approval of the bill included Jeantel Manigat and a committee of the house of representatives, of which Guillaume Manigat was president, made the following comment: 'The appeal made to foreign capital by the establishment of factories of all kinds for the processing of our products will achieve the economic revolution which must revive our unhappy country'.[46]

It is curious to read Janvier, who had elsewhere warned of the dangers of foreign investment and ownership of land and had urged his fellow citizens to develop the country with local capital,[47] praising Salomon as 'the first Haitian head of state to have seriously opened his country to French capital'.[48]

In his public pronouncements Salomon laid considerable emphasis upon the way in which economic dependence is likely to undermine the effective political independence of the country, and we have no reason to doubt his good faith in this matter. He listed some of the imported products which Haitians could very well manufacture for themselves. 'Must we for ever remain tributory to the foreigner, and even at his mercy, for our food?' he demanded.[49] In a speech to the legislature he ascribed the troubles of the country to its isolation and to internal dissensions which 'have diverted our attention from the growing danger to which our political independence has been exposed by the material dependence into which we have allowed ourselves to fall with respect to the foreigner'.[50]

Yet a politician cannot be judged solely by his explicit intentions. There can be no doubt that the founding of the *Banque Nationale*, Article 5 of the agrarian law and the search for US or French protection together represent the most significant invitation to foreign intervention in the affairs of nineteenth-century Haiti, and contributed in a major way to create the conditions which made the US invasion of 1915 possible. Whatever Salomon's intentions, the consequences of his policies by no means enable us to describe him as a fierce defender of national independence.

COLOUR AND CLASS

The two further claims about Salomon – that he was the man who regrouped the blacks into an effective party and was a proletarian class leader – can be dealt with more briefly. There is no doubt that he was associated with the cause of the blacks from 1843 onwards. The National Party – of which he was the recognised head from the mid 1870s on – was predominantly black in its composition and leadership (though like its rival, the predominantly mulatto Liberal Party, it contained leading members of the other colour). Salomon was generally known as *mangeur des mulâtres*, but it was an epithet he rejected, pointing to the fact that his own children were mulattoes. Although the National Party was composed principally of blacks, it was an elite party, representing the interests of a rural black landowning class and of a small black urban elite. Divisions developed between the different elements in this alliance after the defeat of the Liberal invasion, and Salomon's regime was eventually overthrown by a black group from Cap Haïtien. He can hardly therefore be said to have effectively consolidated the blacks in any permanent way, nor can it properly be argued that he was a proletarian leader. He was himself from a major landowning family and the class which he had led in the risings of 1843–4 was that intermediate class of middle and small landowners which has played such a crucial role in Haitian political developments. While Salomon had support from the masses in the capital from time to time, this was only because he was marginally less arrogant and exclusive than were his mulatto opponents. His government had never managed to secure the unqualified support of the people of the Cap.

CONCLUSION

It may therefore fairly be concluded that the claims made on behalf of Salomon and the National Party by latter-day *noiriste* writers are not substantiated by a study of the available evidence. While it is no doubt important for the politician to propound legends of the past in order to reinforce his claims in the present, it is at least part of the historian's work to question these stylised accounts and, where appropriate, to demolish them.

3   Biology and the Politics of François Duvalier

'Colour prejudice', wrote Jacques Roumain, 'is the sentimental expression of the opposition of classes, of the class struggle; the psychological reaction to a historical and economic fact: the unbridled exploitation of the Haitian masses by the bourgeoisie.'[1] The contemporary Haitian poet René Depestre agrees, and attacks those versions of the *négritude* ideology which imply 'the absurd idea that the Black man is a man endowed with a particular human nature.'[2] It is not the fact of belonging to a particular race, nor the colour of the skin, nor the shape of the nose, he insists, which determines the culture of a people, but the concrete conditions of society as they have developed historically in the life of that people. Racial differences are, objectively speaking, of no significance, and a belief in their importance is simply the result of ideology. Racial prejudice, theories of racial superiority, and notions of significant racial differences are seen as the emanation of a false consciousness, which itself is ultimately to be explained in terms of class conflict. While racial differences are thus subjective or ideological, class differences are said to be objective; there are real significant social consequences stemming from class divisions which do not depend in any way upon the consciousness of the persons involved.

In contrast to this position, many writers have insisted that racial differences are fundamental, and cannot be explained simply in terms of economic forces. In response to the question, 'Are you a racist?' René Piquion declared in 1935 'Yes I am, and this is perhaps one of the reasons I am not a communist. Anyone who is a racist is not a communist.'[3] Some writers have gone further and have positively asserted that racial factors, rooted in biology, have influenced or determined the psychological characteristics of the different races, and have in this way affected the

48

varying social, economic and cultural institutions and arrangements which are to be found in the world. If biological factors
determine the psychology of a person, and if his psychology will
determine how he behaves, then it will be important for the
politician to be aware of those biological factors which influence
social psychology. In this chapter I shall examine the ideas of Dr
François Duvalier and the group of thinkers with whom he was
associated, on the connection between biology and politics, and
relate these ideas to the earlier racial theories of Gobineau.

RACE AND POLITICS IN HAITI

On 1 January 1804 Jean-Jacques Dessalines had declared Haiti
an independent country; in the previous year he is said to have
torn the white strip out of the French tricolour, leaving a flag of
blue and red (which was later to become black and red). The red
came to represent the small but powerful mulatto group, while
the blue (or the black) stood for the mass of black citizens. From
the earliest days there has been tension between these two
groups. The mulattoes have in general been educated, literate,
Roman Catholic, French-speaking, and relatively rich; the
blacks have mostly been poor, *Kréyol*-speaking, voodooist, illit-
erate, and uneducated. The coincidence between colour and
class is not complete – there has always been a small black elite,
and some poor mulattoes, but these are rare exceptions and are
dealt with in the *Kréyol* proverb: *nèg riche sé mulât; mulât pov sé nèg*
(a rich negro is a mulatto; a poor mulatto is a negro). Divisions
among the population are thus superimposed in such a way that
the two groups have sometimes loosely been referred to as castes
rather than classes. During the early years of independence Haiti
was known to the outside world largely through a number of
inaccurate and fanciful writings, and was pictured as brutish,
uncivilised, and devoid of culture.

Referring to the situation in Haiti (as he conceived of it) in
support of his racial theories, Arthur de Gobineau declared in
1853: 'The manners are as depraved, brutal and savage as in
Dahomey or among the Fellatahs'.[4] After a preliminary excur-
sion into journalism, Gobineau (1816–82) had become de Toc-
queville's official secretary at the French Ministry of Foreign
Affairs in 1849. He remained in the foreign service for many

years, working in Switzerland, Persia, Greece, Brazil, and Sweden; he retired in 1877. Gobineau is sometimes called the father of racist ideology.[5] He maintained that whatever the origin of the human race, 'it is certain that the different families are today absolutely separate'.[6] The black race is at 'the foot of the ladder',[7] and is 'incapable of civilisation'.[8]

In the face of these attacks, a number of Haitian writers at the end of the nineteenth century set out to show that there is no innate difference between the races, and that people of all races are fundamentally equal. In 1885 Anténor Firmin wrote *De l'égalité des races humaines*; in the previous year Louis Joseph Janvier had written his essay *L'égalité des races*; and at the turn of the century Hannibal Price published *De la réhabilitation de la race noire par la république d'Haïti*. The argument of all these writers was that black people are fundamentally the same as Europeans, and that differences between the races are only superficial. 'Men are everywhere endowed with the same qualities and with the same faults, without distinction of colour or of anatomic form,' wrote Firmin.[9] The theory of racial inferiority, insisted Price, is to be understood as the ideology of a slave-owning society, put forward to justify its social system.[10] These writers tended to play down the African element in Haitian culture, and to emphasise its links with movements in Europe, and it would be quite wrong to think of them as the grandfathers of *négritude*.[11] Janvier argued that Haitian institutions were not of African origin, but emanated from France and England; the country should therefore develop according to the European model. Price stated that although the Haitian was African by blood, he was French in spirit. Firmin asked whether the Haitian mentality followed a Latin or an Anglo-Saxon discipline, but did not concern himself with the African contribution to Haitian culture.

With the American occupation of Haiti (1915–34) there was a new awakening of national consciousness. There was a widespread resentment against this foreign invasion. Numerous journals and reviews of the period reflect this resentment. Connected with the nationalist movement was a revival of interest in the African past. Writers like Arthur Holly, J. C. Dorsainvil, and above all Jean Price Mars, maintained that Haitian culture and institutions are predominantly of African origin, and that the religious and folklore customs of the Haitian masses form a valuable link with the past. 'If we submit these traditions to a comparative examination,' wrote Price Mars in 1928, 'they reveal immediately that, with respect to the greater part of them, Africa is their country of origin'.[12] Holly went further and argued that this African culture was an inevitable result of the fact that the bulk of the Haitian people belonged to the negro race. 'Each race', he asserted, 'has its particular genius which is reflected in its psychological aptitudes'.[13] It was, he went on, important to conserve these traditions and it was therefore quite wrong to allow European teachers to control the educational system in Haiti. Holly believed that the true cultural and religious life of the black people of Haiti was preserved in the voodoo cult, which should therefore be accepted as a valid national institution.[14] Haitians should not be ashamed of their African origins, for all speculative and positive sciences find their origin in African civilisation.[15]

Price Mars developed his ideas in numerous ethnological writings; poets like Jacques Roumain and Carl Brouard also reflected a new appreciation of Africa.[16] In 1929 a group known as the *Trois D* began to meet; its leaders were Louis Diaquoi, Lorimer Denis, and François Duvalier. Diaquoi (1907–32) was born in Gonaïves and attended the college St Louis de Gonzague in Port-au-Prince. He was active in journalism and seems to have made a lasting impression on his contemporaries in spite of his death at an early age. Denis (1904–57) was born in Cap Haïtien, the son of a senator. After studying law in the capital, he became a qualified *avocat* in 1929. He acquired an interest in ethnology, and was director of the Bureau d'Ethnologie from 1946 until his death in 1957. Duvalier (1907–71) was born in Port-au-Prince and raised by Duval Duvalier, a justice of the peace. After studying medicine he became interested in public health, and was for some years associated with the anti-malaria and anti-yaws campaigns, which were supported by the United States government. In the meanwhile he had also become interested in ethnology, and together with Denis wrote a number of studies in this field. He strongly supported the black middle-class government of Dumarsais Estimé, who was elected in 1946 after a military coup had terminated thirty years of mulatto rule; later he became a cabinet minister under Estimé. This regime was, however, overturned by the military in 1950, and Paul Magloire became a *caudillo*-styled president. Duvalier returned to the practice of medicine, and was one of Magloire's opponents. In 1956 Magloire was forced to flee the country, and after over a year of provisional governments, Duvalier was elected

president in September 1957. He proclaimed himself a disciple of
Estimé and the spokesman of the rising black middle class and of
the peasant masses; his principal rival was Louis Déjoie, who
came from the mulatto elite. Duvalier was proclaimed president
for life in 1964, and was later given power to nominate his
successor. His son has now followed him as president for life.

Duvalier, Denis, and others continued to discuss the implications of ethnology for the culture of Haiti. Duvalier, in a poem
written in 1934 represented the plight of the African in the New
World:

> I then recalled the route traversed by my ancestors of distant
>   Africa—
> The sons of the jungle
> Whose bones during 'the centuries of starry silence'
> Have helped to create the pyramids.
> And I continued my way, this time with heavy heart,
> In the night.
> I walked on and on and on
> Straight ahead.
> And the black of my ebony skin was lost
> In the shadows of the night.[17]

Duvalier argued that the Haitian people, being of predominantly
African origin, should follow with sympathy and interest the
struggle which was going on for African independence and unity.
Haitians should,

> reject all the bundle of mistaken ideas according to which we
> have lived from 1804 to the present day: 1. the belief in a
> savage Africa with which we have no affinity; 2. the belief . . .
> that we are in the *avant garde* of black civilisation because we
> are a free and independent people, more developed and more
> intelligent; . . . all that collection of stupid colonial prejudices
> which handicap us.[18]

THE BIOLOGICAL BASIS

Among the ethnologists of the thirties in Haiti there was disagreement about the origins of cultural and social differences

among the races. As we have seen, Holly believed that these differences were biologically determined, and he demanded of his fellow intellectuals what their position on this question was. J. C. Dorsainvil disagreed with Holly, arguing that, 'the differences between men come from a difference of culture created by differences of *milieu*'.[19] More recently, Joseph Baguidy denied the existence of significant psychological differences between the races,[20] and Emmanuel C. Paul maintained that one of the most significant advances in the discipline of ethnology has been a dissociation between biology and culture; consequently less emphasis is placed upon the link between 'race' and 'civilisation' than was the case previously.[21] Duvalier and Denis, on the other hand, seem to have accepted the basic position of Holly, and indicated a biological foundation to cultural differences among the races. Duvalier explicitly accepted part of Gobineau's thesis that there are distinct races in the world, and that the distinction is basically a biological one. 'Is it not true,' he asked in 1935, 'that the most recent conclusions of bio-psychology confirm at every point the classification of Gobineau?' It is, he went on, according to the laws of heredity that the specific characteristics of the ancestors continue to reproduce themselves in an unbroken line in the psychology of their descendents.[22] He agreed with Gobineau that the black races are distinguished by their *sensibilité, subjectivisme* ,and *rythme*, qualities which manifest themselves in poetry, music, and dancing. 'La sentimentalité, conditionne toutes les activités du Noir'.[23] In a later essay Duvalier and Denis quoted L. S. Senghor in support of their position, and used the term of Frobenius, *païdeuma,* to describe the way in which black people enter into relationship with the external world. The writings of the German ethnologist Leo Frobenius exercised considerable influence upon black writers of the late thirties; one of his principal works was translated into French and published in 1936 under the title *Histoire de la civilisation africaine*. The first number of the Martiniquan review *Tropiques* edited by Aimé Césaire contained an article on Frobenius.[24] Another member of the *griots* group, Kléber Georges Jacob, also insisted on the importance of studying the 'anthropo-biometrique' type to which the Haitian people belong,[25] and maintained that there is such a thing as 'une psychologie raciale' which is closely related to these biological factors.[26]

The idea that there is a peculiarly African way of relating to the external world and of understanding the world, has, of course, become a familiar part of the *négritude* ideology. 'In contrast to the classic European', writes the president of Senegal,

> the Negro African does not draw a line between himself and the object; he does not hold it at a distance, nor does he merely look at it and analyse it. After holding it at a distance [*sic*], after scanning it without analysing it, he takes it vibrant in his hands, careful not to kill or fix it. He touches it, feels it, *smells* it.[27]

Again, Senghor writes of a sense of communion, the gifts of myth-making and of rhythm which characterise the black races.[28] In some places Senghor implies that these features are the result of environmental factors: geographical, economic, social, cultural, and political;[29] elsewhere he points to the 'physiopsychologie du Nègre' as the factor which explains the African 'métaphysique'.[30] There seems to be much in common between this version of *négritude* and the idea of Lévy-Bruhl that primitive people have a 'prelogical' mentality – a position which the French anthropologist himself renounced in his later writings.

Duvalier and Denis thus insisted that there is a fundamental difference between the psychology of black people and the psychology of whites, and that this difference has its roots in biology. They agreed with Dorsainvil that there had been a mixing of the races, and that four-fifths of the Haitian people are of mixed blood.[31] Nevertheless it is possible to say that the Haitian people are of predominantly African stock, and that they therefore share in the basic unity manifested by the black people of the world. It is in this context that Duvalier saw the voodoo cult, which both reflects and perpetuates the spiritual life of the masses; what is more it has played a crucial role in the social and political life of the Haitian people.[32]

Duvalier thus accepted Gobineau's contentions that is is possible to distinguish certain races in the history of mankind, that in spite of racial mixtures these groups have retained a specifiable identity, and that there are a number of psychological characteristics which are peculiar to the races. He further agreed that the black races are distinguished by the importance which they attach to the senses, and by their practice of understanding by association with, rather than by detachment from, the external world. He disagreed, of course, with Gobineau's belief that the black races are inferior.

SOCIAL AND POLITICAL CONSEQUENCES

After having asserted the biological basis of psychological differences among the races, Gobineau went on to maintain that these peculiar psychological characteristics of the different races have social consequences, and that the form of government suitable for one racial group is unlikely to be appropriate for other groups. He argued that differences in national character were similar to differences between the major races, for he seems to have thought of nations simply as sub-divisions of the races. Gobineau made the familiar assertion that political institutions which are suitable for one society cannot usually be exported; Hegel, Burke, Coleridge, de Maistre, and others had said the same. 'Bad institutions', wrote Gobineau,

> are those which, however well they work on paper, are not in harmony with the national qualities or caprices, and so do not suit a particular State, though they might be very successful in the neighbouring country. They would bring only anarchy and disorder, even if they were taken from the statute book of the angels.[33]

If institutions cannot usually be transposed from one nation to its neighbour, even less can they properly be exported to countries where an entirely different *race* predominates. Gobineau pointed to Haiti and to the Sandwich Islands as two examples of 'governments formed on European models by people different from us in race', and criticised the results of such experiments. In Haiti, he argued, the political institutions are copied from Europe and 'nothing African has remained in the Statute law'. All attempts to treat an African like a European are sure to fail, and it would be infinitely preferable to allow the black man to 'return quite freely to the despotic, patriarchal system that is naturally suited to those of his brethren on whom the conquering Mussulmans of Africa have not laid their yoke'.[34] Gobineau

would heartily have endorsed that commonplace of undergraduate essays, that one cannot successfully impose the Westminster model of parliamentary democracy upon the countries of the
'third world'!

Duvalier and Denis again accepted the basic contention of
Gobineau that the social, psychological, and cultural peculiarities of African people implied a different political system from
those which have evolved in a European context. Haiti presents
'the sad spectacle of a people, singularly lively at the time of its
original ethnic integrity, on the point of abdicating its historic
mission'.[35] Too often Haitians try to copy European customs
and habits, assuming that these are 'cultured' and 'civilised'.[36]
The same was true of the colonised territories of Africa, though
the authors compared British colonial policy favourably with
French 'assimilationism'. The former, they claimed, allowed for
an emphasis upon African culture, and for the continuance and
growth of specifically African institutions.[37] The *griots* movement
set out to elaborate a social doctrine which was specifically
Haitian. Duvalier stated that the group sought to detect 'the
bio-psychological elements of the Haitian man, in order to
extract the material for a national doctrine'.[38] He insisted that it
is wrong to seek outside the country for solutions to Haitian
problems; satisfactory solutions must be peculiarly Haitian. 'It
is', he wrote, 'altogether unscientific to confer, according to our
good pleasure, this or that form of government on a human
group.'[39] Duvalier insisted, in agreement with Gobineau, that
many of the problems of contemporary Haiti could be traced
back to colonial times. The social structure of the country in the
1930s was nothing but 'un prolonguement de la société
coloniale'.[40] He called for a revolution in values and for a real
transfer of power in the community. But this could be accom-
plished only by a rediscovery of the traditions and beliefs of the
Haitian masses. Just as it is inappropriate to introduce political
institutions from overseas, so it is wrong to import foreign
ideologies. 'As far as we are concerned,' he declared in 1967,

> the doctrine of our forefathers existed before marxism. I wish
> to say succinctly that we in this island of the Caribbean have
> nothing to learn from anyone. We do not stand in need of any
> doctrine or teacher in the way of political philosophy for we
> believe that we can be set as examples for others.[41]

What is the nature of that political system which is particularly appropriate to the African mentality? Many black writers have insisted on the importance of the organic community in Africa, and on the emphasis which Africans place upon co-operation rather than on competition. They have argued that the individualism which has characterised Western Europe since the reformation is unknown in the traditions of Africa, and, where it is present, it is an intrusion which has accompanied the colonial occupation. Senghor considers this co-operative element in African life, and sees it as one of the foundations of his doctrine of African socialism. In Haiti, ethnological writers have pointed in this context to the institution of the *Combite* – a system of community action where neighbours and relations will combine to work for one member of the community when he needs it, and where he is expected to help others in similar projects when necessary.

Some black writers have argued that traditional African government was fundamentally democractic, and not, as popularly believed, despotic and authoritarian. Jomo Kenyatta, Sylla Assane, Ndabaningi Sithole, and others have emphasised the traditional democracy of African civilisations.[42] While most black writers insist on the sovereignty of the people, many of them have developed a populist ideology, which combines ideas of the need for leadership with a belief in the popular origin of authority. There was among many of the *griots* writers of the thirties and forties in Haiti a conviction that the African mentality of the people required strong political leadership or even dictatorship. Carl Brouard stated that democracy is inappropriate for a backward country,[43] and K. Georges Jacob referred to democratic and republican institutions as window-dressing designed to mislead the masses.[44] Price Mars was quoted by Diaquoi to the effect that the democractic formulæ enshrined in Haitian legal and constitutional documents were devoid of sense; being out of harmony with the customs of the people, they only served to justify the exploitation of the masses by the elite.[45] Diaquoi himself referred to such institutions as freedom of the press, free elections, a constitutional opposition, and democracy itself as 'sordid tinsel',[46] while René Piquion maintained that Haiti needed a strong dictatorship reinforced by a mystique of authority which can sanctify force even in the eyes of those it crushes.[47]

These criticisms of democracy were often combined with an

idea of the leader who reflects and crystalises the will of the people. Duvalier himself rarely attacked democracy explicitly, but gave it a populist flavour; he spoke of 'a dynamic democracy adapted to our mores and to our mentality'.[48] Again and again he pointed to Kemal Ataturk as the model of a leader, who strengthened the personality of the new Turkey, by showing the Turkish citizen the importance of his ethnographic roots and thus giving him a new national pride.[49] He also saw in Ataturk the prophet of women's liberation.[50] Edward Shils, in his monograph on *Political Development in the New States* notes the prevalence of populism among political intellectuals in the new states.[51] He also sees 'Kemalism' as providing a potential ideology for modernisation, but goes on to say that as far as he is aware Kemalism has few explicit proponents in the 'third world'.[52] Duvalier was certainly one of them. A recent apologist of Duvalierism also quoted with approval Sukharno's belief that liberal democracy is a caricature of popular participation in government.[53]

Duvalier insisted that his own power derives from the people. 'Haitian people', he declared in 1964,' you are the source of my power.'[54] He clearly saw himself in the role of the 'hero', who represents the interests of his people, and leads them into a new era. Immanuel Wallerstein has drawn attention to the role of the hero in a number of African countries.[55] Senghor has also, in recent years, emphasised the importance of leadership, and almost seems to echo Gobineau, when he writes:

> The presidential regime expresses the spirit of Negro African philosophy which is based not on the individual but on the person. The president personifies the Nation as did the Monarch of former times his people. The masses are not mistaken who speak of the 'reign' of Modibo Keita, Sékou Touré or Houphouet Boigny, in whom they see, above all, the elect of God through the people.[56]

This emphasis upon the importance of leadership is by no means a distinctive feature of African political theory, and is, of course, present in a number of European political ideologies, particularly fascism. I have drawn attention elsewhere to the way in which religion is used to strengthen the Duvalier regime.[57]

CONCLUSION

In this chapter I have attempted to show how Duvalier and a number of other black writers agreed with Gobineau in rejecting the assertion that there are no significant objective differences between the races. They insisted that certain social characteristics of black people are a direct result of psychological peculiarities which themselves depend upon biological factors; these characteristics cannot therefore satisfactorily be explained in terms of class conflict alone. Racial differences are objective, just as class differences are said to be objective. A politician must therefore understand those psychological and biological factors which are important in determining the culture of the people they have to deal with. It is no accident that Duvalier is known as 'Papa Doc'.

Earlier I pointed to the distinction which is sometimes drawn between subjective and objective divisions in society. Differences of economic class are held to be 'objective', having significant consequences which are quite independent of people's beliefs; racial differences on the other hand are believed to have no such important objective consequences. We have seen how Duvalier and those who agreed with him challenged this distinction by claiming that racial differences too are objective. It would also be possible to question the distinction from another point of view: perhaps those who make distinctions of this kind fail to recognise the subjective aspect of class relations. The whole class structure in a capitalist state depends upon a number of subjective factors, such as the belief that contracts will be honoured and that the courts will take steps to enforce them, the acceptance of legal currency, and a whole set of other beliefs and assumptions. Again we may doubt how much the mere fact of a person's being in a particular relationship of employee to employer will tell us about his behaviour; or rather, the very notion of persons being in a particular relationship involves something more than the notion of *things* being related to each other. This something more is consciousness. That is why Marx insisted that the economic system 'is not a thing but a social relationship between persons mediated through things'.[58] Nor will we be able to predict with certainty the legal, religious, and cultural arrangements of a state without taking account of the subjective interpretation of

the situation which is held by the persons involved. This subjective understanding and assessment on the part of those concerned will surely be influenced by the objective situation which
confronts them, but there is no automatic or mechanical link. If
there were we would not find ideological disagreements among
members of the same economic class. 'Marx and I are ourselves
partly to blame,' lamented Engels towards the end of his life, 'for
the fact that the younger people sometimes lay more stress on the
economic side than is due to it.'[59]

4 East Indians and Black Power in Trinidad

While Haiti was founded explicitly on a racial basis, as a homeland for African people, Trinidad has always prided itself on its ethnic pluralism. Even the whites came from different European countries – France, Spain, Britain and Portugal. The two major racial groups in Trinidad are Indians and Africans, with the former making up something like 38 per cent of the population.

During the late 1960s a number of the Caribbean islands were the scene of black power movements of protest. This chapter will look at the course of events in Trinidad which culminated in the crisis of February–April 1970. It will emerge that although much of the movement's rhetoric and symbolism was ethnic – specifically concerning race and colour – the protest must be seen as a complex phenomenon in which issues of race, colour, age, economic class and social status were all involved. In this respect the black power demonstrations in Trinidad share some basic characteristics with protest movements in Haiti discussed in a later chapter. I shall be concerned especially with the efforts made by leaders to forge a united front with East Indians and with the reactions of various sections of the Indian population.

The term 'black power' was popularised in the USA in the early sixties, and was associated with the adoption by a large section of the negro community of a more militant attitude towards the racial situation than had been common in an earlier period. It was assumed that 'black' referred to any one who was wholly or partially of African descent. The ideology of the black power movement owed a great deal to the writings of Caribbean intellectuals of a previous generation. Among French-speaking writers, Jean Price Mars, Aimé Césaire, and Frantz Fanon must be mentioned; among English-speaking West Indians, Marcus Garvey, Henry Sylvester Williams, George Padmore, and C. L.

61

R. James stand out. These writers were concerned with the plight of Africans, both in Africa and in the New World.

The ideology of black power as it developed in the USA during the sixties was flexible, and at times it was suggested that 'black' might legitimately refer to all oppressed persons throughout the world, occupants of the so-called 'third world'. Negro activists of an earlier period, connected with such organisations as the NAACP and the Urban League, had already associated the negro struggle with a world-wide battle against oppression; in this matter the influence of W. E. B. Du Bois had been crucial. 'We stretch our hand across the sea,' declared Roy Wilkins, 'to the new independent state of India. We hail the Indonesians in their struggle for liberty. We are one with the Africans in the effort to throw off the yoke of colonialism. . . . The race problem . . . has assumed world-wide proportions.'[1]

In the mid-sixties Stokeley Carmichael and those associated with him were very keen to link the black power movement with other radical movements in the third world. Carmichael insisted that Castro was one of the blackest men in the hemisphere, and that, 'we got brothers in Africa, we got brothers in Cuba, we got brothers in India, we got brothers in Latin America, we got brothers all over the world.'[2] The young black power leaders were actually attacked by more conservative negroes in the United States for their cosmopolitanism:

> The 'black' creation of these earnest young people is but a tail to another's kite. It is tied to Castro, to Chile and to South America, to Peking and to God knows what else. It is not a movement by black people for the improvement of black Americans here in America.[3]

Nevertheless, in spite of this international and inter-racial dimension, black power in its United States context necessarily remained Afro-centred, or rather, negro-centred.

The black power ideology needed some important modifications before it could successfully be imported into the eastern Caribbean. In the first place, *political* power is in the hands of black people in Barbados, Trinidad, and Guyana. The black power movement in the eastern Caribbean has therefore concentrated not upon political and legal matters, but rather upon economic, social, and cultural factors, emphasising the crucial role played by 'the white power structure' in these fields. The leaders of the movement in Trinidad insisted, with Gordon Lewis that, 'the possession of political sovereignty. . . is, in fact, of negligible value, since it is rendered largely nugatory by the surrender of large slices of economic sovereignty to outside forces, both financial and political.'[4]

Secondly, in Trinidad and Guyana there is a large proportion of East Indians. In Trinidad the racial composition of the population, according to the 1960 census, was 43.5 per cent negro and 36.4 per cent East Indian, and since 1960 the percentage of Indians has increased.[5] In Guyana over half the population is of East Indian descent. The movement has thus had to face the problem of relations with the Indian population. Does 'black' mean African, or non-white? Are Indians black or not? So far as the term 'black' has been used in the past it has generally been understood as referring to persons of predominantly African descent. Until recently the term was rarely used at all in 'polite' Trinidadian circles. Africans were called 'dark', 'creole', or 'negro'. Most Indians do not think of themselves as black, and it is only by a conscious effort that African leaders of the black power movement have been able to use the term in such a way as to include Indians. All too often they slip into using the term to refer to Africans alone. This emerges particularly in speeches, but also there is an ambiguous use of the term 'black' in writings like Walter Rodney's *The Groundings with my Brothers.*[6]

In Guyana, where Africans are only about 36 per cent of the population, there is considerable emphasis upon the importance of unity among Afro-Guyanese themselves. The African Society for Cultural Relations with Independent Africa (ASCRIA) was founded by Sidney King (Eusi Kwyana is the African name which he has adopted) and others; it believes that Afro-Guyanese unity and the reconstruction of African identity is an essential preliminary to unity with East Indians. Nevertheless they maintain that Afro-Indian unity is the ultimate objective. 'Indian Guyanese!' they declare 'Long-term salvation does not lie with European power centres, North Atlantic or Warsaw alliance. Away with European destiny. Think of yourselves as part of the black people of the world.'[7] Also Walter Green has stated that 'Black power is black people – all non-white people which include East Indians.'[8] During his recent visit to Guyana, Carmichael seems to have accepted the view of black power as a two-stage affair. He stated in his address at the University of Guyana that,

> a clear concept of black power in Guyana would mean the black people moving with the Indians to set up a government which really controls the economic interests of Guyana for the benefit of the masses of the people in Guyana.[9]

There is, he declared, no point in Indians and Africans fighting each other, because neither group really controls power in the community. Earlier on in his address, however, he insisted that ·'the highest political expression of black power is Pan-Africanism'. He distinguished black power from Guyanese power, and asserted that black people throughout the world must recognise Africa as their mother-land, and join together to fight the imperialism of the West. Not all radicals in Guyana accepted Carmichael's position. Members of the Ratoon Group – a recent outgrowth from the New World movement, which is composed mainly of intellectuals and professionals – who had invited Carmichael, were sometimes embarrassed by the statements of their guest.

In Trinidad the leaders of the black power movement were practically unanimous in their expressed desire to include East Indians as full partners in the movement. Although one occasionally finds in speeches and in pamphlets the kind of equivocation in the use of the term 'black' that we have already noted with respect to Rodney, there was, during the months of February to April 1970, a determined effort to include Indians in the movement. There is a long history of suspicion and even of hostility between Indians and Africans in Trinidad. With the ending of slavery, large numbers of indentured labourers were brought to Trinidad from India to work principally in the sugar fields. They were prepared to do work at a level of remuneration which the newly liberated slaves rejected. This plentiful supply of cheap labour tended to depress wage levels, and Indian immigration was believed by many Africans to be the principal cause of low wages. Suspicion between the races was often encouraged by the colonial power, and the local white residents welcomed Indian immigration insofar as it tended to counteract the growing power of the negroes. Intermarriage between Indian and African has become less uncommon than it was, but it is still very much the exception. Suspicion between the two groups is very widespread. The black power leaders underestimated the importance of these feelings, and failed to do the necessary groundwork among the Indian community. Some of the leaders of the movement recognised the need for such groundwork, but the movement grew so fast among the young negro masses in the towns, that there was little opportunity to do the slow and painstaking work which was necessary in the villages of central Trinidad.

The black power rising of February to April 1970 was caused by a number of factors. In the first place, unemployment among young people has been very high. In the age group 15–19, 35 per cent of the labour force was unemployed in 1967; and in the age group 20–24, the figure was 20 per cent.[10] Secondly, there has undoubtedly been unjust racial discrimination in Trinidad, both in social life, and what is more important, with respect to job opportunities in the private sector. Thirdly, a growing nationalism, particularly on the part of the young, is evident in recent years (although Lewis certainly overstates the phenomenon when he writes of 'an all-embracing nationalism . . . of a peculiarly marked intensity').[11] This nationalism has involved attacks upon the domination of the economy by foreign interests. Many of the black power leaders were graduates or undergraduates of the University of the West Indies (UWI), and the St Augustine campus of the university has provided a centre of radical activity in recent years. Nevertheless the movement became a political force only when these students went into the community and helped to organise the masses. Another factor which led to the explosion was a widespread belief that the established political parties were unable or unwilling to take the kind of radical action demanded by black power leaders. Neither the People's National Movement (PNM) government, nor the principal opposition party (the Democratic Labour Party – DLP) appeared to take seriously the growing discontent in the country. Both parties have failed to build up effective youth sections, and the absence of young people from party politics has been a striking feature of Trinidad life in recent years. The government of Dr Williams had been in power since 1956, and showed distinct signs of old age; it had lost touch with the masses. A few years ago the government could have relied implicitly on support from the army and from urban groups like the steelbandsmen; these were seen almost as sub-sections of the PNM and were composed largely of young negro Trinidadians from the poorer urban areas. During the recent crisis, however, neither of these groups was prepared to support the government.

The black power movement of February to April 1970 was essentially led by and composed of young West Indians of predominantly African descent. Less than 15 per cent of the persons detained by the Trinidad Government under the state of emergency proclaimed on 21 April were over thirty years of age, while the age of the rank and file was very much lower. Also, of the fifty or so persons detained, all except five were of predominantly African descent; only two were of predominantly Indian origin. Nevertheless the leaders of the movement were certainly aware that only an Afro-Indian alliance of radicals could hope successfully to challenge the government of Eric Williams. In trade union terms, this meant an alliance between sugar and oil. The Oilfield Workers' Trade Union (OWTU) has been extending into a number of industries other than oil in recent years, and has been making alliances with unions whose leadership is also politically radical. The OWTU has been particularly eager to extend its influence into the sugar industry, but this has been resisted by the combined efforts of the PNM government and the All Trinidad Sugar Estates and Factory Workers Trade Union led by Bhadase Sagan Maraj. Also head of the most important hindu group in Trinidad, the Maha Sabha, Maraj enjoyed a position of considerable power among Indians of the sugar belt; he was Representative for the Chaguanas constituency, and made frequent appeals to the racial and religious loyalties of Indians. Afro-Indian unity has been the policy of *Vanguard* (organ of the OWTU) since its inception. George Weekes (president general of the OWTU) and other leaders of the black power movement were clear that they could succeed only if they could get Indian support, though the rank and file of the movement often failed to see this. Many of the associations and groups supporting the marches and demonstrations were explicitly Afro-orientated: there was the Afro-Association of Trinidad and Tobago (centred at Couva), the African Unity Brothers (of St Anns), the African Cultural Association (of St James), while the largest group in the South, the Universal Movement for the Reconstruction of Black Identity (UMROBI) directed its manifesto to 'all black people who consider themselves Negro, African or of African descent'. The National Joint Action Committee (NJAC) founded by Geddes Granger, David Darbeau, and others early in 1969 was theoretically interracial, but its numerical support came largely from east Port of Spain, where the population is almost entirely of African descent. Probably less than 1 per cent of those who attended the marches and demonstrations of February to April 1970 were of Indian origin.

THE CRISIS OF FEBRUARY TO APRIL 1970

On 15 October 1968 Walter Rodney, a Guyanese lecturer in the University of the West Indies at Mona, Jamaica, was declared a prohibited immigrant by the Jamaican government, and the ensuing protests and demonstrations gave a new impetus to radical forces throughout the English-speaking Caribbean. A number of intellectuals joined together in Trinidad to form a newspaper, *Moko*, and some months later *Abeng* appeared in Jamaica. On 26 February 1969 a small group of students, headed by Geddes Granger, prevented the governor-general of Canada from entering the St Augustine campus of the UWI in Trinidad; this was a gesture of solidarity with West Indian students who had been arrested in Canada for the part which they allegedly had played in the partial destruction of the computer centre at Sir George Williams University in Montreal. (The students had occupied the centre in protest against the university's failure properly to investigate their charges of racial discrimination by university officials). This event was followed later in 1969 by a bus strike during which a number of radicals were arrested; there were also further disturbances at the university. Clive Thomas, another Guyanese lecturer at Mona, was declared an illegal immigrant by the Jamaican government, and the university was apparently unwilling to appoint him to a position at St Augustine. At the same time there was also a dispute arising from the university's action in effectively removing another lecturer from its staff. The Student Guild led by Carl Blackwood declared a boycott of classes and they were supported by the West Indies Group of University Teachers who called on its members to cease teaching. Eventually the administrative buildings were taken over by the students, and a public enquiry was instituted by the Trinidad government.

Carnival 1970 was marked by a number of 'old mas' bands dedicated to a black power theme. 'King Sugar' presented by the UWI depicted the iniquities of the plantation system, and 'White Devils' attacked the dominance of white values in the community. Other bands carried pictures of American black power leaders including Rap Brown and Stokeley Carmichael (himself born in Trinidad). On 26 February 1970 a small but significant demonstration took place in Port of Spain when students and other young people marched in support of the West Indian students involved in the Sir George Williams incident. They entered the downtown branch of the Royal Bank of Canada, and demonstrated inside the Roman Catholic cathedral. Early on the following morning eight of the leaders were arrested on a number of charges and were initially refused bail. The first major demonstration took place on Wednesday 4 March, when over 10 000 people marched to Shanty Town in a gesture of solidarity with the eight. On the following day, outside the court house where the eight were being tried, a large group of black power supporters was forcibly dispersed by the police; they went on a small rampage, smashing the windows of eight or nine downtown stores, including three which belonged to Indian families. On the same evening a fire bomb did damage to another prominent Indian store in San Juan. The leaders of the movement quickly recognised the danger of alienating Indian opinion, and they organised a massive demonstration on the following day, marching to San Juan under the banner of Afro-Indian unity. Nevertheless, much harm had already been done, and the events of the previous few days were to be exploited by those who saw racial unity as a challenge to their interests. 'These people', declared B. S. Maraj,

> have done considerable damage to business property owned by Indians. . . . These wanton and lawless acts do not show that the black power movement has any sympathy, brotherliness or incorporation with the Indians of this country, as it pretends to profess [sic].[12]

The leaders of the NJAC made a determined effort to rebut these charges. Outside one large Indian store Granger declared, 'There is a move afoot to make the Indians believe that we are against them. We are not against them. We consider every

Indian our brother.'[13] Perhaps the most dramatically conceived demonstration, and from the point of view of this chapter, the most significant, was the march to the sugar belt, organised by the NJAC. It was declared to be a demonstration of solidarity, by the largely urban-dwelling African youth of the movement, with the 'suffering and exploited' Indian sugar workers. Outspoken opposition to the march was voiced by Maraj, who saw it as a challenge to what he conceived to be his own prophetic role in County Caroni; he must also have seen it as a further step by the OWTU to infiltrate the sugar industry. 'What is their motive now?', he demanded. 'For the last 100 years the sugar workers have been working under trying conditions, and *these people* did not see it fit to help. . . . Having broken, burned and looted Indian business places, how can they show love for these Indian people?'[14]

Granger attacked the statement made by Maraj as a threat designed to divide Indians from negroes 'in the interests of the power structure',[15] and he announced that the projected demonstration would be held in spite of these threats. Maraj insisted that the intention of the organisers to enter the sugar fields 'without any invitation from either the workers or the workers' representatives' infringed the rights of the sugar workers. 'I and others will be there,' he added ominously, 'and may God help us after.'[16] The original intention of the NJAC was that the demonstrators should spend a day cutting cane alongside the Indian cane cutters, but this plan was wisely modified; the demonstrators would instead march through the area and would hold meetings at various points on the route. An unexpected and somewhat bizarre note was introduced into these events, when the Roman Catholic archbishop of Port of Spain announced that he would join the marchers, but almost immediately reversed his decision.

The Caroni march eventually took place on Thursday 12 March. On the previous day a number of Indian students from UWI had visited many of the villages through which the marchers were to pass, in an attempt to convince the local inhabitants that the demonstrators had no hostile intention towards them. They found that many of the villagers genuinely feared that the marchers intended to do mischief. Not all the students who went out on this mission were in favour of the demonstration, but they felt that, if it was going to take place, then the best thing to do would be for Indians to quieten the fears of the villagers and also to join the procession themselves, in order to avoid the appearance of a racial confrontation between predominantly African demonstrators and a largely Indian population. I am informed that over one hundred armed Indians were strategically placed out of sight along the route of the march. The demonstration eventually took place without any major incident. The black power supporters walked over thirty miles from Port of Spain to Couva.

Further demonstrations and meetings took place throughout Trinidad and Tobago in the following weeks, and a number of business places and private homes were destroyed by fire bombs. There was clearly a disagreement within the cabinet on how to deal with the situation, and on 13 April 1970 the deputy prime minister, A. N. R. Robinson, resigned. On 18 April the governor-general, Sir Solomon Hochoy, left Trinidad 'on holiday', and the chief justice, Sir Arthur McShine, was appointed to act in his place. It is widely believed that Hochoy refused to sign a declaration of emergency, possibly for fear that reprisals might be taken against the Chinese community. Nevertheless the governor-general's disappearance during the crisis was perhaps a trifle surprising. On the following day there was a strike of sugar workers at Brechin Castle, which was supported by the NJAC. Efforts were made by Maraj to get the strikers back to work, but he was only partially successful. A joint demonstration of sugar workers and workers from other industries was planned for 21 April, but in the early hours of that day a state of emergency was declared, demonstrations were banned, and many of the black power leaders were arrested.

THE TRINIDAD BLACK POWER MOVEMENT

As I have already indicated, the black power movement in Trinidad was composed of a number of different groups, each with its own way of looking at things. Some groups, like UM-ROBI (led by two school teachers, graduates from the UWI, Mona) tended to be rather more interested in social and cultural factors than in radical economic reforms, though the economic factor was not ignored. The Trinidad Black Panthers were quite prepared to work with the government, while those groups associated with the NJAC called not only for a change of government, but for an entirely new political and economic system. After having issued, half-way through March, their rather modest statement of demands, the Panthers were denounced by the bulk of the movement as compromisers; they in turn accused their critics of being 'academic'.[17] From this point on the Panthers, who represented only a small fraction of the movement, played no further part in the demonstrations. All supporters of the movement agreed in rejecting the dominance of 'white values' in the community, and were united by a common acceptance of certain symbols, rather than by an agreed ideology, or programme of action. The clenched fist, the cry of 'power', the dashiki (Afro shirt) and the fat-head (Afro hair-cut), the red, black, and green flags, the use of 'brother' and 'sister': these were the things which united the movement. George Weekes, whose own background in social protest goes back further than that of most leaders of the movement, began to address a black power meeting: 'Friends and comrades'. . . . 'None ah dat', shouted some of the listeners, 'we are brothers and sisters.' 'Brothers and sisters', Mr. Weekes continued.[18]

Leaders like Weekes, Granger, Darbeau, and Nunez insisted that the dominance of European cultural values in Trinidad society was only a reflection of the fact that the economy was controlled by the 'white power structure'. 'It is easy', declared Darbeau,

> to see the effects of this mental colonization in the way we dress. Our whole life-style in fact attests to the thoroughness of the brainwashing. We suffer these problems because no serious attempt has been made to transform the colonial economy.[19]

Values have been twisted by colonialism, they argued; the people have been taught a preference for things imported. 'To be modern', observed V. S. Naipaul, 'is to ignore local products and to use those advertised in American magazines.'[20] Trollope had made a similar complaint about Jamaica one hundred years earlier: 'But it is to be remarked all through the island that the people are fond of English dishes, and that they despise, or affect to despise, their own productions.'[21] Black government, the leaders of the movement insisted, is different from black power;

political decisions are dictated by economic pressure groups, 'so that our own government is no more than devoted puppets of the white foreign capitalist bastards and local white capitalists.'[22] The movement directed much of its fire against the black middle classes – 'Afro-Saxons' as they were sometimes called – who had adopted white values, and had accommodated themselves to a system which involves the exploitation of the mass of black people in the interest of the whites. No significant change could take place in society while these 'black whites' continued to hold local power.

The radicals in the movement rejected the political system which they believed to be a mere reflection of the economic situation. 'We regard Her Majesty the Queen, Her Government, Princess Alice, Her Dukes and Lords', wrote Granger, 'as nothing more than monkeys on our back.'[23] Statues of colonial governors – thieves and pirates – should be removed from public places, and highways should be renamed. They rejected the idea of forming a political party and attempting to attain political power through constitutional means; a third party is 'a third fraud'.[24] There is 'too much government', declared Granger, 'Too many damn Ministers, junior Ministers, Senators, Representatives, City Councillors, County Councillors, Village Councillors, not to mention Boards, Committees and Political Parties.'[25] Minor reforms, like the institution of an ombudsman, the declaration of a republic, or the presence of new men in the cabinet, will not succeed in ending the corruption in the country: 'Nothing but a complete change of the system, of our way of life, could end this corruption.'[26] The NJAC's journal, *Liberation*, published in June 1970, declared that the association has 'rejected the contemporary political system including elections and party politics'. Like Rousseau,[27] they attacked a system in which 'professional politicians come to the people once in five years to beg for another five year term'. 'The interim is spent,' they add, 'in a round of cocktail parties selling out to the enemies of the people.'[28] The system of parliamentary democracy does not allow for a participation by the masses and it leads to a divorce between political leaders and their black brothers.[29] The movement was characterised by a populist belief in the possibility and desirability of mass participation in politics. 'Power to the people', was perhaps the favourite slogan of the movement. It is no answer simply to change masters: 'We do not need any masters.'[30] What is more, parliamentary democracy on the

Westminster model reinforces racial divisions in countries like Trinidad and Guyana.[31]

Among certain leaders of the radical wing of the black power movement there was evident a kind of 'Jacobinism': a search for perfection and purity, a refusal to compromise, a determination to create an entirely new society, an absolute rejection of present arrangements:

> Would we not shatter it to bits, and then
> Remould it nearer to the heart's desire?

There is the belief in the purifying effects of violence, not as an end, but as a means to a revolution in values, a view of revolution similar to that of Proudhon, Sorel, and other quasi-anarchist writers. 'Revolution', they write,

is the fundamental structural change brought about by a *conscious* effort to effect *necessary* change. . . . Blackman who is conscious realizes that in *revolution there can be no compromise.* Compromise has resulted in the evolutionist, the reformist and the liberals betraying basic principles, so that confrontation with the white power structure may be avoided.[32]

The more radical of the leaders saw the necessity for a confrontation with the government and with the whole establishment. 'This is war', cried Granger, in Woodford Square, 'We are going to show them that the will of the people is the will of God.'[33]

Another characteristic feature of anarchist theory was present in the movement; there was a call for individual self-discipline, and at times a somewhat puritanical rejection of luxury. 'We must buy the minimum of clothes,' wrote Brother Damla, 'and forget all luxuries. We must forget that there are places with sweet jerseys and fancy pants.'[34] Granger advised his hearers to abstain during the crisis from dancing and rum drinking and from anything that is not absolutely necessary, while Darbeau urged his readers to engage in soul searching and self examination: 'New faces in office tomorrow will not change the situation. If we examine our own lives, we will understand why. Day after day we betray the same values for which we criticize the current stooges in office.'[35] One of the 'seven pillars' of UMROBI states: 'that constant self-analysis is to be the basis of strength'.

Religious institutions in the country, particularly the Roman

Catholic church, were attacked as bolstering up the white power structure and as perpetuating white values. The Roman Catholic church is the largest and most powerful religious body in the country, and it has been more or less controlled by Irish Dominican priests, and white Trinidadian laymen. In 1968 a Trinidadian was appointed archbishop; he comes from a well-known family and is of predominantly European descent. In 1970 the Anglican church elected a black bishop, though it too, until recently has been dominated by European clergy. In the Presbyterian church, Canadians have played a leading role. 'The Catholic Church', declared *Vanguard*, 'is the supreme embodiment of all that is distorted in our value system.'[36] According to many leaders of the movement the church has taught the black man to worship white values, and meekly to accept the oppressive system which holds him down: 'Blessed are the meek, says the white priest to their black flock, for they shall inherit the earth. Yet the wealth of the earth belongs to the violent whites who retain it by greater violence.'[37] Other black power leaders insisted that Jesus was himself a revolutionary 'outsider', and that, 'When the Church returns to its original function of being a movement for the oppressed masses we will be able to accept it as an integral part of a new society.'[38]

As we have already noticed, symbols rather than ideology united the movement; but most of the symbols were associated with African or with American negro traditions. Almost all the leaders of the movement were, however, committed to the idea of Afro-Indian unity, and to an interpretation of black power which could include the Indian masses. As early as April 1969, an NJAC statement had included Indians among 'black people'.[39] This position was reiterated many times during the early months of 1970: black people are all the oppressed people of the third world. The movement went on to exclude 'black-skinned persons who treasure white values . . . who behave white', such men are not be accounted 'black brothers', for they are traitors to the black man.[40] Other writers from the black power movement, however, sometimes used the term 'black' to mean African. Aldwyn Primus, of the Black Panthers, tended towards this interpretation.[41] Three other writers in 1968, discussing the relevance of the black power movement to the West Indies, clearly interpreted black power to mean Afro-power. 'Black power', they wrote, 'amounts to Negritude with socio-economic and political dimensions.'[42] The possibility of Indian participation is something of an after-thought. 'Black power in the West Indies', they maintained, 'will lead directly to a reassertion of the positive qualities of the African element in the population, and indirectly, by its search for new cultural norms in a multi-racial community, to the assertion of Asiatic values as well.'[43] Black consciousness and Afro-Carib consciousness are clearly believed to be more or less the same thing.[44] Nevertheless, during the early months of 1970, Afro-Indian unity was the avowed concern of the black power leadership. Murray himself, one of the three writers quoted above, saw the Caroni march as 'a gesture of unity with the Indian' on the part of the African youth.[45]

Although the leadership was fairly united on this matter, it was not unusual for the rank and file to treat Indians with a certain degree of suspicion, if they tried to associate with the movement. One Indian carrying a banner which called for: 'Power to the black man', had it snatched from him by a negro youth, with the words 'Give me that, you mamaguy yourself'.[46] Incidents of a similar kind could be recounted.

INDIAN REACTIONS

As might be expected, the Indian community reacted in a number of different ways to the black power movement. Many of the values of the movement were different from those which most Indians had come to accept, and the symbolism did not make them feel at home. Discussions of racial and national characteristics can often be misleading, but may contain elements of truth. The Indians in Trinidad are generally believed to be socially conservative, to place a considerable emphasis upon the importance of political stability, and on the protection of property; individual initiative is admired, and it is generally felt that hard work on the part of the individual, supported by his family, ought to be rewarded materially. Nevertheless, it should be remembered also that Indians in Trinidad are perhaps the most depressed racial group, from an economic point of view. The average annual income of an Indian is considerably less than that of a negro, and central Trinidad (inhabited mainly by Indians) has not yet enjoyed the kind of prosperity which has

been evident in the north and in the south since the Second
World War. Thus there is plenty in Trinidad with which Indians
are discontented, but, generally speaking, the black power leaders failed to channel this discontent into the movement.

Almost all middle-class Indians, in the professions and in
business, were totally opposed to black power. Not only was it
seen to be a movement composed predominantly of negroes, but,
much more important, it was clearly advocating sweeping
changes in the social and economic structure of the country, and
thus challenging the privileged position which they held. Their
reaction to the movement was very much the same as that of
other bourgeois racial groups: French creole, Portuguese, English, Chinese, Syrian, and negro.[47] As we have already noted, B.
S. Maraj and those associated with him were also actively
opposed to the black power movement, though for different
reasons. Its call to working-class Indians in the sugar belt to join
with the poor negroes in the towns threatened the very basis of
his power. The movement was claiming that racial and religious
loyalties (which Maraj and others have been able to exploit in
the past) are less important than the economic exploitation
which these rural Indians suffer together with the African poor.

The majority of Indians looked with a certain detachment and
with some suspicion upon what was going on. They saw a
confrontation between the black power movement and the government as an affair which concerned negroes. The demonstrators were negro, the police were negro. 'Let these bloody niggers
kill each other off' was the sentiment expressed to me by a group
of young Indians who were discussing the movement at the back
of a hindu temple in Tacarigua. These Indians were apprehen-
sive about the long-term aims of the movement. One Indian
student put it as follows:

> Let the Black Power advocates take control . . . Then what are
> we going to have?. . . . White capitalists kicked out, Chinese
> kicked out, Syrian capitalists kicked out! Who is going to
> follow next? The Indians of course.[48]

Other Indians insisted that they do not consider themselves
'black', they 'do not feel the negro stigma of blackness'.[49] An
Indian writer as sympathetic to the black power movement as
Brinsley Samaroo, agreed that Indians 'do not regard them-

selves as black'.[50] Samaroo (a university lecturer) together with a number of the Indian students from UWI, accepted many of the aims of the black power movement, and associated themselves with it at certain points, without committing themselves totally to it. As has already been noted, many of these students prepared the way for the Caroni march of 12 March, and also took part in the demonstration. Yet they were critical of certain aspects of the movement, and obviously did not feel themselves to be fully involved.

The response of the DLP – the main opposition party – was ambivalent. The party, which was predominantly Indian in composition, had been divided for some months. A minority of the old DLP in the house of representatives seemed to accept the leadership of Maraj, while the majority recognised Vernon Jamadar as leader. This majority group issued a number of statements during the crisis, which were moderate in tone, and which recognised the right of people to make demonstrations of protest against the government. They called for dialogue with black power leaders: 'This is not the time to quiet dissent by a display of force. We wish to advise the protestors that disciplined peaceful demonstrations will achieve their object.'[51] Most of the black power leaders were not, however, interested in dialogue with the traditional political parties, and this applied quite as much to the opposition parties as to the PNM. Even the Tapia House Group, led by Lloyd Best, which affects a certain radical posture, was spurned by the movement: 'Best and Co. are so far away from the masses that they do not see that it will take more than a dictionary to bridge the gap.'[52] The nearest the DLP came to associating with the black power movement was a rather timid clenched fist salute given by the acting leader of the party as he walked out of the house of representatives on Friday 13 March 1970.

There were a small number of Indians who actively associated with the black power movement. These were lead by Chan Maharaj, a relation of veteran politician Stephen Maharaj. His organisation, known as the National Freedom Organization, centred at Arouca, took part in most of the major demonstrations, while Maharaj himself appeared regularly on the platform alongside NJAC speakers. He was particularly prominent in the march to San Juan, and attacked the position taken by Bhadase Maraj:

It seems to me that Mr. Maraj does not really understand the
Black Power struggle that is now going on. . . . I must make it
clear to him that the fight is not an African against Indian. It
is a fight against exploitation and political oppression upon
the black people of Trinidad. . . . It seems to me that is the
only way for many politicians to remain in power – division of
the races.[53]

Maharaj, however, spoke for only a small minority of Indians,
though it is possible that this number would have grown if the
black power movement had not been cut short by the state of
emergency. The Caroni march had certainly made an impression upon Indian opinion, and there was the real possibility of an
alliance between the sugar workers and some of the urban trade
unions in connection with the Brechin Castle strike of 19–21
April; it is likely that the possibility of such an alliance convinced
Williams that he should have a state of emergency proclaimed
when he did.

Certainly the failure of the black power movement to engage
the active support of large numbers of Indians was one of the
causes of its downfall. If it had been able to rely upon support
from the masses of Indians from its inception, it would have
presented an even more serious challenge to the government
than it did. Nevertheless, this was not the main reason for the
government's survival. The immediate salvation of the government, in the face of the army revolt, was due to the loyalty of the
coastguards and of the police. An equally important factor was
the support given to the government by the large group of
middle-class Trinidadians, and by a considerable section of the
urban working class. One of the factors which the black power
movement seems to have underestimated was the role of the
working class. Most urban workers with regular jobs were not
prepared to support a movement which might have put their
jobs in danger. When the state of emergency was declared, very
few workers came out on strike, and dock workers even organised their own 'police' force to guard the docks. Many workers
joined the volunteer police force during the early days of the
state of emergency.

The black power movement cannot, then, satisfactorily be
understood simply in terms of class or race. There was certainly
a strong racial component. Much of the rhetoric of the leaders

was directed against 'white capitalist bastards', but the immediate objects of their wrath were the government and the Trinidad middle class, most of whom were black. Although the radical white undergraduate would not have been quite at home in the demonstrations of February to April 1970, it would have been his class more than his colour which would have made him unacceptable. One young man who was prominent in a number of the demonstrations, carrying a flag or a banner, was of predominantly European origin, with fair hair and light complexion; but he was completely accepted, as he came from a poor family, and had shared the hardships of bad housing and unemployment with his black brothers. If the demonstrators came across someone in a collar, tie, and jacket, he was seen as an enemy, whatever the colour of his face. (Was not Stokeley Carmichael greeted in Guyana with cries of 'take off your tie'?) And yet it was not simply a class affair. *Vanguard* was misrepresenting the situation when it saw the crisis, in marxist terms, as 'a confrontation between the bourgeoise [*sic*] and the masses'.[54] We have already seen that large sections of the labour movement supported the government throughout, and to say that these people *must* have been bourgeois at heart, is only to turn *Vanguard's* assertion into a tautology. If we must use marxist terminology, the movement is more accurately to be seen as a rising of the *lumpenproletariat* – though this represents only part of the truth.

V. S. Naipaul concludes his chapter on Trinidad in *The Middle Passage* (first published in 1962) with some prophetic observations:

Some weeks after the news of Lumumba's death I came upon a procession in one of the main streets of Port of Spain. It was an orderly procession made up wholly of Negroes. They were singing hymns, which contrasted with the violence of their banners and placards. These were anti-white, anti-clerical and pro-African in an ill-defined, inclusive way. I had never before seen anything like it in Trinidad. . . . I thought then that it was a purely local eruption, created by the pressures of local politics. But soon, on the journey I was now getting ready to make, I came to see that such eruptions were widespread, and represented feelings coming to the surface in Negro communities throughout the Caribbean: confused feelings, without direction; the Negro's rejection of the guilt he has borne for so long; the last, delayed Spartacan revolt, more radical than Toussaint L'Ouverture's; the closing of accounts this side of the middle passage.[55]

Part III
Economy

5 Economic Dependence and Political Autonomy, 1804–1915

By the solemn declaration of independence on January 1 1804, Haiti became the first post-colonial state of Latin America. The black and coloured generals assembled in Gonaïves declared their determination to 'renounce France for ever and to die rather than to live under her domination'. One of the problems facing the new government was how to secure and maintain an *effective* independence. There are certain social factors which might be said to be necessary conditions of such a real political independence or at least conditions, the absence of which will seriously frustrate this objective. Among the most obvious are the development of an indigenous culture and the formation of a national economy. In this chapter I shall consider the concern of Haitian politicians and publicists with the economic conditions necessary for political autonomy.

*** ***

AUTARKY AND ECONOMY

The concept of national autonomy is in certain respects similar to that of individual liberty.[1] Just as liberty can meaningfully be discussed only in the context of particular situations, so national autonomy makes sense only in relation to concrete factors which limit or might limit the possible courses of action open to a state. Although we might properly assert that an individual is freer than another (insofar as there are more courses of action open to

83

him in a given situation than to his fellow) or that a particular
individual is freer now than he was previously (insofar as all the
courses of action which were previously open to him are still
open, and more), it is difficult to conceive of what might be
meant by asserting that an individual is totally free. Similarly,
for a nation to be absolutely autonomous, it would be necessary
for that nation to have no relationships with any external body,
for all relationships constitute some kind of restriction upon
national autonomy as they do upon individual liberty. Autonomy, like liberty, is a matter of degree.

Many political thinkers have argued that a satisfactory degree
of national autonomy implies a considerable measure of economic independence. Some have gone further and have suggested
that economic self-sufficiency is a necessary condition of such
economic independence. Aristotle stated that the *polis* should be
of such a size as to permit *autarkeia*; a good state is one which is
culturally and economically self-sufficient. Thomas Aquinas
agreed that a city that is able to satisfy all its vital needs is more
dignified than one that is economically dependent upon its
neighbours. This theme of autarky was particularly evident in
the writings of the German romantic nationalists of the early
nineteenth century. Hegel characterised autonomous states as
'units whose needs are met within their own borders', while
Fichte wrote a treatise on *The Closed Commercial State*. In all these
cases it is significant to note that the notion of the ideal political
unit is closely related to the current conceptions of God, whose
perfection is thought to involve self-sufficiency.[2]

Contemporary nationalist writers from Latin America and the
Caribbean, though not all accepting the ideal of autarky, insist
that their countries must move significantly in the direction of
economic independence if political independence is to be more
than an empty symbol. Many of these countries have received
the formal trappings of political independence while remaining
economically dependent upon a former metropolis, or having
liberated themselves from the grip of one master find themselves
economic thralls of another. Of modern radicals in Jamaica, Rex
Nettleford writes 'In their eyes the gains of political independence are all but negated by the economic satellisation of the
country by North America'.[3] As we have seen, the leaders of the
Trinidad black power movement agreed.

INDEPENDENCE AND ECONOMY: THE PROBLEMS

When Haiti achieved political independence in 1804, certain positive steps were taken in the direction of economic independence. Land belonging to former colonists was nationalised, and the government attempted to control foreign trade, to protect local industry and to diversify agriculture. Nevertheless, as the nineteenth century proceeded, foreign economic involvement in Haiti increased and the United States occupation from 1915 to 1934 carried forward in a more radical manner tendencies which had long been evident. Since the assassination of Jean-Jacques Dessalines, the first head of state, in October 1806, the ruling groups in the country have been unwilling to take steps necessary for maintaining national autonomy, frequently preferring to invite foreign intervention rather than allowing their opponents to gain power. The way in which the idea of race provided much of the inspiration and incentive for a true autonomy, while deep social divisions closely related to colour led to continual erosions of this autonomy, is the theme of a recent book.[4]

Many Haitian writers have put forward theories and ideas about the nature of their country's under-development and dependence and it is quite wrong to think, with A. O. Hirschman, that there were no 'indigenous theories, ideas or views' about the nature of Latin America's relative economic stagnation in the nineteenth century. Although Haitian writers of the period often adapted economic theories originating in Europe, they did so as a response to their post-colonial experience and their ideas can in this sense be called 'indigenous'.[5]

Throughout the nineteenth century there were three key issues of economic policy that concerned Haitian publicists and politicians. The first was the question of land tenure, the second was the desirability of attracting foreign capital and encouraging or permitting foreign immigration, and the third was the role which the state can and should play in the process of economic development. The three subjects are, of course, closely related.

With respect to the first, there was disagreement in the early years on whether it should be the object of the government to maintain or restore the plantation system of agriculture which had prevailed in the colonial period. By the end of Boyer's presidency this issue was effectively settled; with some notable exceptions plantation agriculture had declined and only half-hearted attempts were made to restore it after 1843. A further issue in connection with land tenure was the constitutional article prohibiting the foreign ownership of land. The desirability of this provision was a matter of almost continuous debate throughout the century, though the change was not formally effected until after the US invasion.

Closely akin to the question of the foreign ownership of land was the debate on the need for foreign capital in order to achieve economic development. Many of those who advocated the encouragement of foreign investment were, for obvious reasons, outspoken in their demands for repealing the prohibition of the foreign ownership of land. It was argued that without the legal guarantee provided by ownership, foreigners would be unwilling to risk capital investment in industry or in infrastructural enterprise. A cognate issue was that of immigration. In the early years there was the proposal that indentured labourers should be imported to maintain plantation agriculture, while towards the end of the century and up to the US invasion there was considerable controversy centred on the arrival of large numbers of Levantine migrants.

The third issue of economic policy that absorbed the attention of Haitians in the period was the proper role of the government in regulating or encouraging economic activity. In the years following independence it was mainly a question of whether the government should prohibit or control imports in order to encourage local products. Later on however, politicians and theorists debated such questions as whether the government's proper role included the founding of agricultural banks and whether the government should actively participate in industrial development, either on its own or in collaboration with private investors.

The US invasion of 1915 put an end to the possibility of economic independence or political autonomy. While the façade of political independence was maintained, under a client president, there was little attempt to disguise the fact that all effective decisions were taken by the US administration. The occupation did, however, lead to a nationalist revival. The patriotic movements united Haitians of different colours and classes in a common determination to rid the country of 'les blancs'. Since 1930 Haitian governments have paid lip service to ideas of economic nationalism, but little has been done to restrict the activities of foreign companies operating in the country. Recent developments have, if anything, increased Haiti's dependence without stimulating significant economic growth.

THE COLONIAL ECONOMY

The French colony of Saint-Domingue was the most profitable European colony in the latter part of the eighteenth century. Its principal *raison d'être* as a colony was to supply France with those tropical products – sugar, coffee, cotton, indigo – which could not easily be cultivated in Europe. The economic life of the colony was in fact a mere appendage to that of the metropolis. The agricultural system was entirely geared to supplying the French market, while most of the food, clothing and luxury items were imported from France. Strict control was maintained by France over the commerce of Saint-Domingue and harsh penalties were prescribed for those who infringed the laws prohibiting colonials from engaging in foreign commerce.

By the end of the eighteenth century the indigenous Indian population had practically died out or had been killed off, and the colony was populated largely by immigrants (voluntary or involuntary) or by first or second generation descendants of such immigrants, known as *créoles*. As we have noted in a previous chapter, the slaves outnumbered the whites by more than ten to one, with an intermediate 'caste' of free coloureds somewhat less numerous than the whites. Many of the plantations were owned by men who in no sense thought of themselves as belonging to Saint-Domingue; the ambition of these men was to return to France with the fortune they had made in the colony. There was little conception of Saint-Domingue as having an interest of its own, distinct from that of France. The colonial whites had, as a result, little loyalty towards the territory, recognising a common interest as planters or merchants but not as Saint-Dominguois. This is not, however, to say that they did not resent certain aspects of metropolitan control nor seek a degree of autonomy for the colony.[6]

The attitude of the free coloured, or *affranchis*, as they were called, was different. Saint-Domingue was their home and it should not be forgotten that perhaps a quarter of the properties were owned by the free coloureds. Many of the *créole* slaves also thought of Saint-Domingue as their home, though in general the *bossal* slaves (those born in Africa), like the whites, saw Saint-Domingue as a place of sojourn; their home was Africa.

It is impossible to trace here the course of the revolution in Saint-Domingue which commenced in 1789, following events in Paris, and which culminated in the declaration of independence thirteen years later. These years of violent struggle, which involved all sections of the colonial population as well as French, British and Spanish troops, destroyed much of the agriculture. Sugar mills, plantation houses and irrigation systems were ruined; many owners and managers fled and newly liberated slaves began to squat on vacant land. The new government under Dessalines was faced with a formidable task.

* * *   * * *

INDEPENDENCE AND ECONOMIC POLICY: THE EARLY YEARS

It soon became clear that political independence, if it was to be effective, had implications in the economic sphere. In fact Toussaint Louverture had already modified the commercial policy of the colony during the period when he was governor-general under the semi-autonomous constitution of 1801. In particular he had been eager to develop trading relations with Britain and the USA, thereby reducing economic dependence on France.

Jean-Jacques Dessalines became the first head of state and was soon named emperor. He was a black former slave and was concerned to defend the interests of the mass of predominantly black *nouveaux libres* against the pretentions of the predominantly mulatto *anciens libres*. He opposed the latter in their attempts to seize vacant properties, particularly in the South, and was assassinated in October 1806 partly as a result of such policies. The country split into two parts: the northern state (which became a kingdom in 1811) was ruled by Henry Christophe, while the South and West became a republic presided over by Alexandre Pétion. For a short period the South under André Rigaud seceded to form a third state and for the whole period the region of La Grand'Anse formed an autonomous region. On the death of Pétion in 1818 Jean-Pierre Boyer succeeded to power in the republic, and after the suicide of Christophe two years later Haiti was once more united.

TRADE AND COMMERCE

With the declaration of independence, French property was confiscated. Furthermore the imperial constitution of May 1805 stated categorically that 'no white man (*aucun blanc*), whatever his nationality, can set foot on this territory as master or proprietor, and is unable in the future to acquire any property'. This constitutional provision formalised the situation which had existed for over a year; in fact in August 1803 Dessalines had made it clear to the British that after independence land ownership would be restricted to nationals and that whites would be confined to the towns.[7]

Despite his prohibition of foreign ownership, Dessalines fully realised the importance of foreign trade and encouraged the overtures made by British and United States agents. General George Nugent, governor of Jamaica, opened negotiations with the black general early in 1804, seeking a commercial agreement. His messages were conveyed by Captain Perkins, a Jamaican mulatto officer, who was well-known in Haiti. The Americans were not slow in following the lead of the British and their envoy arrived in Gonaïves at the begining of September in the same year. During the first two years of independence, the USA was Haiti's most important trading partner and one Haitian, writing anonymously in the official *Gazette*, warned against the danger of United States imperialism. Owing to its proximity, as well as to the frequent visits of its citizens to the ports of the empire and to 'the pretentions to which these might give birth', the USA, he warned, might in the future be a greater threat to Haitian independence than were the countries of Europe. Because of pressure from the French government, however, whose diplomatic support the Americans needed in their dispute with Spain over the details of the Louisiana purchase, an embargo was placed by the US government on commerce with Haiti in February 1806.[8]

When it was suggested to Dessalines that the fierce policy he pursued towards the former French colonists would jeopardise his trade relations with other white countries, the emperor replied: 'Such a man does not know the whites. Hang a white man below one of the pans in the scales of the custom house, and put a sack of coffee in the other pan; the other whites will buy the coffee without paying attention to the body of their fellow white man.'[9] The imperial constitution proclaimed commerce to be, after agriculture, a principal source of wealth, and guaranteed protection to foreign merchants. Yet commerce was closely controlled. In November 1805 the government 'wishing to assure exclusively to Haitian speculators the benefits resulting from the exploitation of salt', and 'desiring to favour the prosperity of this branch of internal commerce' forbade the importation of salt.[10] According to the law, captains of ships were forbidden to sell retail, and goods could be imported only by licensed merchants. By a decree of 2 September 1806, Dessalines imposed a 10 per cent tax on all imported goods and, in an attempt to raise further revenue, set a tax on exports of coffee and other goods.[11] This policy was attacked by the group which assassinated the emperor in October 1806.

After the death of Dessalines, Henry Christophe was proclaimed provisional president, but the constitution under which he would have had to operate was not at all to his liking. In particular, the powers of the president were too narrowly circumscribed. From 1806 until 1820, Haiti was split into two hostile states, the North under Christophe and the South and West under Alexandre Pétion. The republican constitution of December 1806 retained Dessalines's famous prohibition of foreign ownership. Many republican spokesmen were eager to maintain this prohibition which Hérard Dumesle referred to as '*le boulevard de notre indépendance*'.[12] Guy-Joseph Bonnet also had argued that Haiti must continue to restrict the ownership of land to nationals as long as the country remained economically weak and industrially backward.[13] At the same time the republican government encouraged exports by modifying the duty on coffee and other products which had been imposed by Dessalines. The assassins of the emperor, in their manifesto of 16 October 1806, attacked the commercial policy of 'this stupid man', and the new senate urged foreign merchants to 'continue coming without fear to find in our ports those goods which your climate denies you, giving us in exchange the fruits of your industry'.[14] In February 1807, a senate decree promised to protect foreign comercial property and to maintain public order[15] and, in the following

April, Louis Auguste Daumec, in his report to the senate, referred to the moral benefits of trade, arguing that it is by commerce that 'ferocious people have become mild and humane'.[16] Foreign merchants, although allowed to establish premises in the republic, were restricted to certain specified ports and were forbidden to operate in the interior.

Christophe went even further in the direction of encouraging foreign trade, issuing a proclamation on 24 November 1806 which abolished all restrictions and all exclusive concessions in foreign commerce which had been introduced by the emperor. 'Each will be free to sell and buy on the conditions which he believes to be the most advantageous.'[17] He stated that all the energies of the country were being turned towards the production of goods for export.[18] The policy of the northern state in its early years was thus one of free trade, and the encouragement of foreign speculators. Quite soon, however, the policy was modified and Christophe introduced a tax on imported white sugar, in order 'to encourage national manufactures' and to give to the sugar industry 'all the protection possible'.[19] The 1807 constitution of the northern state omitted the prohibition of white ownership of land, and included an article which had the opposite effect: 'The government solemnly guarantees to foreign merchants the security of their persons and their property, and assures them of the most effective protection.' (article 41) Leading spokesmen of the northern state, like Baron de Vastey, attacked the republic for its prohibition of foreign ownership of land, stating that this article was 'unjust, impolitic and contrary to the laws of polished nations'. The northern kingdom, he continued, forbade *French* ownership because France was still at war with the Haitian people, but he believed that foreign immigration and investment were in the interests of the country.[20] In fact, Thomas Clarkson found it necessary to warn King Henry against foreign penetration of the country, suggesting that the right of foreigners to own property should be restricted to the trading cities of the coast.[21]

A growing number of merchants, many of them British, had established themselves in the principal cities of the republic and of the northern state. The Comte de Limonade, foreign secretary of the kingdom, stated that foreign merchants who respected the laws of the kingdom would be welcome.[22] These merchants looked forward to the occasional visits of Sir Home Popham and his British warships to Cap Henry (Cap Haïtien), visits which, according to W. W. Harvey, not only 'served . . . to produce in the minds of the natives a favourable impression towards the whites, they also tended to ensure a continuance of their peaceable and respectful behaviour'. More importantly, they facilitated the efforts of these merchants to recover debts owed to them by local residents.[23] Throughout the century, Haitian ports were host, often unwillingly, to similar visits from foreign fleets which rarely failed to produce an impression, though not always a favourable one.

Owing partly to US and French embargo on trade with Haiti, the British achieved a near monopoly of Haitian commerce. A British order in council of 14 December 1808 had authorised trade with both the northern state and with the republic. By 1814 the British were in a strong enough position to persuade Pétion to reduce import duties on British goods from 10 per cent to 5 per cent.[24] J. B. Inginac took credit for this reduction in duty, claiming that it had had a lasting and beneficial result for Haiti.[25] In July 1817 the senate confirmed this privileged position of British goods, in spite of US pressure. Most of the foreign commercial houses of the republic were by this time British.

THE PLANTATION SYSTEM

While the politicians of the republic and of the kingdom recognised the importance of foreign commerce at least in the short run, changes were taking place which would have a crucial effect upon the nature and extent of external trade in the future. The end of slavery and the resistance to forced labour on the part of the population led to a gradual break-up of the plantation system. There was on the part of the former slave population an understandable dislike of labouring on large plantations, even if these were owned by the state or by black and coloured proprietors.

Toussaint and Dessalines had attempted to maintain the large plantations intact and were able to exercise sufficient compulsion to ensure that enough labourers remained on the estates to keep them going. In an ordinance of October 1804 the emperor deplored the movement into the towns, pointing to the fact that the growing urban sub-proletariat would constitute a politically 'dangerous' group; he proposed a census of the population and decreed a limit on the number of servants an urban household could employ.[26] Other Haitians had opted for emigration; Dessalines imposed ten months imprisonment on captains of foreign ships found carrying such fugitives and the death penalty on the would-be emigrants themselves. With the emperor's death and the dividing of the country, the governments of Haiti were faced with a choice between employing forced labour and breaking up the old estates. On 31 March 1807 a law was passed in Christophe's northern state which provided for the sale of land to the people, though this law was not put into effect for more than ten years owing to 'important circumstances', which were not specified.[27] Only a few days later, the republic began to enact legislation which was to result in the granting and sale of state land.

The idea of breaking up the old plantations and distributing the land in smaller lots goes back to Polvérel's proclamation of 27 August 1793. Not only was emancipation decreed, but there was also provision for dividing vacant plantations and conquered Spanish land among the newly liberated slaves.[28] The republican law of 20 April 1807 was designed to prevent the creation of small peasant properties by prohibiting the sale of estates smaller than ten *carreaux* (about 13 hectares), except in the case of the enlargement of already existing plantations. By a decree of December 1809, however, Pétion made grants of land to retired soldiers ranging from five *carreaux* for privates to 25 *carreaux* for colonels. Further laws were passed from 1811 onwards providing for the distribution of land to military officers and to civil servants. During the presidency of Pétion, over 150 000 hectares were distributed or sold to more than 10 000 persons.[29] Certainly the principal beneficiaries were the (predominantly mulatto) officers of the republican army, but the land reform represented a radical departure from the plantation system.

Pétion's proposals for land distribution met with considerable opposition in the senate. Bonnet believed that they opened the way to even further fragmentations, and viewed with alarm the consequent decline in the production and export of sugar.[30] The precise reason for Pétion's insistence on land reform is a matter of dispute, but is almost certainly more complicated than the president and his supporters suggested. Pétion himself argued that a growth in the number of proprietors would strengthen the state.[31] Lepelletier de Saint Rémy put the position somewhat differently, stating that Pétion found it necessary to create a group of grateful dependents and also, by means of these reforms, to 'assure the supremacy of his caste over that of the blacks'.[32] Jean Price Mars and Leslie Manigat have in more recent years developed these arguments.[33] The widely accepted view that Pétion effected a 'democratisation' of land tenure and that 'plantations disappeared' needs challenging. A number of larger estates were handed over to high ranking military officers who spent much of their time supervising them. General Marion, for example, the commandant of the *arrondissement* of Les Cayes was frequently absent for considerable periods; though claiming to be on government business in Port-au-Prince, it was well known that he was in fact engaged in supervising 'a part of his immense estates'. The French consul estimated that his annual income was at least 600 000 francs and that Borgella was even richer.[34]

If the break-up of many of the large plantations was to some extent a natural and unintended consequence of the ending of slavery and the difficulty of imposing forced labour, it was also a deliberate policy on the part of certain politicians in the two states. Baron de Vastey, for example, who was in charge of agricultural policy in the kingdom for many years, insisted that the country should aim to achieve self-sufficiency in foodstuffs, moving away from an exclusive concern with 'colonial productions' to a situation where agriculture is divided between objects of subsistence and trade. He argued that 'a nation must be able to supply herself with everything she principally wants. If she depends for subsistence on foreign markets, she has no more her independence in her own hands.'[35] Colonialism which had been based on exploitation, first of gold, then of sugar and coffee, was a thing of the past, and should no longer dominate the economy of the country.[36] Pétion also urged the peasants to grow subsistence crops, particularly those which could be conserved,[37] although his successor became alarmed at the number of workers who had left the plantations, and at the consequent decline in the production of export crops.

In his 1819 circular *Pour la répression du vagabondage*, Boyer urged that more emphasis be placed upon the production of sugar, coffee, and cotton,[38] and later he drew attention to 'the pernicious custom which many people have contracted of abandoning work on estates and devoting themselves to cutting wood which does not belong to them'.[39] A foreigner who visited Haiti from 1818 to 1819 also observed how the growth in small properties had led to a clearing of land, particularly on the mountain sides.[40] The government's concern about the falling number of agricultural labourers, and the growth of squatting is reflected in the infamous Rural Code of 1826, which attempted to tie labourers to the estates on which they were currently working, and to re-establish the semi-feudal system of labour relations which had been introduced by Toussaint Louverture. The injunctions of religion were invoked by Boyer to condemn indolence and laziness, vices which were encouraged by the colonial oppressors in order that they might better subjugate the population.[41]

* * *   * * *

CONTROVERSIES IN THE BOYER ERA

At Pétion's death in 1818, Jean-Pierre Boyer became life president; with the death of Christophe in 1820 and the subjugation of La Grand'Anse in the previous year, the whole of the western part of the island was united under one government. Boyer marched into the Spanish part of the island in 1822, and ruled over the whole of Hispaniola until he was removed from office by the revolution of 1843. In the early part of this period, Boyer's efforts were mainly directed towards securing the full legal recognition of Haitian independence by the great powers. He made it clear to the United States government that any significant development in commercial relations between the two countries depended upon recognition. British goods imported in US ships were no longer to benefit from reduced tariffs, and there was a general rise in import duties in 1819. British recognition of some of the newly independent states of Latin America, and her continued refusal to recognise Haiti resulted in 1825 in the end of Britain's privileged commercial position in Haiti. Boyer ascribed foreign hostility towards Haiti and the refusal to invite Haiti to the Panama Congress of 1825 to 'the absurd prejudice resulting from colour differences'. The president was undoubtedly right in his assessment of foreign motives.[42] Trade with the USA had by 1820 recovered somewhat, and the black republic was importing such commodities as salt fish, meat, flour, rice and tobacco from the USA. Imports from Britain consisted principally of manufactured goods, particularly fabrics, while the French supplied luxury items like wine, liqueurs and perfumes. During the 1820s, however, imports from the USA fell from $2 270 601 in 1820 to $823 178 in 1830; this was due partly to an increase of Haitian trade with France following French recognition of Haitian independence in 1825. Exports to the United States also declined in this decade, though not to the same extent.[43]

After the fall of Napoleon in 1814, the restored royalist government in France had begun to seek a settlement with the former colony of Saint-Domingue. Pétion and Christophe were both absolutely firm in rejecting anything less than a recognition of full independence.[44] The former was, however, willing to pay an indemnity to the dispossessed French planters, and also to sign a trade agreement which would give preference to French goods. Pétion wrote to the French agent: 'I propose to Your Excellency . . . to establish the bases of an agreed indemnity which we shall solemnly engage to pay, accompanied by any just guarantee that may be required of us.'[45] No agreement was reached in 1814, and two years later another delegation arrived in the Caribbean, headed by Vicomte Fontanges and Charles Esmangart. Again they received the same reply. Esmangart was convinced that the political independence of Haiti would have to be recognised, but pointed out to the French government that a treaty could be negotiated which would restore economic and commercial dominance to the former metropolis.[46] Another agent was sent from France, and in 1823 Boyer sent a representative to Europe for discussions with Esmangart. Eventually agreement was reached. Haiti was to pay an indemnity of 150 million francs to the dispossessed planters, and although her ports were to be open to vessels of all nations, customs charges on French ships would be half those paid by ships of other nations. 'On these conditions,' declared the French king, 'we concede by this ordinance to the present inhabitants of the French portion of Saint-Domingue the full and complete independence of their government.'[47]

These terms, which after some initial objections were accepted by the Haitian government, had important consequences. In the first place, they opened the way to French domination of the commerce of Haiti for half a century; secondly, they placed heavy financial burdens round the neck of the black republic. Attempts to raise the money from Haitian farmers and business-men met with resistance. The French consul in Les Cayes records that only one Haitian commercial house contributed anything significant towards the payment of the debt. In order to pay the first instalment of the indemnity, the Haitian government had to raise a loan in France of 24 million francs. The Haitians found it impossible to pay further instalments, and in 1838 an agreement was reached to reduce the amount payable from the outstanding 120 million to 60 million francs to be paid over a period of thirty years. Haiti had still not repaid the 24 million franc loan of 1825. Boyer's agreement thus landed the country in serious financial involvement with the former metropolis, signifi-cantly limiting her economic independence.[48]

Hostility towards France was almost universal. The French consul in Les Cayes recorded a conversation which he had heard outside his house between a black and a mulatto:

> You are very confident, said the former, because you have there (pointing a finger at my house) *your master who protects you*; but never forget what I am telling you; we, my brothers and I, shall soon put everything in its place: we are the only true children of Haiti.

The consul went on to say how the mulatto in turn accused the black of wishing to hand over the country to the French and concluded that 'France does not have a true friend among the natives of any colour'. The United States consul in Haiti also noted the general antagonism towards France.[49]

Even prior to the indemnity of 1825, and the resulting finan-cial entanglements, there was concern among a certain class in Haiti about the activities of foreign businessmen in the country, and the implications which this might have for national auton-omy. In 1820 local merchants had attempted to persuade Boyer to modify the law in such a way as to restrict further the activities of foreign capitalists and middle-men. Boyer received the group 'with that urbanity for which he was well-known', and issued instructions to government officials that the law against foreigners engaging in retail trade be strictly enforced.[50] Local businessmen were still dissatisfied, and in May 1821 they organised themselves into two chambers of commerce, the *Cercle de Commerce Haïtien*, in the capital, and the *Chambre de Commerce National*, in Cap Haïtien.

Later in the same year, a number of speakers in the legislative assembly argued that new restrictions should be imposed upon foreign merchants. Pierre André led the attack and was supported by others. 'Who is there among us,' demanded Jean-Baptiste Nicolas Saint-Martin during the same debate, 'who, since the time of our political independence, has not remarked with sad countenance, that our submission and dependence has been complete in the commercial sphere?' Having chased away the enemy during the revolutionary war, he went on, Haitians were now faced with an invasion of foreign merchants seeking to profit from the wealth of the country. It was nothing less than 'a colonial system of commerce' which was developing. The banner of commercial independence must, he insisted, be raised.[51] A lively debate took place between those who wished the country to pursue a policy of import substitution and those who defended the traditional emphasis upon the export of primary products. There was a significant group in the republic who favoured the latter policy, asserting that Haiti should concentrate on the export of such crops as sugar, coffee, cotton and indigo, and should continue to import cloth, manufactures, machinery and luxury goods from abroad.[52]

The government was basically committed to preserving what was left of the plantation system, as is clear from the provisions of the Rural Code. Nevertheless Boyer also attempted to satisfy the economic nationalists. A law of 1825 reasserted the principle that the permits necessary for all who wished to trade in the country would cost more to foreigners than to locals. In 1828 he instructed commandants of the *arrondissements* to ensure that enough *vivres* (crops for local consumption) were grown on each plantation to feed the residents.[53] Yet these feeble gestures failed to quieten the demands of his critics who argued for a much more dynamic policy of protection for new industries and for local tradesmen, together with a real move away from dependence on the export of colonial products.

French merchants replied to these arguments, and one of them, Martelly, published a letter from the celebrated French economist J. B. Say, which stated that the economic nationalism advocated by André and Saint-Martin would be detrimental to the prosperity of Haiti. The journal, *Le Propagateur Haïtien*, joined the battle on the side of the economic nationalists. James Franklin, a British businessman resident in the country, suggested that in any case Haiti was becoming an unfruitful field for foreign investment or involvement, and that foreign capitalists would be well advised to avoid investing in the country. According to Franklin, not only was there a declining interest in foreign trade but there was a deliberate attempt by Boyer 'to keep his people ignorant of artificial wants', a prospect which was horrible for the commercial adventurer even to contemplate![54]

The debate about the proper role of foreign capital and about the wisdom of protective tariffs continued throughout the thirties. In 1831 the pro-government journal *Phare* defended the moderate protectionism of Boyer, while the *Feuille de Commerce* called for a more open commercial policy, and a determined effort to attract foreign investment. What, demanded Fruneau, was fettering agricultural development and hindering the establishment of manufacturing industries and commercial houses? The absence of capital. And who is able to supply this want except the foreign investor?[55] In fact, the protectionist policy of the government was not even designed to encourage the growth of local industry, but simply to shield established concerns owned by its supporters from foreign competition. On the other hand, the nationalist writers associated with the journals *L'Union* and *Le Républicain* assailed Boyer for his failure to adopt a dynamic policy of economic development. Just as in the literary field these men wished to encourage the growth of an indigenous tradition, moving away from the francophone orientation of most Haitian literature up to this time, so in the economic field they demanded policies which would free Haiti from excessive dependence upon foreigners. In agriculture, they argued for diversification, so that the country would become self-sufficient in foodstuffs while developing new crops for export.[56] They recognised, however, that any expansion in agriculture was likely to come up against a shortage of labour. One result of Pétion's land reforms had been that agricultural labourers had left the large estates and had settled on their own land. One writer suggested the introduction of indentured labourers from India, along the lines of the scheme which was just beginning in British Guiana. *L'Union* of 30 August 1838 published a letter from Calcutta

Economy

giving details of the indentureship system. These Haitian liberals were even more concerned with industrial development, which they viewed as the key to national prosperity and progress. After all, was it not the industrial genius of Britain which had made her mistress of the modern world?[57] Eugène Nau lamented the fact that Haiti, which was richly endowed with natural resources, should have to rely on foreign nations to supply such simple items as bricks, glassware and pottery. Yet he was full of hope for the future; he saw a new interest in agricultural and industrial growth, and called for the establishment of a development bank which would facilitate the building of factories to produce bricks, essential oils, paper and soap, to supply not only the home market but also the other islands of the Caribbean and even Europe. If this were to occur, Haiti would become 'one day a people powerful and truly independent'; then the country would be respected in the eyes of the world.[58]

THE 1843 REVOLUTION

Opposition to the Boyer regime increased. The most vocal section was led by Hérard Dumesle and David Saint Preux, and was centred in the lower house of the legislature. The chief organ of opposition during the early forties was *Le Manifeste*, which was controlled by Dumai Lespinasse. In 1841 an anonymous article in the journal argued for the retention of the prohibition of the foreign ownership of land in face of increasing pressure to change the law. The constitutional provision was wise 'because, in uprooting the colonial regime and all the evils which followed, it constituted the basis of our nationality'. Opponents of the prohibition were arguing that its repeal would lead to an influx of foreign capital, which was necessary for the revival of agriculture and for industrial development. The anonymous author rejected these arguments, insisting that

> We can then and we must by ourselves progress in civilisation and accumulate capital . . . It is precisely because we have no capital and because our civilisation is backward that this measure (i.e. repeal of the prohibition of white ownership of land) is impracticable in the political circumstances in which we find ourselves and which we shall soon improve.

The author went on to point out that foreign ownership would lead to the gradual absorption of smallholdings into the larger estates which would readily have fallen into foreign hands; the plantation system would return and 'Haiti would once more become in a certain sense a colony, no longer solely of France, but of Europe, and would be the sad theatre of the ambition and rivalry of different peoples.'[59] In 1842 the newspaper attacked the tendency of the French consul to intervene in the internal affairs of Haiti in such strong language that legal action was taken against the author, Dumai Lespinasse.

The group associated with *Le Manifeste* thus strongly supported the revolution of 1843 which overthrew Boyer. The new constitution retained the prohibition on foreign ownership: 'No white man can acquire Haitian nationality nor the right of possessing any landed property in Haiti (article 8).' This principle was, however, being undermined by foreigners marrying Haitians and thereby gaining effective control of property. The black nationalist president Pierrot (1845–6), in an attempt to prevent this means of circumventing the law, issued a decree in September 1845 depriving Haitians of their right to own property on marrying a foreigner. This measure, however, had no lasting effects.

The revolution of 1843, which was largely engineered by a group of mulatto politicians, was followed by a peasant rising in the South, led by the Salomon family. This was inspired partly by the fear that the new government would attempt to suppress small landholdings in the interest of the larger estates. The government firmly denied that this was their intention, and in order to passify the rebels and to prevent further discord they agreed to abolish all taxes on the export of local agricultural and industrial products: 'Whereas the end of the revolution has been to protect equally all industries and particularly agriculture, this inexhaustible source of national wealth, it is right to free it from a tax which hinders its development and prosperity.'[60] The government also imprisoned members of the Salomon family, and a new outbreak occurred again in the South, led by Louis Jean-Jacques Acaau, who called himself '*chef des reclamations de mes concitoyens*'.[61] The government of Charles Hérard fell, and a series of short-lived governments ended in 1847 with the election of Faustin Soulouque to the presidency. After several ballots had failed to produce a president, the black general was suggested as a compromise candidate by a group of mulatto politicians which included the Ardouin brothers. These men believed that in Haiti a black man should reign and that mulattoes should rule; the president should thus be a figurehead. This strategy became known as *la politique de doublure*.

The new president, however, surprised his supporters by having a will of his own; in 1849 he was proclaimed emperor. Soulouque's finance minister was the formidable Salomon *jeune*, who later became head of state himself in 1879. Salomon arranged a government decree setting up *magasins d'état* for the sale of necessities and creating a state monopoly in the buying of coffee. The purpose of this decree was to ensure a fair price to the peasants, to cut the power of foreign and local merchants and to boost government revenue. The decree alienated foreign merchants and led to consular protests from Britain and France. The pressure was sufficient to persuade the government to suspend the operation of the law only ten days after it had been passed. Coffee was freed from state control, but fixed prices were maintained for imported goods. This compromise was, however, prejudicial to US merchants and the commercial agent asked his government to send a fleet of warships. The request was not acceded to, but the Haitian government agreed to abolish the 10 per cent surtax on American goods. A gradual increase in US exports to Haiti followed this action.[62] The system was modified in 1850 when state agencies were established at the principal ports of the country to handle the export of coffee and to purchase all imports, which they would then resell to merchants at fixed prices. It is clear that Salomon's plans to control trade and protect the peasants against exploitation by local and foreign merchants were largely ineffective owing to diplomatic and consular pressure on the government. 'Soulouque,' wrote British diplomat Sir Spenser St John, 'gained the good opinion of many of our countrymen on account of the protection which he generally accorded to foreigners, and a supposed predeliction for the English.'[63]

LAND OWNERSHIP AND ECONOMIC DEVELOPMENT

Soulouque fell, and was succeeded in 1859 by Fabre Nicholas Geffrard. The question of the foreign ownership of land remained a live issue throughout the period. A Jamaican who was 'Chemist and Geologist to the Republic of Haiti' stated in 1861 that any attempt to change the laws restricting whites from owning property in the republic would have 'very evil consequences', and would imperil the whole Geffrard regime. The 'enlightened portion' of the Haitian people believed that these restrictions should be removed; 'the masses of the people,' he went on, 'are not prepared for so momentous a change'.[64]

In 1860, an anonymous tract was published in Paris under the title *De la gérontocratie en Haïti*. It was probably written by two Frenchmen, Vieillot and Labordère, who had spent many years in the country. The writers asserted that the mulattoes were the racial group most suited to the Caribbean, and that neither white nor black would survive long in the climate. The pamphlet also argued in favour of European immigration, affirming that the presence of hard-working, disciplined monogamous white peasants in Haiti would have a beneficial moral effect (presumably these unfortunate migrants would last long enough to breed with the local blacks!). From this basis the authors developed an attack upon the prohibition of foreign ownership of land in the republic, which was attacked as the most absurd plank in the policy of the 'ultra-blacks'.[65]

In reaction to this anonymous pamphlet and to similar arguments, Edmond Paul enunciated in the early 1860s a coherent theory of economic autarky. Paul was born in 1837 at Port-au-Prince, the son of General Jean Paul, who in 1847 was a leading candidate for the presidency. Although from a black family, Edmond Paul was closely associated with the predominantly mulatto Liberal Party, and in the 1870s was one of the leaders of the party in the legislative assembly. In 1879, with the victory of the National Party, he fled to Jamaica, but returned to Haiti after the fall of Salomon in 1888 and became a senator in 1890. 'His speeches, his writings, even his political errors,' writes Placide David, 'all his pragmatism, stemmed from his dream of national recovery, which he had made the sole end of his life.'[66] Paul insisted that the law against white ownership of land raised two fundamental issues: *what is a nation?* and *what is legisation?* He argued that Haiti, as an independent nation, symbolised black dignity and the equality of the races; these principles lay at the basis of the idea of Haitian nationality. 'To accord the right of property to whites,' he maintained, 'while colour prejudice is still prevalent, would be to renounce the end which the nation pursues.' When colour prejudice is a thing of the past, and when there is no longer a significant opposition between the interests of black and white, only then should Haiti think of modifying its law on this matter. Is it not the case, he demanded, that throughout the world and 'up to this day, the prosperity of the whites is founded on the degradation of the blacks?'[67] The consequences of modifying the prohibition of foreign ownership would be the end of the small landholder; economic slavery and the tyranny of money would replace the legal slavery of former days. Paul told his readers that they should concern themselves not only with the abolitionist writers of a previous era, but also 'with Hugo, de Lamartine, de Lamennais, Michelet and Madame George Sand, who have depicted the sufferings of the white proletariat'.[68] Such a condition would come about in Haiti if the legal restrictions on foreign ownership were removed. The Haitian state is thus, for Paul, based upon a belief in racial equality and human dignity; an influx of foreign capitalists would undermine this conception. Furthermore it is the purpose of legislation to preserve the integrity of the nation, and this is what the law against foreign ownership did. The problem of foreign ownership did not, of course, arise in the case of American negroes, whose immigration was encouraged by President Geffrard, nor in the case of Indian indentured labourers, whose virtues were extolled by A. Monfleury during this period. Africans and Indians could become citizens after a year's residence.[69]

The significance of Edmond Paul derives in part from the fact that he linked his ideas about the foreign ownership of land in Haiti to a dynamic theory of economic development. Very often writers who defended the prohibition were concerned simply to guard the vested interests of the *gérontocratie*. Paul saw the matter in the larger context of the accumulation of capital. Strongly influenced by the French economist Michel Chevalier, he argued that the government should play an active role in the economic development of the country by encouraging the growth of local industries, and furthermore that such a programme could be financed basically from within the country itself. The role of foreign capital should be subordinate. In the first place, he observed that much local capital was exported and invested in Europe where it was thought to be safe. He criticised the lack of patriotism in these Haitian investors, but argued that the government could do much to remedy the situation. He did not believe that the government should in normal circumstances directly take on the role of entrepreneur by itself; intervention of this kind 'can be justified only by the complete abdication of private initiative'. Direct subsidies to private industry are by themselves insufficient to stimulate economic growth, and 'wake the people from their long slumber'.[70] What, then, is the role of the government in economic development? Paul suggested that the state should go into partnership with private enterprise in those areas where development is needed, and be willing to take much of the burden of risk which is involved in the growth of new industries. If the government did this, it would 'in one move increase job opportunities, inspire confidence in local capital and attract foreign investment'.[71] He was thus prepared to accept, at least as a temporary measure, a limited role for foreign capital, so long as it was subordinate to local capital.

Paul was fully aware that national autonomy requires economic independence, that economic independence implies economic growth, which depends upon industrialisation, a necessary condition for which is the accumulation of capital. This is, as we have already noted, to be achieved partly by government partnership with private investors, local and foreign. This participation by the government would encourage private investment. The necessary state capital could be raised by extra taxation and by increased duties on imported goods. This latter step would not only raise capital but would provide protection for newly founded local industries.[72] Paul suggested legislation on the subject of protection. The preamble reads:

Whereas since the formation of Haitian nationality up to the present day, Haiti has remained tributary to foreigners with respect to the most important necessities of life of the inhabitants . . .

Whereas the principle of free trade, while it is applicable to those states whose interests are tied up with it and therefore inseparable from it, is fatal and must be considered as such, when it is a question of states which are at the mercy of other states . . .

Whereas the system of protection, wisely administered, will be the source of our material prosperity and at the same time the practical solution to our independence . . .

Paul concluded by suggesting articles which would protect local industry, by prohibiting the import of goods which could well be produced locally. Furthermore he insisted that the absence of industry was tragic not only from the standpoint of material well-being and national independence, but was fatal 'for the development of our intelligence'.[73] Edmond Paul practised what he preached and, with a colleague, he established in 1865 a soap manufacturing company.

Another step which the state should take to stimulate economic growth was the encouragement of technical and scientific education. It is all very well for a country to boast of a rich literary tradition, but 'in our epoch a nation counts for more in the world by its industrialists than by its writers'. With such dependence upon foreign countries for relatively simple manufactured goods as soap, candles, ink, paper, cooking oil, bricks, shoes, clothes, glasses and so on, can Haiti afford poets? 'Today what we need are engineers, builders, industrialists, science teachers.'[74] Paul asserted that it was clearly against the interests of the rapidly developing metropolitan countries to encourage this kind of development in Haiti. They were concerned to get coffee, cotton, sugar and other primary products; they were quite prepared for the blacks of Haiti to have 'academies, museums, conservatories, observatories, gardens, theatres and a palace'. However, they did not want to see a programme of scientific and industrial education which would lead to economic development in countries like Haiti.[75] This view of Edmond Paul's was echoed in Haiti by Frédéric Marcelin [76] and is similar to the plea of the Venezuelan writer Andrés Bello, who had written in 1836, that 'it is not enough to turn out men skilled in the learned professions; it is necessary to form useful citizens.'[77] A strong emphasis upon classical rather than technical education seems to have been a characteristic feature of colonialism.[78]

There is in the thought of Edmond Paul a strong current of Saint Simonism – a belief in the virtue of industrialists, and in government by experts replacing that of politicians. The opening sentence of one of Paul's volumes proclaimed: 'The era of politics is past,'[79] and the author went on to claim that industrialisation will mean the dethroning of the political in favour of the technical. 'Power to the most competent' was the slogan for the future.[80] This theme was also characteristic of writers like Justin Dévot and L. J. Marcelin in the next generation, and reappeared in the 1930s and 1940s particularly in the writings of Jules Blanchet. More importantly, from the point of view of this chapter, Paul saw industrialisation as the means whereby Haiti could achieve economic self-sufficiency together with an increased standard of living.

Edmond Paul also insisted that agriculture should not be neglected during the process of industrial development. For too long Haiti had 'wallowed in the colonial rut', and it was time that the agriculture of the country was reformed and mechanised. Industry is, he maintained, necessary for the support of agriculture.[81] Also, the small farmers of the country should be encouraged by government action, rather than being harassed by excessive taxation. No class has suffered more from government policy than the peasant producers of coffee. These men have never been treated as citizens and their resulting discontent was a principal cause of insurrectionary movements.[82]

The reforms in the Haitian economy which Edmond Paul advocated were, he believed, urgently required if the country was to be saved from underdevelopment and dependence upon other countries. This economic dependence would in turn lead to increasing political intervention in the internal affairs of Haiti. Vital decisions affecting the black republic would be taken, not at home, but on the banks of the Seine and the Thames. It is economic and financial considerations which determine the course of political events: 'Stocks and shares have won or stopped battles. They controlled the Eighteenth Brumaire!'[83] He claimed further that political intervention would end with annexation, and he viewed with alarm President Salomon's creation of the National Bank in 1880, depending, as it did, largely on foreign capital. It would become, he asserted, a Trojan horse which would 'vomit onto the country' foreigners who were bent on annexation. Boyer Bazelais, the leader of the Liberal Party, also attacked the government on this issue: in founding the Bank, Salomon had 'handed over our country to the Whites'.[84] The warning was prophetic. United States financial interest in the reformed National Bank was one of the factors, though not, as we shall see, the principal factor, behind the American invasion of 1915 and the nineteen years of military occupation.

Haiti of the late nineteenth century was thus predominantly agricultural, with the great mass of the population working on fairly small plots of land and growing mostly crops for local consumption, together with small quantities of coffee for export. The pattern of inheritance had led to the division of property into smaller and smaller units and some farmers found it necessary to supplement their income by seasonal work on the larger estates. Much of the labour, including coffee picking, was done by women who also dominated the rural markets. Many of the *spéculateurs* who bought coffee from the peasants and sold it to the export houses were women. The retailing of imported goods was also controlled by women. 'The Haitian women', wrote one foreign observer, 'are really commercial'.[85] By the end of the nineteenth century a few small industries existed to supply the local market with such things as shoes, soap and building materials; most of these were, however, under foreign management. Cuban and Italian immigrants pioneered the development of such small manufacturing firms. In 1885 the US consul reported,

> In the churches, the schools, the commerce, the trade and the chief business enterprises, as the national bank, the tramway company, the coffee cleaning factories, the soap and match-making establishments, the persons who occupy the commanding places, furnishing brains, culture, skill and money, are foreigners.[86]

INCREASING METROPOLITAN INTERVENTION

As the nineteenth century progressed, Haiti was the scene of increasing foreign intervention. Often the cause was some loss suffered by foreign businessmen resident in the country. During the rising in Cap Haïtien against Geffrard led by General Silvain Salnave in 1865, for example, the property of a certain German businessman was destroyed. The cause of the destruction was the bombardment of the city by the British, whose ambassador, the notorious Sir Spenser St John, was sympathetic to the cause of Geffrard. The businessman, together with another German who had suffered a similar loss at Miragoâne, claimed compensation from the government. By 1869 Salnave saw the ways things were going and referred to the growing influence of European merchants in Haiti as a reason for seeking closer ties with the USA.[87] The claims of these foreign merchants were not accepted by the government and in 1872 German frigates appeared in Haitian waters, seized two Haitian ships and demanded £3000 compensation. The government of Nissage Saget agreed to pay the sum, but when the ships were returned, the Haitian flag had been desecrated by the Germans. In the 1880s, there was also a threat of British intervention to protect the interests of the Maunder family.

Large numbers of German merchants had established themselves in the principal cities of the republic, and by 1885 much of the country's trade was carried by German vessels. 'Haiti,' wrote Georges Blondel, 'is in the process of becoming a colony of Hamburg.'[88] Léon Laroche pointed out in 1885 that almost half the large commercial houses in Port-au-Prince were owned by Germans, and that this pattern was repeated in other trading cities of the republic. Furthermore these merchants had become deeply involved in Haitian politics, giving financial backing to particular candidates who were thought to be favourable to their interests, and supporting revolutions. 'We are dupes of their politics,' he declared, 'victims of their intrigues, slaves of their capital.'[89] One of these Germans, Emil Lüders, was convicted on a charge of assaulting the police, and his appeal was dismissed. In December 1897 two German warships appeared off Port-au-Prince demanding compensation for Lüders, a letter of apology to the German emperor, and a twenty-one gun salute to the German flag.[90] The government contemplated resistance, but eventually submitted to these demands. A further case of German intervention occurred during the struggle for power between Nord Alexis and Anténor Firmin in 1902, when a German ship carrying arms for Alexis was seized by the *Crête-à-Pierrot*. The Haitian vessel, normally under the command of a British officer, had been taken over by Admiral Hammerton Killick, acting on behalf of Firmin. The Germans sent a warship, the *Panther*, to capture the *Crête-à-Pierrot*, but Killick blew up himself and the Haitian flag ship rather than hand it over.

Anténor Firmin, as foreign minister under President Hyppolite, had already tried to deal with the problem of foreign merchants. In 1889 the government issued a decree stating that foreign citizens applying for a licence to trade in Haiti must sign an agreement to forgo the right to claim compensation from the government for losses incurred during political or civil disturbances. Strong consular resistance was encountered. British consul Zohrab reported the following to the Foreign Office in London:

> This law, if permitted to stand, will oblige all foreigners to close their offices, stores, or shops and leave the country, or, if they submit and remain, to speedy ruin, for it is nothing more than an open invitation to the lower classes of Haitians to burn and pillage, of which from their hatred of the 'whites' they will take advantage.[91]

The Haitian government was unable to enforce the provision and thus remained open to demands for compensation from foreign merchants, and to the threat of military intervention in support of these demands.

On some occasions military intervention by the USA and by European powers in Haitian affairs was more directly caused by political or strategic factors. The USA, for example, was interested in establishing a naval base at the Môle St Nicolas, at the northwest tip of the country. In 1903 the Americans secured a naval base at Guantanamo Bay in Cuba and became less interested in obtaining the Môle. Nevertheless it was an object of US policy to prevent other nations from securing a base in Hispaniola. Washington was particularly concerned about the growing influence of the Germans in Haiti. US minister in Port-au-Prince, H. W. Furniss, wrote to secretary of state Philander C. Knox, 'Everyone knows of the complicity of the German merchants in Haiti in the Leconte revolution and they also know that the Germans financed the Simon revolution of 1908 and the others before it, and doubtless will finance all those to follow.'[92]

The United States policy of 'dollar diplomacy' was specifically designed to increase American financial and commercial involvement in the economies of Latin American countries, in order to gain political control, thus minimising the political involvement of European nations in the affairs of these republics. The US minister in Haiti at the turn of the century. W. F. Powell, was particularly energetic in pushing American commercial interests in the country. He strongly criticised his country's neutrality during the Lüders affair: 'I think that our government is rapidly losing its influence with the people of these small republics,' he wrote, 'they look to the United States as their protector from unjust aggressions. . . . This is the first time in my life I have ever had cause to be ashamed of being an American.'[93]

Powell reported in 1898 that 'American capital is about to seek an entrance into Haiti to develop its resources.' A company was being formed to improve water supplies, another for the export of timber, and plans were being laid for railway construction.[94] In the following year the Haitian Exploration Co. of New York obtained concessions to develop copper mining, in 1905 a concession for the construction of a railway from Gonaïves to Hinche was made to two Americans, and five years later the McDonald contract (which granted concessions to a US company for railway development together with the right of exploiting lands on each side of the railway line), marked the beginning of significant US penetration of the Haitian economy. At the same time, there was a determined attempt by the USA to gain control of the *Banque Nationale*. In his detailed discussion of these movements, Leslie Manigat points to the years 1909–11 as marking a crucial stage in Haiti's move from the European to the United States sphere of influence.[95]

HAITIAN RESPONSES

P. F. Frédérique, Rosalvo Bobo and other nationalists attacked the provisions of the McDonald contract and the journal *La Discipline* pointed to the way in which United States interests had so penetrated the economic and political life of the neighbouring Dominican Republic that Washington now exercised 'an indisputable right of sovereignty' in that country. Such would also be the fate of Haiti.[96] At the turn of the century, although Haiti was the object of increasing foreign intervention – commercial, political and even military – the constitutional article prohibiting foreign ownership of land was retained. During this period, there was a lively controversy among Haitian publicists on the wisdom of maintaining this provision of the constitution.

The suggestion was even made that Haiti should agree to some kind of foreign protection, though this was definitely a minority opinion. Such a step, insisted Demesvar Delorme, would be as serious as a return to slavery. While most Haitian writers of all parties and colours would have agreed with

Delorme that national independence must be maintained at all costs, they disagreed about the necessary conditions for effective independence. Delorme himself lamented the absence of individual initiative in Haiti, pointing out that this had resulted in a decline in agricultural production and in capital investment. He concluded that the government must play a positive role in the economic development of the country. A continued decline in the economy might lead to the total loss of political autonomy.[97] Delorme, however, refused to be pushed into a total and dogmatic insistence on the continued prohibition of the foreign ownership of land. In reply to a tract by Alexandre Delva, demanding a change in the law on this matter, Edouard Pinckombe, a fervent member of the National Party, had urged Delorme to take a positive stand against foreign ownership. Delorme was rather non-committal, arguing that this law was *'une mesure transitoire'*, and that there should be a gradual modification of the absolute prohibition. Foreign capital would, he believed, aid the development of the country and would not necessarily be inimical to national independence.[98] The National Party had no agreed position on the question of foreign ownership, though 'Ultra-Nationals' (as they were called) like Pinckombe and Janvier, were strongly opposed to any change in the law.

Louis Joseph Janvier was one of the most forceful and outspoken Haitian writers on the subject of national independence. He asserted that political independence is the first goal which should be pursued by Haitian governments, and that there are certain economic preconditions for the achievement and maintenance of such independence. He wrote that

> Political liberty is an asset inferior to national independence. Nations will easily sacrifice the first for the second. They rightly prefer a national dictatorship, no matter if it is tyrannical and unintelligent, to foreign domination, even if this were the most gentle in the world, the most likely to enrich.[99]

Haitians must recognise, he contended, that economic domination by a foreign power will inevitably lead to the loss of national independence. No part of the Haitian territory must therefore be alienated to foreigners. In answer to the argument that rapid economic growth can be achieved only by attracting foreign

capital and by making significant concessions to foreign companies, Janvier partially agreed; the country must therefore be
prepared for a slower rate of growth. The fields, forests and
mines of Haiti must be developed by the citizens of the country,
and 'we must keep the heritage which has been passed on to us
by the Haitians of the past unencumbered by all mortgages, free
from all humiliating contracts, so that it can be transmitted
intact to Haitians of the future'.[100]

Janvier cited Egypt as an example of a country which wanted
to develop too rapidly, and had sold itself to foreign capital; it
would soon find that it had lost its political autonomy. Janvier
argued, as Edmond Paul had argued in an earlier generation,
that it is possible to raise capital within Haiti, and that this could
form a satisfactory basis for economic development. Popular
banks and credit unions should be established in the republic to
encourage saving and to make loans. More of the large estates
should be divided among the peasants.[101] Janvier became one of
the spokesmen for the *piquets* – those peasant irregulars who had
from time to time taken up arms, (and when they had no arms
had used wooden pikes, from which they derived their name) in
order to assert their rights.[102]

Janvier insisted that national economic development requires
an appropriate ideology. The Roman Catholic religion, he
argued, encourages loyalty to an outside authority, thus undermining the sense of patriotism. It should therefore be replaced
by '*Haïtienisme*' as the national religion, with ecclesiastical officials subordinate to the government. He suggested that this kind
of Erastian protestantism would be more easily adopted than
Roman Catholicism by people of the African race. Furthermore,
Roman Catholicism leads to a carefree and irresponsible attitude
towards work. Protestantism, on the other hand, could become
'a powerful factor of social development in Haiti',[103] and lead to
progress:

> The protestant is thrifty, a respecter of the law, a lover of
> books, a friend of peace, rich in courageous hope and persever-
> ance. He is self-reliant, knows how to turn immaterial forces
> into material capital. He suppresses carnival and the festivals
> which are as numerous as they are costly, and which tire and
> diminish man's productive capacity . . . Everything which
> trades, cultivates, manufactures, earns, gets rich, prospers, is
> protestant.[104]

It must have been with some disquiet that Janvier, a fierce supporter of the National Party, saw the setting up of the *Banque Nationale* in 1880, largely financed as it was by French capital. However the purpose of the Salomon government was to use the National Bank, over which it would have some control, to undermine the small foreign-owned finance and credit agencies which had sprung up within the country and whose operations the government found it difficult to regulate. This could be the only justification for the setting up of such a bank in the eyes of a nationalist like Janvier. Not only did Janvier argue that economic development should be based upon local capital, but he also expressed a strong preference for the small peasant proprietor. He praised Dessalines, Christophe and even Pétion for their actual or intended distributions of land to the peasants, and stated that the history of France confirmed the fact that ownership of land by small farmers would result in increased productivity.[105] Salomon's land law of February 1883 was hailed as wise and just (though its purpose was to increase exports rather than to provide land for subsistence farming), and Janvier claimed that the invasion of Haiti by a group of predominantly mulatto exiles later in the same year was a direct consequence of this land law. Janvier was, however, somewhat inconsistent in his economic nationalism and praised Salomon for having been the first head of state to have opened the country to French capital.[106]

The economic theories of the National Janvier are thus quite similar in many respects to those of the Liberal Paul, and the confrontations on the issue of foreign ownership of land and foreign capital appear to cut across party and colour divisions.[107] The francophile mulatto Liberal Léon Laroche attacked Janvier's conception of 'Haiti for the Haitians' as relevant only as a protest against slavery in an earlier period, arguing that in his own day it was a serious mistake which could lead to the increasing isolation of the country.[108] We have already noted Laroche's hostile comments on the power of German merchants in the republic. This pro-French and anti-Anglo-Saxon position was also adopted by the black poet Emmanuel Edouard, who characterised the Anglo-Saxon race as rapacious, unscrupulous and narrowly egotistic. He went on to persuade French financiers and merchants to 'undertake the peaceful and economic conquest of Haiti'. French investment in the black republic would, according to Edouard, be in the interests of both parties.

Let us suppose that in a country many more goods are produced than are consumed. All the existing outlets having become, for no matter what reason, inaccessible or insufficient, and production not being held back, owing to social exigencies, a time will necessarily come when all the goods have accumulated and the factories are overstocked; this country will find itself in an untenable position. An hour will come, whether one wants it or no, when unemployment will hit all, or a certain number of, industries . . . Such will become the position of France. The term colonial politics is often used at the present time, and this is not without reason. It is not for the stupid pleasure of submitting savage or recalcitrant nations to western civilisation that France spends its gold and the blood of its soldiers in Asia and Africa . . . In squandering money and arms abroad, France wishes to prevent the cannon of civil war from sounding in her own cities and countryside.[109]

On the other hand, Hannibal Price, a mulatto Liberal, argued strongly against the dogma of free trade and in favour of a limited protection for local industry.[110]

Roche Grellier, a black economist, accepted the need for attracting foreign capital into Haiti during the 1890s. Without this influx there could be no industrial development, and he claimed that one of the most urgent problems facing the country was to modify the legal restriction on foreigners which inhibited investment.[111] He denied that this financial involvement with foreign countries would in any way endanger national independence, though he criticised the ostentatious consumption patterns of the Haitian bourgeoisie as constituting an obstacle to economic growth.[112] Joseph Justin, another publicist of the period, also insisted that the old prejudice against foreign ownership must be abandoned in the interests of progress and civilisation; the ignorant mass of Haitian peasants would benefit from contact with more enlightened foreign proprietors.[113] Justin argued, however, that Haiti must free itself from all foreign interference in its internal affairs, and that Haitian law should deal more harshly with foreign residents who engaged in political conspiracy. Yet he failed to recognise the close connection between economic dependency and political intervention. A change in the laws concerning foreign ownership of land would not, he believed, endanger national autonomy. 'On the contrary,' he stated, 'I persist in believing that our country will not truly prosper until it opens its doors to foreign capital and credit.'[114]

Writing in the same period, Justin Dévot took a different view of the situation. In his *Cours élémentaire d'instruction civique et d'éducation patriotique*, Dévot stated that the founding fathers of national independence had been wise to prohibit foreign owner-ship of land and that this prohibition was necessary in order to permit the development of Haitian nationality. 'What they feared,' he declared, 'was the monopolisation by rich foreign companies, American for example, of a great part of our land, and the transfer of these lands . . . into hands which were hostile to our autonomy.'[115] Like Edmond Paul, Dévot had considerable faith in the role which social science might play in the economic and political development of the country.[116] L. J. Marcelin, E. Mathon, L. C. Lhérisson and others of this period emphasised the role of scientific experts in determining state policy, and pointed to the economic basis of social and political structures. Marcelin stated that 'the salvation of Haitian society resides in a renovation of the economic regime.'[117] Marcelin's book, *La lutte pour la vie*, published in 1896, was an attempt to produce a systematic and comprehensive work on the natural and social sciences along the lines of Herbert Spencer's synthetic phil-osophy. Marcelin and his friends founded the *Ecole Libre Profes-sionelle*, 'where young Haitians would be able to learn useful trades, and principally those which do not exist in Haiti at present.' During the opening ceremony in January 1893, the young Sténio Vincent (who was to become president of the republic some thirty-seven years later) claimed that the ills of Haiti stemmed from the absence of organised work and appro-priate training. The consequent lack of opportunity for the mass of the people led many into revolutionary activity. Vincent saw the founding of the school as a means of combating this 'immi-nent public danger'.[118] The idea of increased social mobility and of a growing middle class as means for achieving political stability is not of recent origin in Latin America.

Frédéric Marcelin, who had been one of the few prominent mulatto supporters of Salomon and the National Party, and was finance minister under Hyppolite from 1892 to 1894, argued in *Une évolution nécessaire* that Haiti should recognise the part which the USA had come to play in the Caribbean. According to

Marcelin, Haiti and the other small nations of the Caribbean must come to terms with US influence in the region. Haiti ought to repeal its prohibition of foreign ownership of land, which Marcelin called its 'great wall of China'. Foreign immigrants and foreign capital are necessary conditions for economic development.[119] Anténor Firmin agreed with this call for a change in Haitian attitudes towards foreigners. In the constitutional debates of 1889, he had been influential in the decision to liberalise the naturalisation laws, and later, writing from exile, he insisted that the prohibition of foreign ownership was a serious obstacle to the economic development of Haiti.[120] In the years leading up to the US invasion of 1915, opinion in Haiti moved increasingly in favour of allowing foreign ownership of land, and of encouraging foreign investment. Even a nationalist like Rosalvo Bobo, who opposed the McDonald contract, was in favour of increased US investment in the country.[121] Popular opinion on the corruption and lack of patriotism in contemporary politicians was reflected in *Kréyol* songs such as the following:

> *D' un coté Sam égorgeant la Nation*
> *Lui a voté plus de dix-sept millions,*
> *De l'autre coté Leconte avec Défly*
> *Aux étrangers tapé vendre le pays.*

> *Soyez maudits a jamais*
> *O cochons généraux*
> *Nan point crime plus noir*
> *Que de ruiner un peuple.*

On the foreign ownership of land the elite of the country was thus deeply divided, and many of the arguments of an earlier generation were reproduced in the columns of *La Revue de la Société de Législation* in the early years of this century. As already indicated, the influence of the USA and Germany was replacing that of France. A powerful group of intellectuals associated with the government of Nord Alexis (1902–8) welcomed this development, asserting that Haitians were basically Anglo-Saxon rather than Latin in temperament and that they should follow the pattern of civilisation found among the protestant nations of the north. The francophiles responded in favour of maintaining a classical form of education and of retaining close links with

France, but Nord was hostile to the French who had backed his opponent Firmin in the civil war of 1902.[122]

* * *   * * *

THE SEQUEL

In addition to the foreign influences discussed above, there was in the closing decades of the nineteenth century and up to the US invasion of 1915, a major influx of middle eastern migrants. I deal with this migration in Chapter 8, but here it is necessary to emphasize the way in which the presence of many thousands of foreigners in Haiti led to a further erosion of national independence.

Many of the Levantine immigrants were of British, US or French nationality, and even those of Turkish nationality looked to the French embassy for protection. Efforts of the Haitian government to expel or to restrict the commercial activities of these migrants were frustrated by foreign intervention on their behalf. In 1912 the British government informed Washington that unless US pressure were brought to bear on the Haitian government to change its hostile policy towards the Syrio-Lebanese, the British would themselves take unilateral action to protect British nationals among them. President Wilson replied that any government has the right to exclude undesirable aliens or to restrict their activities, and pointed out that similar restrictions have been introduced in a number of British colonies. The Syrio-Lebanese colony began to look to the US embassy rather than to the French for protection, and in 1912 cabled Washington to request intervention on their behalf. This was not acceded to, but it was no doubt with considerable satisfaction, three years later, that the middle eastern colony in Haiti watched the disembarkation of US marines in Port-au-Prince. Successive unstable Haitian governments had been caught between pressures from local residents and from important business interests (particularly German and French) to restrict the activities of Syrio-Lebanese merchants on the one hand, and diplomatic pressure particularly from the British and Americans to protect these aliens on the other. The Syrian question is a powerful reminder of the way in which a large foreign colony within a small state can become the occasion for foreign political intervention in the affairs of that country.

The period from 1880 to 1915 thus saw increasing foreign involvement in the affairs of the black republic. Large sectors of the economy had come under the control of non-nationals and this led in turn to political and military intervention by the great powers. Haitian publicists of the period, as we have seen, expressed differing opinions on these questions. Haiti was in a strategic position, situated in the gateway to the newly built Panama Canal; even before the construction of the canal, the USA and Germany in particular had been interested in establishing a naval base at the Môle St Nicolas. Salnave in 1865 and Salomon in 1883 had offered such a base to the USA in exchange for financial aid, diplomatic support and protection. In the early years of the present century the USA had acquired a base at Guantanamo in Cuba and had invaded and occupied a number of small states in the region. The invasion of Haiti in July 1915 was part of a general strategy for control of the Caribbean region by the US government.

I have discussed elsewhere the causes and consequences of the US invasion and occupation of Haiti. Briefly it can be said that the principal reason for this action was to secure the strategic control of the region and to prevent further foreign penetration. A closely related factor was the desire to see established in Haiti a stable government which would provide a suitable climate for private US investment. This was reinforced by a misguided belief that such intervention was part of a moral obligation resting on the USA to improve the condition of the people of the region.

The policy of the occupation was to enforce the repayment of national debts to foreign creditors and to encourage investment by the US firms. To this end the constitution which was imposed upon the Haitian people in 1918 omitted the long-standing prohibition of the foreign ownership of land. A number of US companies took advantage of the change, and were granted concessions of land. Estimates of the area of land leased or sold in this way vary considerably. Perhaps the figure of 43 000 acres in 1927 is the best estimate, though further concessions were made in later years. The lands in question were mostly state land, which had for generations been occupied and cultivated by peasant farmers whose eviction caused hardship and indignation. Haitian nationalists protested against the steps being taken, though Percival Thoby admitted that such penetration of foreign capital was at least in part a consequence of an extended campaign conducted by Haitian writers and politicians to open the country to such exploitation.

The attempt to introduce a plantation economy was not a great success, partly due to stubborn resistance on the part of the peasants and to the complicated system of land tenure. Many foreign firms found themselves involved in long and costly legal battles and a number withdrew from Haiti after having suffered losses. In addition it is important to remember that plantation agriculture is not necessarily more efficient than the small farming traditionally practised in the country. As one geographer has observed 'a square mile of plantations supports fewer people than a square mile of comparable productivity used for peasant farms'.[123]

US Marines withdrew from Haiti in 1934 and since that time, despite a few feeble gestures in the direction of economic nationalism by the governments of Dumarsais Estimé and François Duvalier, Haiti has remained economically weak and dependent. The trend in recent years has, if anything, been towards an even greater dependence on foreign, particularly United States, aid.

6 Holding the Purse-Strings: Women in Haiti

Monsieur Edouard Tardieu was leader of the Christian Social Party in the election of 1946 and edited the party's newspaper, the columns of which were filled principally with reports of his speeches. On the back page, however, a regular feature was an advertisement for Madame Tardieu's grocery shop. While he was upstairs writing political speeches, she was downstairs managing the family business and making sure that their budget could support the political adventures of her husband. This is not entirely atypical of the situation among the elite in Haiti.

It is also the case that among the masses women play a key financial role. With the rural inhabitants whose way of life reflects the African origins of the people perhaps more closely than in any other island of the Caribbean,[1] women also occupy an important position in the economy. In the present chapter I shall sketch the part played by women in the life of the country and will suggest that, although they suffer from various kinds of oppression, the functions they fulfil in the economy and particularly in the financial affairs of Haiti, give them at different levels a potential power which has scarcely been exploited. All I am able to do here, however, is to give the briefest outline of the situation and a guide to some of the relevant literature.

THE EARLY YEARS

In colonial Saint-Domingue men outnumbered women both among the white colonials and the slave population. Efforts were made by the French administration to encourage white women to migrate, and a number of women were recruited from Paris gaols. The policy met with limited success and by the time of the revolution of 1789 white males still outnumbered females in the

121

colony. Among the slaves imported from Africa, men predominated by over two to one, though this position was of course modified with the birth of creole slaves. By 1796 on many sugar estates women outnumbered men, owing to the fact that a high proportion of those who had left the plantations as maroons or 'brigands' were men. Jean Fouchard suggests that the maroons, in their raids on the plantations, made special efforts to encourage women slaves to join them, but he estimates that in the final decades of the eighteenth century, only 15 per cent to 20 per cent of the maroons were women.[2]

During the revolutionary years (1789-1803) women played an important role, not only by supporting the soldiers in various ways, but also by joining their ranks. The gallant part played by Marie Jeanne, a mulatress from Port-au-Prince, in the defence of *La Crête à Pierrot* has become part of the national legend and has led to her adoption as *'le symbole de la femme soldat'*.[3] Suzanne Simon (wife of Toussaint) and Claire Heureuse (wife of Dessalines) actively supported their husbands.

For many years after independence Haitian governments found it necessary to maintain a large standing army which took men away from agricultural work. Much of the food production fell into the hands of women, who in these early years probably outnumbered men by three to two. Visitors to Haiti in the nineteenth century witnessed to the fact that women did much of the manual work in the countryside. 'The females', wrote Jonathan Brown in 1837, 'perform most of the labor.'[4] Sir Harry Johnstone, at the beginning of the present century, was similarly impressed, and the Haitian writer Jean Price Mars maintained that the women in the peasant communities had been reduced to the level of 'farm animals' or 'work tools' by their husbands.[5] Yet foreigners were also struck by the way in which women managed shops and generally dominated local commerce.[6] They were active as coffee *spéculateurs*, buying from producers and selling to the export houses in the ports; they also bought and sold imported dry goods. They were, according to a US observer, 'free to follow any business they may choose, unrestricted by public opinion'.[7]

The central role played in the economy of the country by women from the poorer classes is reflected in the active part they occasionally played in political conflicts. Much of president Salnave's support, for example, came from the working class women of the capital. The British minister in Port-au-Prince reported home (with evident disapproval and alarm) in 1868 that Salnave had secured support from bands of market women who paraded through the streets on his behalf brandishing butchers' knives.[8] Salnave also appointed two women to the rank of general in the regular army.

While, among the peasants and the urban working class, women were thus not entirely quiescent in the nineteenth century, the story is rather different for those of the elite. Generally they were expected to supervise domestic arrangements and to look after the children. Within the family, however, they often played a powerful role. As Roger Gaillard has pointed out in his fascinating account of bourgeois life in Jérémie at the end of the nineteenth century, the elite families were related to each other by a vast network of intermarriage. At all costs there must be no marital relationships contracted with those of a lower class or of darker skin (which usually meant the same thing). This discipline was rigorously enforced by the aging spinsters of the family who 'having heroically chosen celibacy rather than polluting their blood, vehemently stood guard'.[9] Yet, despite their power within the home, their social role was a severely limited and limiting one. Price Mars denounced his fellow men for having maintained women of the bourgeois class in oppression as 'instruments of pleasure and objects of luxury'. The style of life they lived was narrower than that of the domestic servant.[10] This attitude towards women on the part of the elite is clearly reflected in many Haitian poems where women are frequently portrayed as existing merely for the pleasure of men.[11]

In the capital, girls schools had been opened by the Religieuses de Saint Joseph de Cluny in 1864 and by the Filles de la Sagesse in 1875, but there was virtually no possibility in the period prior to the Second World War for Haitian women of the elite to pursue an independent career.[12] As late as 1941 James Leyburn could write (somewhat short-sightedly as it turned out) that 'a women lawyer or doctor would be unthinkable in Haitian society'.[13]

POPULATION AND FAMILY STRUCTURE

Population statistics, like most statistics in Haiti, are not entirely reliable, but it is probable that women still outnumber men. This is partly due to the fact that a high proportion of Haitian

emigrants to the USA, the Dominican Republic and the Bahamas are males. Many women have moved into Port-au-Prince
from the countryside in recent years, as the job opportunities in
light manufacturing industries, in assembly plants and in
domestic work are better than they are for men. In fact the
report of a recent enquiry states that there are only 647 males to
every thousand females in the capital.[14] As Dawn Marshall puts
it, 'More men migrate to foreign countries, while more women
migrate within Haiti'.[15]

Among the mass of the Haitian poor there are a number of
different patterns of family structure. The most stable form of
relationship is marriage, usually celebrated in church. This
involves cohabitation, economic interdependence of the partners
and a high degree of commitment to one another. *Plasaj,* a form
of common law marriage, is more widespread. Though legally
less binding, it is in practice a stable form of relationship which
gives rise to certain customary and even legal rights and obliga-
tions. In his classic work on the life of the Haitian peasant, Price
Mars described the formalities which precede *plasaj.*[16] There are
other forms of relationship, known as *viv avek, fiyanse* and *rinmin,*
implying less economic interdependence of the partners, a
weaker form of commitment and not usually involving cohabitation. The latter two may lead on to marriage or *plasaj.*[17] Many of
these sexual unions are not exclusive and polygamy is widely
practised. In a survey undertaken in Petit Goâve in 1977 20 per
cent of the female respondents said that their current partner
was also having sexual relations with another woman (this is
of course no conclusive indication of the actual situation, where
the number may be higher — or lower — but it does give some
indication of expectations and assumptions about these
relationships.)[18] With the system of *plasaj,* the female partners
are often *plasé,* or 'placed' (the term is significant) so that they
are able to supervise the various, often widely separated, plots of
land which comprise the patrimony. Suzanne Comhaire Sylvain
suggests three further reasons for the prevalence of polygamy in
Haiti: the fact that working wives increase the family income; the
larger number of children produced; and prestige which a polygamous male acquires from his fellows.[19] It should however be
noted that while the total number of children fathered by one
man increases with polygamy, it appears that unstable unions
are associated with low fertility rates among women.[20] But we

ought not to assume that there is a simple causal relationship between stable unions and live birth rates or that all polygamous unions are unstable.

Family arrangements vary from one part of the country to another. Caroline Legerman points to the contrast between the situation of a peasant community in the South, on the one hand, where marital relationships are relatively stable and where 'the elementary and extended family were functioning units' and the unstable mating patterns found, on the other hand, both in a rural area where wage labour predominates and in an urban slum. The 'mother-orientated' family, in which the man plays a marginal role, common in other Caribbean islands,[21] was evident in the latter two cases but not in the stable peasant community in the South. This suggests that the 'matri-focal' family is less a consequence of the African heritage of Caribbean blacks than of the prevailing economic and social conditions.[22]

ECONOMIC ROLES

As has already been noted, women have played a vital role in the Haitian economy since independence. In 1972 it was estimated that 55 per cent of the female population was active in the labour force. This, as Mats Lundahl points out, is significantly higher than most countries of the 'third world' and is exceeded only by Lesotho.[23] Among the poorer sectors of the population in Haiti – as in some other countries of the Caribbean, and in parts of Africa and Latin America – women play the role of entrepreneur.[24] They often start in a very small way by selling a few hands of bananas; they use the profit to buy some dry goods, a few tablets of soap, some boxes of matches, handkerchiefs and so on, which they then sell either in the market or in such places as bus stops and terminals. Anyone who has visited the terminal at La Salines will be vividly aware of the existence of these pedlars. When they have accumulated a small amount of capital they may go in for more ambitious forms of commerce, perhaps buying coffee from small producers and selling to wholesalers or even direct to the export houses. These women are popularly called *madam sara* (from a migratory bird of that name which attacks supplies of food, particularly millet).[25] She often covers large distances, travelling normally by *tap-tap* (trucks converted into buses.) *Madam sara* is 'the agent that establishes contact between urban consumers and rural producers.'[26] Alfred Métraux has given a description of the activities of a typical *madam sara:*

> A woman of Jacmel bought avocadoes, poultry, pork and syrup in the Marbial market. She sold this produce at Jacmel; there she was careful to buy oranges, rice, maize and large beans which she went to sell at Port-au-Prince. In the capital she obtained the local blue cloth for clothing, Siamese cloth, trousers, blouses, dresses, soap and hardware or haberdashery articles, which she disposed of in the 'mornes'; after which she recommenced the whole series of purchases and sales.[27]

Although terminology is not always used consistently, the women who operate on a smaller scale are known as *revendeuses*, who mostly sell retail. The situation is complicated by the fact that the *madam sara* frequently also acts as a *revendeuse*. In recent years *madam sara* has internationalised her activities and travels to Miami, to San Juan, Puerto Rico, or Santo Domingo, returning to the Aeroporte François Duvalier, carrying boxes and bags which overflow with her purchases. International factors have further impinged on the activities of these merchants insofar as many of them are able to augment their capital with money which has been remitted from relations working abroad.

Women also dominate the vegetable and fruit markets throughout the country and it is they rather than their spouses who deal with the family cash. A single file of women (often including girls in their early teens or even younger) carrying huge baskets of fruit and vegetables on their heads, is a familiar sight in the countryside, on the routes into the market towns or junctions. In the evening they can be seen returning with their baskets full of cooking oil, kitchen utensils, *clairin* (white rum) and tins of condensed milk, which have been purchased at the market with some of their proceeds. Yet despite the vital role played by the peasant woman in the economy of the family, she rarely has a say in family decisions; 'she must obey without discussion and without question, otherwise she is beaten'.[28] It should also be observed that men dominate the export markets for coffee and sisal and that possibilities for women to move into new spheres of commerce are severely limited.[29]

The urban working class, as I have already observed, includes a large female component. In the years following 1946 women played a part in the growing trade union movement and there was a women's section of the *Mouvement Ouvrier Paysan* (MOP). Women in fact predominated in a number of the smaller unions. Many of the new industries in the capital employ a majority of women, who are paid even less than men. In Port-au-Prince it is often the case that the woman of the family is the principal breadwinner.

Among the urban middle class and the elite, women are also economically active, though to a lesser degree. They frequently man (if this is the right word!) the cash desks in the Port-au-Prince shops and in many cases they manage the business. One of the striking features of a Port-au-Prince shopping street is the number of stores operating under the name of women: 'Madame Derenoncour', 'Madame T. Baker' and many more. In other cases the women look after the whole financial and accounting side of a business. I remember being struck by the way in which the woman would sign the cheques for the family with which I stayed. The husband ordered the building materials but she paid; in restaurants she paid the bill. In another elite family the woman teaches foreign languages, in yet another she gives music lessons; all suggesting a degree of economic independence. There are in Haiti today a number of women doctors, lawyers and academics. In many of the more traditional elite families, however, the wife is not in paid employment and is expected to preside over the family home. Many of them engage in charitable table works under the auspices of such agencies as *L'Association des Dames de Saint François de Sales*, founded at Port-au-Prince in 1869.

The question, of course, arises in the cases noted above, whether the woman is the mere paymaster or accountant who acts at the orders of the man, or whether she really exercises a significant degree of power in the family. One writer has recently claimed that the degree of economic autonomy enjoyed by women offers them only the illusion of liberty. They in fact act, despite themselves, as 'agents of consolidation of an established exploitative order'.[30] The situation clearly varies from family to family, but my impression is that the woman often has a significant say in family decisions among the elite. It should however be emphasised that this influence is earned by hard work, while the man's strong position is guaranteed by tradition.

CULTURAL AND POLITICAL LIFE

Voodoo is the religion of the Haitian masses and, as in the case of most religions, women are more active participants than men. Although most *humforts* (voodoo temples) are presided over by a man, women play an important role in the cult. In some cases a *humfort* is presided over by a *mambo* (priestess). The anthropologist Alfred Métraux was clearly impressed by the *mambos* he met in Haiti as other foreign visitors have been.[31] Women have also been among the more articulate apologists of the religion and the *humfort* in Paris is run by a woman, Mathilda Beauvoir.[32]

In other cultural activities women have been prominent and have been among the pioneers in the study and practice of folk music and dancing.[33] Lavinia Williams, though born in the USA, has lived in Haiti for many years and her dance school is well known throughout the Caribbean. Christopher Charles has recently drawn attention to the importance of women poets during the past century.[34]

Women generally play little part in public life. Efforts have been made to remedy the situation. *La Ligue de la Jeunesse Haïtienne* was active in the early years of the United States occupation publishing a *Revue*. It was succeeded by *La Ligue Féminine d'Action Social*. This association, founded in 1934 by Madeleine Sylvain Bouchereau and others, organised literacy and domestic classes for women and, in a petition of 1936, demanded improved educational facilities for girls. It actively campaigned for equal rights and in 1950 women secured the vote.[35] Lydia Jeanty, a leading members of the *Ligue Féminine d'Action Social,* was the first woman cabinet minister, in the provisional government of Franck Sylvain in 1957. From 1935 onwards the *Ligue* published *La Voix des Femmes* and in 1938 *La Semeuse* was founded by Jeanne Perez. In the political arena, however, little real change has taken place, and women are hardly involved in explicit political activities. An exception to the rule is Madame Max Adolphe, a high officer in the *Volontaires de la Securité Nationale (tonton macoutes)* and sometime commandant of Fort Dimanche, where political prisoners are incarcerated. She is a former mayor of Port-au-Prince. The political role played by women is indirect, through the influence on their husbands. This is clear from the power of Simon Ovide Duvalier and of Madame St Victor under François Duvalier, and the role played by Michele Duvalier today. Activists of former years, however, lament the apathy among Haitian women in more recent years,[36] as does a younger writer who asserts that 'there is no feminist movement in Haiti today'.[37]

CONCLUSION

Despite the crucial role they play in the economic and financial life of the country, Haitian women still find that they are in certain ways an oppressed and overworked majority. This may lead us to question the judgment of Friedrich Engels that 'the predominance of the man in marriage is simply a consequence of his economic predominance and will vanish with it automatically'.[38]

7 Economic Problems of the Black Republic: a Critical Bibliography

not very insightful or

THE PAST

Until quite recently scholarly writers have largely ignored the social and economic life of nineteenth-century Haiti. Alain Turnier's *Les États Unis et le marché haïtien* stands out as one of the few earlier works to make a real contribution to our understanding of economic policies and practices in the last century. Of late, however, a few Haitian writers have tackled aspects of the subject; outstanding among them has been Benoît Joachim. His thesis at the University of Paris discusses how Haiti, after achieving political independence became economically dependent on European and North American nations and particularly upon France.[1] His general argument is briefly presented in 'Le néo-colonialism à l'essai: la France et l'indépendance d'Haïti.[2] In two further articles he traces this attempt at neo-colonialism back to the 1825 indemnity which Haiti agreed in compensation to dispossessed French planters, as a condition of the French recognition of Haitian independence.[3] In 'Commerce et décolonisation: l'expérience franco-haïtienne au XIXème siècle'[4] he sketches the growth of French economic power in Haiti in the middle years of the century. 'La bourgeoisie d'affaires en Haïti au XIXème siècle'[5] looks at aspects of the social structure of the country.

Some of the material in these articles is brought together in Joachim's book *Les racines de sous-développement en Haïti*. He wrote from a basically marxist standpoint, but his work was built upon solid research and critical insight; his recent death represents a considerable loss to Haitian scholarship. Also concerned with nineteenth-century Haiti is Schiller Thébaud's thesis on the

130

development of agriculture in Haiti. This work, however, deals with the whole period of Haitian independence up to the present day. Also on Haiti's agriculture is Serge Larose, *L'Exploitation agricole en Haïti: guide d'études*. Leslie Manigat's monograph *La politique agraire du gouvernement d'Alexandre Pétion* and his long article on the substitution of US for French domination, during the first decade of this century, contain much important material and can be seen as having set the tone for later scholarly work on the subject. Two recent articles by R. K. Lacerte deal with agricultural policy in this period.[6] A good economic history of Haiti has, however, still to be written.

AGRICULTURE AND ECONOMIC STRUCTURE

Haiti is primarily a rural country and most works on the economy have dealt mainly or exclusively with agriculture. Outstanding are Mats Lundahl's *Peasants and Poverty: a Study of Haiti* and his later collection of essays called *The Haitian Economy: Man, Land and Markets*. Despite their shortcomings, they mark a major contribution to a study of Haitian economic life; their documentation is excellent and the author has made use of a vast amount of published and unpublished material. The historical sections, however, are rather weak and suggest an uncritical reliance on such classics as Leyburn's *The Haitian People*.

In *Peasants and Poverty* Lundahl maintains the controversial thesis that the marketing of agricultural produce is generally characterised by a situation of near-perfect competition. He also insists that astronomical interest rates are a result of high risk and thus to be explained within the framework of classical economic theory. Lundahl ascribes the lack of economic growth and the general decline in standards of living in the countryside to the passivity and corruption of the government and to a system of taxes which make it unprofitable for peasant producers to modify their ways.

In *The Haitian Economy* Lundahl first looks at different interpretations of Haiti's history defending his previously stated view that the country's poverty is due less to external factors than to social and political weaknesses in the internal dynamics of the country. Unfortunately, however, there is little about the role of foreign capital in Haiti, and the author's reference to the

ailing assembly plants as 'the only bright spark in the economy'
(p. 9) is surprising.

While rightly stressing the difference between the system of
land tenure in Haiti and that which prevails in most of Latin
America, the author perpetuates the false idea that plantations
disappeared as a result of Pétion's land reforms, and he fails to
recognise the considerable diversity in the size of holdings. His
statement that land in Haiti is 'relatively evenly distributed' (p.
9, see also p. 76) is quite misleading. The 1971 census figures
suggest that 22 per cent of the land is divided among a mere 3.7
per cent of the farms also that almost half the farms are less than
1.5 acres (.60 hectares) and account for only 14 per cent of the
cultivable land. Furthermore, as Clarence Zuvekas (*Agricultural
Development in Haiti*) has pointed out, the census *understates* the
number and size of large farms; for example it shows no holding
in the West of more than 20 hectares, which is patently false.

Lundahl modifies his earlier thesis that coffee marketing in
Haiti is a classic instance of perfect competition. The important
work of Christian Girault (*Le commerce du café en Haïti, spéculateurs
et exportateurs*) has convinced him that this is not so with respect
to the activities of export houses, but he still wishes to assert
effective competition at the level of the *spéculateurs*. Here as
elsewhere in the book one gets the impression that the author
knows the literature about Haiti without knowing Haiti. Anyone
familiar with the Haitian countryside will recognise that, although there may be many *spéculateurs* operating in a region, each
has strong commercial and customary ties with particular peasant farmers. The latter do not shop around to find the *spéculateur*
offering the best price, but are frequently obliged to sell to one
buyer. That there are a number of buyers in a particular region
does not in itself demonstrate the presence of perfect competition.

Laying much more emphasis upon external factors in accounting for Haiti's plight, is Giovanni Caprio's *Haiti: wirts-
chaftliche Entwicklung und periphere Gesellschaftsformation*. His basic
position is outlined in a review of Lundahl's first book.[7] A
principal issue between these two authors is whether and to what
extent poverty in 'third world' countries like Haiti can be
ascribed to the activity of North Atlantic capitalism. An extreme
position is taken by Jean Luc (Yves Montas) in his book *Structures économiques et lutte national populaire en Haïti*. For him 'imperialism' organises production, fixes prices and 'tells us what to

produce'. This extraordinary reification of imperialism tends to deprive Haitians of any responsibility or initiative and is strangely reminiscent of some classical economists whose 'rational man' merely responds to external stimuli like a robot. An earlier marxist work, *L'économie haïtienne et sa voie de développement*, by Gérard Pierre-Charles, contains some useful chapters but is now rather out-dated. Paul Moral's *L'économie Haïtienne* is also somewhat dated, though his *Le paysan haïtien* remains a classical study of rural life. The chapters by Christopher Clague in Robert Rotberg's book, *Haiti: the Politics of Squalor*, includes helpful data on the economy of Haiti. Wolf Donner's *Haiti: Naturraumpotential und Entwicklung* emphasises the geographical and physical basis of Haiti's economic problems. It has been published in *Kréyol* translation under the title *Ayiti-potansyèl natirèl é dévelopman*.

ECONOMIC DEVELOPMENT AND CO-OPERATIVE ENTERPRISE

Something of a stir was caused a few years ago by a book published from within Haiti, which contained implicit criticisms of the way things were going in the country. In *Enquête sur le développement*, Jean-Jacques Honorat claimed to write without the embarrassment of any 'ism', though clearly influenced by a *noiriste* tradition in drawing attention to '*des particularités ethno-sociologiques de notre peuplement*'. A response, *Haïti: quel développement?*, was published from Montreal by three Haitian exiles, Charles Manigat, Claude Moïse and Emile Ollivier. His later book, *Le manifeste du dernier monde* is a curious mixture of economics and mysticism (not entirely unknown before), where he argues among other things for the application of intermediate technology to the problems of Haiti.

A vast number of aid agencies are at work in Haiti, some merely handing out food aid, others in conjunction with local bodies (often religious groups) are sponsoring many projects. The presence of these groups has led to a considerable literature, often dealing with quite detailed projects. A good general survey is Robert Maguire's *Bottom-up Development in Haiti*. It is a brief essay but is free from the kind of nonsense which inspired O. Ernest Moore in writing *Haiti: its Stagnant Society and Shackled Economy*. Moore believed that the USA has the vocation of 'lifting

Haiti out of the rut'; 'its successful performance', he goes on, 'will be a vivid demonstration of our willingness to help a good neighbour who, because he got off to a bad start in life, has never been able to find his proper place in the world.'[8]

On co-operative enterprises there is the earlier work of Camille Lamothe (*Contribution à la vulgarisation de la pensée coopérative* and *Le mouvement coopératif et la question sociale*) and Marie-Thérèse Vallès (*Les idéologies coopératives et leur applicabilité en Haïti*). More recently Christian Girault has discussed the role of coffee co-operatives in *Le commerce du café* and there is a chapter on 'Co-operative Structures in the Haitian Economy' in Lundahl's *The Haitian Economy*.

A significant feature of the last two decades has been the growth of light manufacturing industries and assembly plants, mostly in and around Port-au-Prince. L. Delatour and K. Voltaire discuss this development in *International Sub-contracting Activities in Haiti,* as does T. K. Morrison.[9] The development of light manufacturing industries is also dealt with in the World Bank report, *Haiti: Urban Sector Survey*. 'État, classes sociales et industrialisation dépendante en Haïti, 1970–1980'[10] by Anthony Barbier deals with some of the wider social implications. In 'Port-au-Prince: dix ans de croissance (1970-1980)' Christian Girault and Henry Godard[11] look at the consequences for urban growth. Girault has also examined the role another important sector of the economy in 'Tourisme et dépendance en Haïti'.[12] On economic relations between Haiti and the Commonwealth Caribbean, Mirlande Manigat has written *Haiti and Caricom*.

8 No Hawkers and Pedlars: Arabs of the Antilles

The islands of the Caribbean are peopled by migrants and their descendants. Colonial adventurers, slaves and indentured labourers were of course the principal sources of population. Nevertheless there have been other significant immigrant groups, including jews, Italians, Spaniards and Levantines. The arabs of the Antilles are numerically insignificant, yet from their ranks today come the prime minister and the president of the appeal court in Jamaica, the presidents of both legislative assemblies in the Dominican Republic and some of the most influential members of the business community in many Caribbean countries. It is therefore surprising that they have received so little attention in the writing of historians and social scientists.[1]

Where did these migrants come from? Why did they leave their native land? When did they arrive in the Caribbean? Which sections of the population left? How were they received in their new homeland? What has been their subsequent history? These are some of the questions which I shall attempt briefly to answer in this present chapter with respect to four West Indian countries. In the Dominican Republic and to a lesser extent in Jamaica, these migrant groups have become involved in every aspect of national life, while in Haiti and Trinidad they generally remain a somewhat isolated minority, marrying within their own ethnic group and (with a few notable exceptions) playing little part in national life. I shall suggest that the contrasting development of these communities in the four countries is to be explained largely in terms of the different social and ethnic composition of these countries.

Although much scorn is poured today upon a crude push-pull theory of migration, critics of the model usually end by adopting it and account for population movements by distinguishing

135

factors in the country or countries of origin which encourage emigration from those in the country or countries of destination which foster immigration. Those rightly wishing to consider these movements in the context of the world labour market still need to examine the conditions of this market as they affect the situation at both ends of the process. The push and the pull may indeed be parts of a single world phenomenon but it is necessary to pay attention to the situation in the countries concerned if we wish to account for particular movements of population.

The arrival of arabs in the Caribbean was part of a larger emigration from the Levant which began in the 1860s and became a major population flow by the 1890s. There are a number of factors accounting for this emigration which I shall not discuss here in great detail. They may be summarised as follows.

Lebanon had been a part of the Turkish Ottoman empire for several centuries, broken only by an Egyptian occupation from 1831 to 1840. The population of Lebanon was fairly equally divided between muslims and Druzes on the one hand and christians on the other. The irruption in 1860 of conflict between two major communities, the Maronite christians and the Druzes (a religious community of muslim origin, dating back to the eleventh century) led to considerable suffering and a sense of insecurity on the part of religious minorities. The Turkish occupation of the Levant also involved a degree of persecution or at least of discrimination against christians. Later, in 1909, Ottoman law was changed to allow for the conscription of christians into the Turkish army. This was very much resented by christians of the region and gave young men a further reason to emigrate.

Lebanon had been for some time the scene of missionary activity, protestant and Roman Catholic. Mission schools taught European languages and encouraged their pupils to look outward and westward. In 1866 the college which later became the American University of Beirut was founded and in 1875 the Jesuits opened the University of St Joseph.[2] The British and French administration of Egypt and the Sudan required persons literate in Arabic as well as in European languages. The relatively developed educational system of Lebanon produced considerable numbers of such persons who were glad to find employment in North Africa. The building of the Suez Canal also attracted workers from various parts of the Middle East including the Levant. Some, like the father of a Dominican psychiatrist I spoke to, began working on the canal and made their way, via Marseilles, to the Americas.

Further factors encouraged emigration. The opening of the Suez Canal in 1869 enabled trade between Europe and the Far East to bypass Lebanon easily, and there was increasing competition from Japanese silk exports. This led to economic hardship among the Lebanese.

Why migrants leave one particular country and go to another is, however, not the only interesting question that may be asked about migratory movements. *How* the migrants moved is also worth asking. Here we may distinguish impersonally organised systems of migration, such as indentureship, from 'chain' migrations where 'prospective migrants learn of opportunities, are provided with transportation, and have initial accommodation and employment arranged *by means of primary social relationships with previous migrants*'.[3] Clearly this categorisation is unlikely to be complete, as the first migrants cannot themselves be instances of chain migration but normally emigrate on their own initiative, and are thus able to constitute the first link in the chain.[4] Levantines who began arriving in the Caribbean in the 1880s were not part of an organised migration but left the Levant on individual initiative. Soon, however, a chain migration was set up, with a host of informal agents facilitating the population flow.

A principal route to the Americas was through Marseilles, where the Levantines took a ship heading westwards. Some of the early migrants did not care where exactly they were going and were prepared to take the first ship heading in the right direction. On arriving in the Americas they would look for a suitable place to settle. One family I visited went originally to Argentina. Not finding opportunities there, they secured a mule and crossed the Andes to Chile. From there they went to Mexico, and owing to the violence in that country, proceeded to Haiti where they eventually made their home. At this time many countries of the western hemisphere were eager to receive settlers and there were few barriers to immigration.

Later migrants usually went to join members of their family or friends who had gone ahead. Successful migrants would often go back for a visit to their home town, perhaps in order to find a wife. On returning to the Caribbean they would bring with them young relations or friends.[5] It is therefore not entirely surprising to find that in Jamaica, for example, a large number of Lebanese families came from a single village just outside Beirut, called Schweifat, and belonged to the Greek Orthodox church; this includes such families as the Hannas, Karrams, Seagas, Shoucairs, Zaccas, Khaleels, and Azans. In the Dominican Republic many families, including the Hachés, the Najri Acras and the Yeara Nassers, come from the Maronite community in Gazhir. The Syrians of the rue Courbe in Port-au-Prince are Greek Orthodox from Tartous. Most of the large Palestinian families in the Antilles, for example the Handals, Marzoukas, Jaars, Mourras, Lamas, Talamas and Issas come from the Latin parish in Bethlehem.

In the course of the migration many Levantines changed their surnames. In some cases they were fleeing from the Turkish police and listed only their forenames on the ship's register to escape Turkish checks. In the small Lebanese villages people were often known by their two forenames. Nellie Ammar's father was Shehadie Khaleel Malick, but was generally known as Mr Khaleel. The Issa family in Jamaica were originally Issa Miladi. Many of the Josephs of the Antilles have dropped their family name. 'Bully' Joseph's father, for example, was originally Louis Joseph Houtonnie, but he was known as Mr Joseph and his children were registered under that name. Some arab migrants even took entirely new names, like the son of Jorge Heded, who adopted the typical Dominican name Lluberes. Again, immigration officials often confused first names with family names.

A further aspect of the subject is the effect of emigration on the communities from which the migrants come. With respect to the Levantine movements under discussion it would be worth mentioning the disruption of village and family life, with the departure of a large proportion of the young men, and the impact of cash sent back by successful migrants.[6]

In this chapter, however, I do not intend to examine in any detail the causes for the migration, the effects on life in the Levant itself, nor indeed the mechanisms which facilitated the departures, but rather to look at how the migrants settled into the country of destination and what has happened to them since. I shall be concerned with four West Indian countries: Haiti, the Dominican Republic, Trinidad and Tobago, and Jamaica. One thing that will emerge in the course of the discussion is the astonishing commercial success of these communities; this is something they have in common. Yet there are striking differences between the role played by communities of Levantine descent in the four countries. I shall suggest that these are to be explained largely in terms of the different social and ethnic composition of these countries.

COUNTRY OF ORIGIN

Although the Lebanese led the migration, they were soon followed by Palestinians and Syrians. Today the Lebanese predominate in the Dominican Republic and Jamaica, while Palestinians are the most significant group in Haiti. The situation is substantially as follows:

Jamaica: Lebanese, Palestinians[7]
Dominican Republic: Lebanese, Palestinians
Haiti: Palestinians, Lebanese, Syrians
Trinidad: Syrians, Lebanese,

West Indians of other ethnic groups generally lump together all Levantine residents calling them 'Syrians' (in the anglophone Caribbean), 'Turcos', or 'Arabés' in the Dominican Republic and 'Syriens' or 'Lezarabs' in Haiti. Among Levantines themselves, however, the distinctions are normally made and it is not unusual to find that a degree of suspicion or even animosity exists between them. Generally speaking the Lebanese are more westernised, while Syrians and Palestinians are more traditionally arab in their cultural and social life. The Lebanese tend to marry people of other ethnic groups more frequently than do the Palestinians or Syrians. There are of course exceptions and it would not be difficult to point to Lebanese families with strong endogamous patterns, who maintain traditional arab customs, cuisine and language. The weekly Arabic radio programme in Haiti, for example, is run by a Lebanese Maronite.

Many Lebanese, however, usually from the Maronite community, deny that they are arabs, insisting that they are 'Phoenicians'. This is more than a semantic distinction and reflects a different attitude towards the current conflicts in the Middle East – a matter to which I shall return. In the 1970s an unsuccessful attempt was made in Trinidad to found a 'Phoenician Society'.

ECONOMIC ACTIVITIES

Most of the migrants had been small landowners or tenant
farmers, though they included some school teachers and small
businessmen. A high proportion were young unmarried males.[8]
The majority arrived in the Antilles with little or no money.
Some began their new life by using the few resources they had to
buy some dry goods or cloth, selling as itinerant pedlars from
village to village and door to door. A few went into banana
production, like Abdulla Younis who, just prior to the First
World War, took over the business which his cousins, the
Abrahams and the Josephs, had built up near Port Antonio in
Jamaica. Some, like Miguel Cury of Cabral in the Dominican
Republic, grew and exported coffee. Others began working in
shops until they had enough money to become pedlars. To the
end of his life old Elias Issa, who had arrived in Jamaica in 1894,
could show the mark on his back made by the box he had carried
as a pedlar. After some years he was able to buy a donkey and
then set up shop in Princess Street, later moving to Orange
Street.

As we shall see when looking at the individual countries, the
arrival of the arabs was generally greeted with considerable
alarm by established merchants and market women. Political
campaigns were directed against them and their stores were
occasionally burned down. Many were forced by popular pressure or by government action to leave the country.

A visitor to Haiti at the turn of the century noted the role of
the arab traders and reflected the popular prejudice against
them:

> The greater part of the trade of the interior is in the hands of
> itinerant Syrian pedlars, of whom there are many thousands
> in Hayti. It is strange to find them in these Western islands.
> They are a race unspeakable, living ten in a room, consum-
> mate cheats; they are usurers and parasites sucking the blood
> from the country and in no way enriching their adopted land
> in return. . . . You meet them in the country districts, dirty,
> under-sized, well-featured people, followed by a boy carrying
> their box of goods.[9]

From retail commerce the arabs moved quite quickly into the
import-export trade, challenging the position of foreign and local

elites. Close links were maintained between arab businesses in various parts of the Caribbean and beyond. In Cuba they founded garment factories, exporting their products to arab merchants in other islands. In the early years they were portrayed as parasites and criticised for failing to invest their profits locally[10] but today large sections of manufacturing industry in the Caribbean are controlled by Levantines. In the Dominican Republic and in Jamaica the sons of businessmen have gone into the professions, particularly medicine and law. With a base in the professions they have moved into academic affairs (in the Dominican Republic), cultural activities and, as we have noted, into politics.

INTERNATIONAL LINKS

Another notable feature of the arab migration is the way in which the families cut across national boundaries. Very often a family would go first to one country and, leaving a brother in charge of the newly founded business, would move on to start business in a neighbouring country. By marriage the international links have been extended. The Handals, for example, are to be found in Jamaica and Haiti (also in Honduras and Brazil); furthermore they are related by marriage to the Daccaretts, Deebs, Hasbouns, Cassis, Talamas, Zarours, Boulos and Jaars. The Llama family in Jamaica is connected to the Lamas of the Dominican Republic and is related in turn to the Issas of Jamaica, who have married with the Abellas, Habeebs, Ganems, Gadala Marias, Shoucairs, Ghisays, and the Salehs. Most of these are Palestinians but some of the Lebanese families have also extensive links with arab families in other countries. The Hannas in Jamaica are related to the Deeb and the Boulos families in Haiti, to the Laquis family in Trinidad and to the Brimos, Zaccas, Fattas, Karrams and Ziadis in Jamaica itself.

These family relationships often lead to commercial links and also make it possible for an individual or a family to move fairly easily from one country to another. During several of the persecutions in Haiti, for instance, Levantines were able to migrate to other countries of the Caribbean. Furthermore many families keep close ties with the Middle East. In the early days the men would often return to their home village to find a wife, whom they would bring back to the Caribbean. Later with growing prosperity they were able to go to the Levant on holiday. Some of the migrants returned to live in the Levant, a few of them taking West Indian wives with them. Other families keep no contact with their relations in the Levant and take little interest in the present problems of the Middle East.

Events in the Levant have had a number of important reverberations among the arabs of the Antilles. In the first place the creation of the state of Israel in 1948 led most of the jews to become isolated from christian arabs. Prior to this date jewish families from the Middle East were generally accepted as part of the Levantine community. Again, more recent events have led to some tension between Palestinians and Syrians on the one hand and Lebanese on the other. The latter commonly blame the other nationalities for the contemporary turmoil in their homeland. As a result of this some of the Lebanese strongly voiced in private conversation their support for Israel's occupation of southern Lebanon. In contrast, Palestinians resent the way in which they believe the Lebanese to have betrayed the arab cause. Many Palestinian families have backed the Palestine Liberation Organisation and have probably made sizeable financial contributions to the cause. A recent number of a Haitian journal has suggested that one particular Palestinian family has given substantial support to the PLO and ascribed the explosion in their family home which killed four persons to the Israeli secret service. However, a leading member of the family denied the suggestions, insisting that the family has always avoided political involvement and is devoted solely to making money.[11]

I wish now to give a brief account of the arab communities in each of the countries under consideration.

JAMAICA

Jamaica at the end of the nineteenth century was a British crown colony, having given up its legislative assembly in the wake of the Morant Bay riots of 1865. Jamaica had been British since the mid-seventeenth century and was a prosperous sugar colony in the eighteenth century. The island was still predominantly agricultural, with a number of large sugar plantations and an extensive peasant population growing coffee and crops for local consumption. Over three-quarters of the food consumed was produced on the island.[12] The great majority of the population was black, with a small brown middle class and some white residents and colonial administrators. Generally speaking colour and class divisions reinforced each other, so that whites tended to be rich and blacks were mostly poor.

Levantine migrants began arriving in Jamaica in the late 1880s. Among the first were members of the Handal family who were also established in Haiti. Another early arrival was George Assab Bardowell, who had been born in Lebanon in 1876 and arrived in Jamaica in 1892. He opened a garment business in Savanna-la-Mar and later moved to Kingston. Other migrants around the turn of the century included Elias Issa from Bethlehem, Racheed Hanna, Shehadie Khaleel Malick, Nasric Gabriel Kalphat, Farid Hanna, Nagib Azan, Rizk Mahfood, Said Nadir Shoucair and others from Schweifat in Lebanon. The Brimo family from Damascus settled near Walderston at a place still known as Syrian Hill.

As in other parts of the Caribbean most of the Levantine migrants began as pedlars and soon set up small businesses in provincial towns. Typical was Louis Joseph Houtonnie who arrived in 1909 and landed with no money. He had come via Cuba and spent all he had on the journey; he slept for a while in the doorway of Rashid Hanna's shop and began hawking dry goods. Soon he was able to establish a small store in Morant Bay. Joseph Matalon, arriving in 1911, was more fortunate and found his uncle Moses in Jamaica already. He was given credit and assistance by a fellow jew, who was a textile wholesaler. Matalon opened a store in Falmouth, selling textiles to small retailers on the north coast. In 1920 he began business in Kingston but this failed during the slump and he returned to the north coast. The family of seven boys and four girls was fairly poor; while in their teens the boys had only two pairs of 'going out' trousers between them and had to arrange a rota for their use!

Elias Azan reached Jamaica in 1909 with his second cousin Nagib, who had lived in Jamaica already but had left after the earthquake of 1907. Elias worked with one of the Shoucairs who had a store in West Queen Street, Kingston. Elias sent for his brother George in 1911 and by 1914 they both had small stores. In 1922 twenty-six members of the family arrived from Lebanon, and four years later their father and mother joined them together with brother Nacif and three girls who soon married. By the thirties the Azans and their in-laws had dry goods stores in Spaldings, Christiana, May Pen, Frankfield, Port Maria, Chapelton, and Kay Valley. Members of the family later opened businesses in Kingston and in Linstead.

By the end of the First World War some concern was being voiced in the colony about the numbers of arabs arriving, and in 1919 a dictation and comprehension test for immigrants was introduced with the object of restricting entry. Nevertheless the Levantines continued to arrive and generally managed to circumvent the immigration barriers. 'These Syrians are up to all manner of tricks', observed the colonial secretary in 1927, when referring to the arrival of Jad Mahfood and Khaleel Hourani.[13] Although the Levantine migration did not cause the same kind of political controversy as we find in independent Haiti, there is occasional evidence of Jamaican unease. A question was asked in the legislative council in 1935, arising from the expulsion of some arab traders from Haiti. 'What steps will the Government of Jamaica take to prevent these foreigners from taking up their abode in this country?'[14]

The Levantine merchants who began in the smaller towns were often able to open stores in the capital and then to engage in wholesale commerce. They also succeeded in diversifying their commercial activities. Some like Joe Joseph moved into real estate; Philip Seaga opened a travel agency, Louis Joseph started a bus service on the north coast, bought 600 acres of land in Portland and owned a bar in Port Antonio. Joseph Issa, son of Elias, went into car sales but the family thought that this was a somewhat disreputable trade and disapproved of the move. Others started small manufacturing industries. In 1935 four 'Syrians' were listed as being involved in manufacturing (of soap and beer), while 144 were running dry goods and grocery stores.[15] Under 'racial origin' in the 1943 census, 834 persons were listed as 'Syrian' and a further 171 as 'Syrian Coloured'. Of these, three-quarters were unmarried and 500 were under twenty years of age. By 1960 the total number of 'Syrians' had increased to 1354, over half of them living in Kingston and St Andrew. By the 1970 census, however, the number of Syrian/Lebanese had fallen to 1007.[16] In the 1950s the Club Aleph was founded as a social centre for those of Levantine origin and flourished for a number of years.

On returning from the Second World War, the Matalon brothers started the Commodity Service Company. Today, Industrial Commercial Developments, controlled by the Matalon family, has over twenty manufacturing and trading subsidiaries, with a turnover exceeding $J 220 million. The fact that they were jews gave them access to the Jamaican business community. Jewish families of sephardic origin were well established and by this time constituted an important sector of the Jamaican elite. Other Levantines lacked this opening, but nevertheless began manufacturing consumer goods. Today the president of the Jamaica Manufacturers Association, Winston Mahfood, is of Lebanese origin. He is managing director of CPM Industries, which also includes Abraham Issa and George Khouri among its directors. CPM manufactures a wide range of goods from footwear to electrical products and envelopes. During the government of Michael Manley some merchants were faced with the choice of going into manufacturing or quitting business, owing to restrictions placed on imported goods. Numbers of arabs took one of 'the five flights to Miami'. Others, the Ammar–Azar partnership for example, began manufacturing some of the items which had previously been imported.

In her consideration of the ethnic composition of the Jamaican entrepreneurial elites, Carol Holzberg finds, however, that there are only two 'Lebanese/Syrian' among a total of thirty eight individuals considered as the top businessmen in the island. The list includes sixteen of European extraction and nine jews.[17] Perhaps the explanation for this is that she has taken the elite from an analysis of the boards of forty public companies quoted on the Jamaican Stock Exchange. Most of the Levantine businesses remain private and family concerns and would not therefore qualify under her criterion. At the height of his power Eddie Hanna, for instance, owned forty-three stores with over four thousand employees, but would not have been included in Holzberg's list of top businessmen.

The category 'Syrian Coloured' suggests that a number of migrants married or cohabited with black or coloured Jamaicans, rather than remaining an exclusive community as they generally did in Trinidad. The father of 'Bully' Joseph, a leading figure in the Jamaica Labour Party for some years, married a coloured Jamaican, as he did himself. Edward Seaga's father married a Panamanian creole. Nevertheless some resistance to mixed marriages was manifested by the more traditional arab families. One Lebanese man told me that his brothers threatened to shoot him if he married a Jamaican. His creole wife observed that they failed to keep their promise!

Many persons of arab or part arab extraction have played an important role in the national life of Jamaica. For years there was great rivalry between the son of Racheed Hanna, Edward (probably the first Levantine child to be born in Jamaica, in 1894) and Abraham Issa, son of Elias. The former, of Lebanese origin, was a leading Anglican and a governor of Kingston College, while Abe Issa was a Palestinian Roman Catholic and a keen supporter of St George's College. They were both members of the legislative council for some time. As Jamaica moved towards independence men like this were gradually incorporated into the 'establishment'. Hanna and Issa became members of the jewish-dominated board of the *Daily Gleaner*. They also joined boards of public companies such as the Industrial Development Corporation and the reconstituted Tourist Board. Edward Zacca, who had been a leading member of the Club Aleph in the 1950s, is today president of the Appeal Court. In the cultural sphere, Bobby Ghisays, a grandson of Elias Issa, writes and produces plays and pantomime.

Edward Seaga is prime minister and leader of the Jamaica Labour Party. I asked him whether being of Lebanese descent was not a problem in a country whose population is of overwhelmingly African origin. He said that in one respect it was an advantage; being a 'Syrian' he did not need to prove his competence. In another way, however, it was a disadvantage; he *did* need to demonstrate his good faith and his genuine identification with the interests of the Jamaican people. He reminded me that his constituency in West Kingston is one of the poorest and roughest in the country, populated almost entirely by black Jamaicans, and yet he was able to secure a massive majority over his PNP rival. We shall shortly return to consider the significance of this phenomenon.

Although Levantine families in Jamaica have generally been accepted by other ethnic groups and identify themselves with the nation, many still maintain links with the Middle East and in their family life perpetuate arab customs. In 1946 twenty-three of the Azan family returned to Lebanon with the intention of settling there. They chartered a plane to Florida and made their way to New York, where they encountered a dock strike. Elias and his brother had to support the family in a hotel for about a month before embarking. After several months in Lebanon they decided that life was more difficult than in Jamaica and returned to the Caribbean. Others lived for longer periods in the Levant. This dual attachment has sometimes led to embarrassment. A member of one of the leading Palestinian family in Jamaica who speaks Arabic in his home and has lived for some years in the Middle East refused to see me with the comment 'I know nothing about these people, I am one hundred per cent Jamaican'.

HAITI

Haiti's independence, achieved after a bitter and bloody struggle, was based upon a conception of race. Independence was for Haitians a symbol of the dignity and capacity of the black or African race. The social structure of Haiti at the close of the nineteenth century was distinguished by the existence of a tightly knit group of urban mulatto families who constituted the major element of the ruling class. In addition to owning large estates most of them engaged in commerce and occasionally in politics. The other section of the ruling class was black and generally rural-based. They were joined from time to time by successful military leaders who may have risen from the black middle class. The mass of the population was black and lived on plots of various sizes which they cultivated for a living. Most of the large businesses were owned by foreigners, as were the small manufacturing firms making such items as shoes. The retail trade was largely in the hands of black women who would travel from village to village with their wares.

By the end of the century Levantine immigrants had arrived in considerable numbers and were challenging the position of the market women. Over a hundred had become naturalised, and by 1903 the British consul estimated that there were six or seven thousand Levantines in Haiti, mostly from Lebanon and Aleppo. The majority were of Turkish nationality, enjoying a degree of French protection; six, including the Benjamin and Btesh families had acquired British nationality; fifteen were United States citizens; and a further 60 or so had forged US papers.[18] W. F. Powell, US minister in Port-au-Prince, estimated the numbers of arab immigrants, somewhat unrealistically, at 15 000.[19]

As traders, these migrants were clearly a great success and this is witnessed to by the fierce hostility towards *lezarabs* on the part of Haitian market traders. This was exploited by political parties who sought popularity by attacking these immigrants and promising to expel them from the country. Bitter campaigns were waged in the press, and there was even a newspaper called *L'Antisyrien*. In 1903 a law was passed to restrict their commercial activities, to make naturalisation more difficult and to prevent the arrival of more of them. Diplomatic pressure, particularly from the USA delayed the promulgation of this law, but it came into force in June 1904. Levantine businesses were attacked by mobs and their owners were physically assaulted. Throughout 1905 press attacks against these 'Levantine monsters' and 'descendants of Judas' continued. Articles in successive numbers of *Le Commerce* called for *'l'extirpation des Syriens'*.[20]

As a result of legislative and popular attacks a considerable number of Levantines left Haiti at this time; the British consul estimated the number at about 900.[21] However the government of Antoine Simon (1908–11) was less hostile than that of Alexis Nord, his predecessor, and the legislation was not rigidly enforced against them. The election campaign of Cincinnatus Leconte in 1911 involved promises to enforce anti-Syrian legislation, and with his advent they again came under attack. This time it was not merely the market women who were feeling the pressure of Levantine competition. During the first decade of the century successful arab merchants had moved into the import-export trade and were beginning to challenge local and foreign *commerçants*. French merchants had put pressure on their embassy not to give effective protection to the immigrants, who then decided to seek US protection for their colony. This was willingly granted by the USA, whose government was keen to reduce European influence in the Caribbean; also many of the arab traders had developed close commercial links with North American manufacturing firms and proved to be one of the principal means by which the USA was able to increase exports to the black republic.[22] Elite politicians like J. N. Léger, Sténio Vincent and Edmond Laforest denounced the Levantines, defending the legislation against them.[23] It is likely that in order to protect themselves some arabs conspired with opposition leaders, and when President Leconte was blown up in his national palace in 1912 they received the blame. Riots in a number of cities led to the destruction of business premises.[24]

By the first decade of the century the arabs had become a part of the Haitian landscape and their presence was frequently noted by foreign visitors. Eugène Aubin who lived in Port-au-Prince from 1904 to 1906 remarked on their energetic commercial activity. He noted the absence of Levantine clergy and the lack of any organisation among them; there was, however, a small restaurant serving arab food. Aubin reported that one Syrian had married a negress and settled down as a voodoo priest in the hills behind Léogane.[25] J. Montague Simpson also noted the important role played by Levantine migrants at this time.[26]

Not surprisingly, the arabs watched the disembarkation of US marines in July 1915 with some degree of satisfaction. During the nineteen years of occupation that followed they were generally left alone to carry on business. A Syrian Commercial Club was founded in 1920 to look after the interests of the colony and to provide a social centre. Migrants continued to arrive throughout this period from Palestine and Syria as well as from Lebanon. Most of those arriving were christians, though there were fifty or so jewish families in Haiti up to the end of the Second World War. After this time most of them emigrated to North America, and today there are very few jews among the Levantines of Haiti. Up to about 1948, when the state of Israel was founded, Levantine jews in Haiti were generally accepted by other arabs. In the 1920s G. J. Bigio was vice-president of the Syrian Commercial Club and the committee included at least one other jew. Among the christians, Melkites, Maronites and Latins found the Roman Catholic church in Haiti to which they naturally attached themselves. The Greek Orthodox found no church of their persuasion in Haiti. Most of them effectively became Roman Catholics, though they would attend the Orthodox liturgy which was celebrated by visiting clerics from time to time in the Anglican cathedral of the Holy Trinity. The few muslim families in Haiti are normally accepted by the christian arabs.

The arabs in Haiti were kept in touch with other arab colonies in the New World by the occasional visit of unofficial roving 'ambassadors' like Dr Habib Estefano, president of the National Arab Academy of Damascus. He visited Haiti in 1924 and was

the guest of the Syrian Commercial Club. A number of receptions were held, at the Parisiana, the Circle Bellevue and in
Gonaïves, Cap Haïtien and St Marc, where he spoke to the
assembled throng. Among members of the Haitian elite who
attended these receptions were Normil Sylvain, André Faubert,
Etienne Mathon and Georges Sylvain. Estefano assured those
present that 'every Syrian resident in Haiti is a Haitian at heart'
and hoped that every Haitian would be a good friend of Syria.[27]
He was, however, denounced in the press as being a United
States agent, and it was also noted that he had recently taken out
Cuban nationality.[28]

The Levantines in Haiti are still very much a business and
commercial group. Some of the younger generation have studied
for the professions, but most of these have emigrated to North
America. Others, like Antonio Handal and Jean-Claude Assali,
have returned after studying abroad to manage the family business. There is today no Levantine club or association in Haiti,
and social life is centred on the family home. Until very recently
young members of the arab community have found spouses from
their own ethnic group. The Haitian mulatto elite has tended to
look down on *lezarabs* and even today they are thought of as
nouveaux riches – lacking in culture and sophistication. A member
of the elite told me with evident satisfaction how one of the now
prosperous arab families had arrived in Haiti with a dancing
bear which, on the payment of a small fee, would perform on the
waterfront. These antipathies are generally reciprocated.

Members of the arab community have not played much part
in the political life of Haiti. It was only under François Duvalier
that a few of them were brought into political office. Rindel
Assad became minister of tourism in 1958 and in the following
year Carlo Boulos was made minister of health. Jean Deeb was
for some time mayor of Port-au-Prince. Recently over a dozen
young arabs were arrested for alleged complicity in an opposition movement. They were soon released but some of them were
warned that they should leave the country.

As in other parts of the Caribbean, there is in Haiti a degree of
animosity between the Lebanese on the one hand and the
Syrians and Palestinians on the other, partly due to the present
conflicts in the Middle East. One Lebanese-born businessman
told me what a wonderful country Lebanon had been in the past
– with hotels, banks, night clubs – it was he told me 'the

Switzerland of the Middle East'. Just round the corner, in La Grande Rue, I spoke to a Palestinian who poured scorn on Lebanese pretentions. Nasser was right, Beirut was 'the whorehouse of the Middle East'!

DOMINICAN REPUBLIC

It is in the Dominican Republic that the Levantine immigrants have become involved in every aspect of national life. The ethnic situation which they found when they arrived in the late nineteenth century was different from that in the neighbouring republic of Haiti in several respects. In 1821 the inhabitants of the Spanish colony of Santo Domingo, which constituted the eastern two-thirds of the island of Hispaniola, expelled their colonial masters. Almost immediately they were incorporated into the republic of Haiti. Resentment against the Haitians grew, and in 1844 the Dominican Republic became independent for the second time. For a short while in the early 1860s the country returned to colonial status under Spain but independence was soon restored. Mulattoes constituted the majority of the population, with a significant minority of whites and blacks. Most people lived and worked in the countryside, producing crops for local consumption and tobacco for export; another major activity was cattle ranching. With the immigration of Cubans in the late 1860s the sugar industry developed rapidly. Sugar, together with coffee and cocoa, became major export crops.

In the 1880s, when the arab migrants began to arrive, the Dominican Republic was considerably less developed than Haiti. Miguel Cury, who began coffee farming in the hills above Cabral in the south-west part of the country used to export his crop through Haiti from where he would import dry goods. As in other parts of the Caribbean, most of the early migrants began as pedlars until they had saved enough money to start a small retail store. By 1900 the Elmudesi family had established itself in the capital and Nemén Terc had opened a store in El Conde; other arab traders settled in this part of the capital – in Duarte and Mella. La Atarazana had become a centre of arab trading with the textile stores of Nicolas Majluta, Jacobo Majluta (*padre*), Nicolas Cheij, David Yabra and Alfredo Yeje's tailor shop.

In the provincial towns the arab traders were becoming a

force to be reckoned with. At the turn of the century Nacif P. Haché, who had begun trading in Puerto Plata in 1886, opened a store in Santiago, the second city of the republic. Also living in Santiago at this time were the Elias, Gobaira, Salomon, Jelu, Sahdala and Sued families. Azua, Barahona, San José and other towns had small colonies of arab families. In San Pedro de Macoris the local tradesmen denounced these new rivals in a petition addressed to the national congress in June 1896.[29]

The census of 1920 states that there were 1187 persons of Syrian nationality in the country. In addition, many hundreds of arabs had been naturalised and some had married Dominicans of other ethnic origins; their children would thus have had Dominican nationality. Also, numbers of arab migrants were of French, British, United States or Cuban nationality. Levantine traders in the Dominican Republic kept in close touch with the large colony of some 10 000 arabs established in Cuba. Attempts by the Dominican government in 1920 to expel Levantine migrants from the country had an adverse effect on the arab manufacturers of Santiago de Cuba, who exported large quantities of cloth to them.

The 1920s and 1930s saw a significant movement of arabs into manufacturing industry following the pattern which was developing in Brazil and in the USA. They also founded social clubs and associations in San Pedro, Santiago, San Francisco de Macoris and in other cities. In the early 1940s two journals were published, *Libanesa* and *La Voz Arabe*, containing articles on the Middle East and on Levantine colonies in the New World. The advent of Lebanese independence in 1943 was an occasion for increased ethnic awareness among Lebanese of the Americas, particularly the Maronites who predominated in the Dominican Republic.

Under the Trujillo dictatorship the arabs prospered and were in general favourably disposed to 'El Benefactor'. Trujillo in turn protected and promoted them. The Sued brothers of Santiago were among his most reliable supporters, and he appointed Dr Jottin Cury as provincial governor. Trujillo's popularity with the arab minority in the country was evident to arabs in the neighbouring republic, and when the dictator visited Haiti in March 1936 he was given a great welcome by the Levantines in Pétionville.[30]

Having achieved success in the commercial and industrial sphere, many arabs encouraged their sons to enter the professions. One of the early medical doctors was Dr Antonio Elmudesi who was dean of the medical faculty of *La Universidad Autonoma* and president of *La Sociedad de Medicina de Santo Domingo* in the 1940s. Today many persons of Levantine or part Levantine descent are prominent as lawyers, architects and civil engineers; also as playwrights, poets, singers and painters.[31] Four of the recent rectors of the National University are of Lebanese descent and the founder of *La Universidad Central de l'Este* in San Pedro de Macoris is Dr José Hazim Azar, whose son is the present rector. The notorious general and presidential candidate Elías Wessin y Wessin is of Levantine origin, as is the Communist Party candidate at the last presidential election, Narciso Isa Conde. Jottin Cury, a government minister under Camaaño in 1965, later played a leading part in the *Partido Revolucionario Dominicano* and Dr Rafael Kasse Acta is a prominent member of Juan Bosch's party (PLD). Jacobo Majluta Azar and Hugo Tolentino Dipp are respectively president of the senate and of the chamber of deputies, while arabs in the present government of Jorge Blanco include the ministers of finance, commerce and sport.

The imposing *Club Libanés-Sirio-Palestino* dominates one side of the Parque Independencia in the capital. The committee's twelve members (including three women) are mostly of Lebanese descent, the great majority of whom were born in the Caribbean. Only four members could speak any Arabic. The young Syrian barman at the club, however, had recently arrived from Puerto Rico where he had lived for five years. In my interview with the committee a number of them made the familiar claim that Lebanese are not arabs but are of Phoenician origin.

Typical of the large Lebanese families in the Dominican Republic are the Curys (see Figure 1, p. 158). Miguel Cury, son of a Greek Orthodox priest, Abdala Cury, from the town of Boz Bina in northern Lebanon, arrived in the Dominican Republic in the mid 1890s. He settled in the western town of Cabral and started a coffee plantation in the village of Polo, situated in the hills above Cabral. He exported coffee through Haiti and began importing and distributing dry goods.

Miguel's first wife, Maria, was Lebanese; she was from a
family with the same Arabic name (though spelling it 'Khouri').
Of their two sons, one married a Lebanese, Margot Elias and the
other married Francisca Fernandez, a Dominican. Of the thirteen grandchildren three married spouses of Levantine origin.
Of the thirty-six great grandchildren only two married Levantine spouses. One of the grandchildren, Nadim, still cultivates
coffee in Polo and has recently started to export coffee from
Barahona, in partnership with some of his sons.

Maria Khouri's brother, Hanna, married Sara Hasim and
had six children. Three of these remained in Lebanon; one
married a Honduran and went to live in Central America and
two, Sadala and Jorge, came to the Dominican Republic. Two of
Sadala's three children now live in Barahona, one keeps a
furniture store and the other a large clothes shop in the centre of
the town. One of Jorge's children owns and manages the best
restaurant in the city.

Miguel's second wife was Fidelina Espinoza, a Dominican.
Only one of their nine children married a Levantine spouse, and
not one of the grandchildren or great grandchildren married
Levantine spouses. Most of the younger generation have left the
region of Cabral but several older members of the family are to
be found running small stores in Cabral and Polo.

Only those branches of the Cury and Khouri family which
have remained in the Middle East have generally married Levantine spouses. With a few exceptions, those who came to the
Caribbean soon began to marry spouses of different ethnic
origins. Although a number of the family are still engaged in
commerce, many have moved into other occupations; the family
includes lawyers, bankers, doctors, civil and chemical engineers,
architects, and a travel agent. Contact with the Middle East is
maintained by some members of the family and two of the
granddaughters of Hanna Khouri, whose family live in Lebanon, are studying at university in San Pedro de Macoris and
staying with an uncle.

When East Indian youths 'play mas' at Carnival in Trinidad
and when we find black creole ladies making and selling roti at
the Curepe junction, we can hardly think of Trinidad's Indians
as a 'marginal' group. Similarly in the Dominican Republic,
with such a degree of participation in all aspects of national life,
the arabs are as clearly 'Dominican' as the next man. Perhaps

the way in which kippies have become a national dish is the kind of confirmation that is needed.

TRINIDAD AND TOBAGO

Trinidad in the late nineteenth century was different from both Haiti and the Dominican Republic in some important respects. In the first place, like Jamaica, Trinidad and Tobago was a British crown colony, where all important decisions were taken either in London or by British officials in Port of Spain. Secondly, the ethnic composition of the population was more complex than in the other three countries. The whites, divided between French and English creoles, composed the upper class. At the other end of the social scale were the black descendants of African slaves and more recent African immigrants. Work on the plantations was done mainly by East Indian indentured labourers. Other important ethnic groups were the descendants of Chinese and Portuguese indentured workers and a considerable number of coloured people of mixed ethnic origin.[32]

The first Levantine migrants were Lebanese and included the Joseph and Abraham families. A few Syrians began to arrive in the years immediately before the First World War, but in 1921, according to a report by the French consul in Port of Spain, there were fewer than 100 Levantines in Trinidad. 'There is no country more xenophobic than Trinidad. . . . ', remarked the Frenchman, 'there is not a single foreign shop in the principal commercial street of the city'.[33] Considerable numbers of Syrians migrated to the colony in the 1920s and 1930s, however. Very often the new arrivals would begin, as their predecessors had done, by hawking dry goods from door to door in the smaller country towns. Old residents of the village of Toco, on the north coast, to whom I spoke in a bar, told me that they remembered these Syrians arriving with their goods. The hawkers had evidently acquired a smattering of the French based *Kréyol* that was still widely spoken in Trinidad at that time. The old Toco residents, who did not themselves understand *Kréyol*, remembered some of the phrases the Syrians had used and asked me their meaning.[34]

By the 1950s the Syrian community, though still fairly small, had become moderately prosperous and well established. Yet its members maintained a low profile, kept very much to themselves and were fairly narrowly occupied in the dry goods trade. In the 1950 volume entitled *Trinidad: Who, What, Why*, only six Levantines are mentioned, all of them concerned with the dry goods business. Writing about 'the Syrian', the editor of this whimsical volume declared, 'unlike the Portuguese and Chinese, he keeps almost exclusively to his race'.[35] A Syrian-Lebanese Club existed in Trinidad at this time, but it fell apart owing to conflicts between the leading families and to apathy on the part of the rest.

By 1960 there were, according to the census of that year, 1591 persons of Syrian ethnic origin resident in Trinidad and Tobago, almost half of them in the capital. The following decade, however, saw a decline of over one-third in their numbers. This was not due to a lack of commercial success; rather it is an indication that numbers of them were able to set up in business or in the professions in the USA or Canada with capital accumulated from their Trinidadian businesses. This tendency to emigrate was reinforced by the signs of popular hostility directed towards them during the 'black power' movement that began in the late 1960s.

Today members of the community have become involved in many industrial enterprises in Trinidad, including construction, garment manufacturing, food processing and canning, brewing, and the manufacture of glazed tiles, steel chairs, paper bags, envelopes and electrical goods such as televisions, refrigerators, air conditioners and light bulbs. The Levantine community has come a long way since 1921, and its members own large stores in the principal streets of the capital as well as maintaining smaller stores in the less salubrious quarters and in the smaller towns. Some younger members of the community are entering the professions in Trinidad but most are still engaged in commerce and industry. One old member of the community lamented the declining interest in commerce on the part of the younger Syrians. Pointing to his son he said reproachfully: 'He go close de business when ah dead'.

The social life of the Levantines is, as in Haiti, centred on the home. The families are often large and gather together for meals on public holidays and for birthdays and other family festivals. It is a generally held belief among the middle-aged and older people that the woman's place is in the home and that the husband is the head of the household, a belief assented to by the women themselves. One younger lady told me that there was some resistance from members of her own family to her entering university; this was not thought appropriate for women. Members of several families meet in private houses to play cards and engage in other forms of gambling. There is today no Syrian–Lebanese club, though there is a Syrian–Lebanese Women's Charitable Association. This group, founded in 1950 to assist less fortunate members of the community, has in recent years raised money for more general charitable causes in Trinidad such as the Lady Hochoy Home for the mentally handicapped. In 1970 a Trinidad Syrian–Lebanese Youth movement was founded; it is popularly known among its members by the somewhat unfortunate acronym 'Tri-Sly'! This group has a nominal membership of about 150, though less than a third are active members. It appears from comments by adults of the community that the main purpose of Tri-Sly is to act as a marriage agency where suitable partners from within the community might be found for their offspring. Some former members of the movement complained to me that the sons and daughters of the large and prosperous families tended to dominate the proceedings and attempted to lord it over the rest.

As has already been implied, the family is the principal social institution binding together members of the community. Frequently disputes within the extended family, rather than being taken to court, are settled by the senior member of the family acting as 'godfather'. The Levantines in Trinidad tend to marry within the ethnic group and, particularly in the case of the larger and more well-known families, there are few cases of exogenous marriages. The family tree (Figure 2) illustrates this point well. The three brothers and two sisters arrived in Trinidad with their parents in the first decades of the century. Of the 349 names on the family tree (including spouses) only 9 married exogenously. There are, in fact, more cases of marriage within the family among first and second cousins than partnerships outside the ethnic group. The eldest brother, who is now eighty-six, told me that he was very much against these exogenous marriages; his 48-year-old son echoed this opinion. When there are marriages outside the ethnic group, light-skinned partners are preferred.

Although it would be true to say that in Trinidad, as in Haiti, there are few if any poor members of the Levantine community,

158

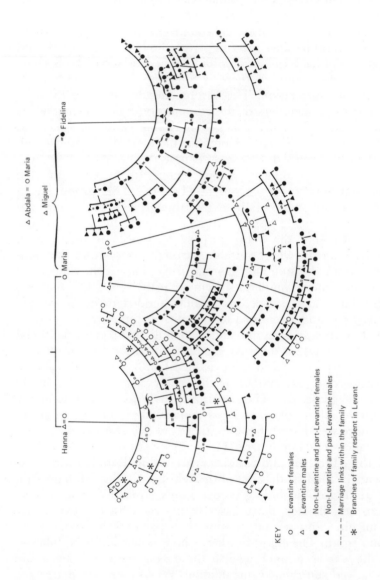

FIGURE 1 *Family tree of Lebanese family from the Dominican Republic*

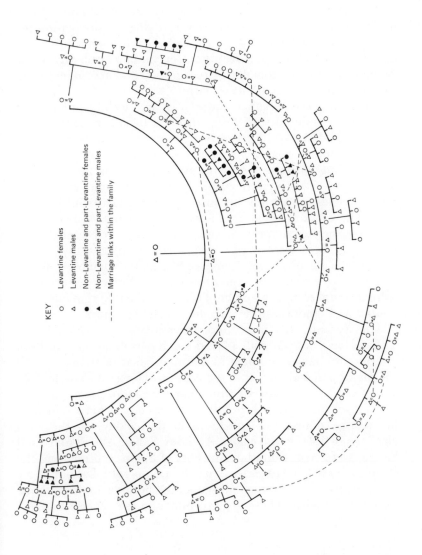

FIGURE 2 *Family tree of Syrian family from Trinidad*

it is nevertheless the case that there are some significant tensions between members of the larger and more prosperous families and their less fortunate fellows. One prominent Lebanese businessman put it like this: 'There is a terrifying division within the community on a class basis'. A young Syrian woman complained about the fate of the less wealthy: 'Certain families living in the Belmont area have gained little recognition and acceptance from the [Levantine] community at large'.[36]

When I asked whether there was any feeling among the Levantine community of being disliked by other, particularly black, Trinidadians the answers given were usually ambivalent. The respondents clearly wished to deny that there was any such hostility, but when pressed by my giving examples, the reply was usually that, if they were disliked, it was nothing to do with ethnic origin, but simply because they were successful in business. The views of Levantines about other ethnic groups tended to follow the stereotypes: the blacks were lazy and wasted their money, Indians were hard-working but untrustworthy. There was, particularly among some of the older members of the community, a distinct hostility towards the French creoles, who were denounced by a member of one prominent Syrian family as 'stupid and ignorant'; they are, he concluded, 'hogs'.

The Syrians, Lebanese and Palestinians in Trinidad and Tobago have not generally played much part in national or local politics and have attempted to maintain good relations with all the major political groups in the country. However, Roy Joseph, a half-Lebanese politician from San Fernando, played an important role in the civic life of the southern city as mayor; in 1950 he became minister of education in the colony. In the local elections of 1960 two cousins, Anthony Sabga Aboud and Fred Sabga, were rival candidates in Port of Spain, representing the People's National Movement and the Democratic Labour Party respectively. The former subsequently became high commissioner in Jamaica. These are exceptions to the general rule.

CONCLUSION

The question is frequently asked with respect to an ethnic minority, how far it has been 'assimilated' by the 'host society', or whether it has become 'acculturated': whether it has adopted the 'values' of the host country. These questions assume a somewhat static conception of the situation into which migrants arrive. It is in fact doubtful whether anything like a 'host society' with common values exists. There are many clubs, associations and societies within the modern state, but there is no such thing as 'society' into which migrants might be expected to integrate. The reifying of relationships within the state by assuming the existence of a 'society' or system of common or shared values leads to endless confusion. Research that has been done on the matter suggests that even in relatively 'homogeneous' countries or groups there is little to suggest a consensus on values.[37]

R. E. Park pointed to situations in which 'peoples of different racial stocks may live side by side in a relation of symbiosis, each playing a role in the common economy, but not interbreeding to any great extent; each maintaining . . . a more or less complete tribal organization or society of their own'.[38] To suggest that such a situation constitutes a 'plural society' is to misconceive the state of affairs. Human relationships within the borders of a legally and politically defined entity like the state do not normally constitute anything like a 'system' or 'society'. Thus when a sociologist speaks of the Syrians of Trinidad as 'outside the system', it is not at all clear what is meant.[39] The Syrians certainly buy from and sell to other inhabitants, attend the same schools, for the most part speak the same language and eat much the same food as the rest of the population. It is this talk about 'society' or 'the social system' that leads some writers to speak of East Indians who constitute over a third of the population of Trinidad as 'marginal'; or even more grotesquely to refer to the Indian population of Guyana and Trinidad as 'historical accidents'.[40]

If however we look at behaviour patterns, it does seem to be the case that, while in Haiti the Levantines have remained fairly distinct, generally marrying within the ethnic group, in the Dominican Republic and Jamaica they have often married outside the ethnic group and have become involved in a wide variety of occupations. In the Dominican Republic, Levantines had by the 1940s become generally accepted by their fellow countrymen. Leadership among them was passing into the hands of Dominican-born Levantines, many of whom were in fact ethnically mixed. Some of these had in turn married Dominicans of other ethnic origins and their children were receiving advanced education and moving into professional positions. The principal reason for this is that nationality among

Dominicans is not as closely tied to racial identity as it is in Haiti. Light-skinned people of mixed race form a majority in the Dominican Republic, which lacks the same tightly-knit mulatto elite, characteristic of her western neighbour. It was therefore easier for the arabs to become accepted as potential marriage partners than it was in Haiti. Being near-white was indeed a positive advantage in the former Spanish colony as it was in the British colonies of the Caribbean. While a foreigner is often given greater hospitality in Haiti than in the Dominican Republic, he also has the impression that were he to live there for a hundred years he would not be accepted as Haitian. In the eastern republic, on the other hand, a foreigner living and working in the country who wished to become accepted as a national, would fairly soon be generally regarded as Dominican. It may in fact be part of the explanation for the more rapid economic development in the latter, that entrepreneurial ethnic minorities, feeling themselves more readily accepted, have invested more of their capital in the country itself rather than, as in Haiti, sending most of it abroad.

As it is instructive to compare the situation in the two parts of Hispaniola, it is also worth contrasting the development of the arab communities in two former British colonies, Jamaica and Trinidad. Racial factors play a much more significant part in the politics of the latter than they do in the former, which has a stronger sense of nationality. If a Jamaican can show that he is genuinely identified with the nation he may be accepted by those of other races or colours. In Trinidad, on the other hand, it is inconceivable that a person of Lebanese origin could become prime minister. Particularly in politics but also in social life, ethnicity is of greater salience, partly because of the large East Indian population which has a strong sense of its separate identity.[41] We find a large number of ethnic groups living side by side but generally remaining distinct: Africans, Indians, Portuguese, Chinese, French and English creoles, together with a considerable number of coloured people of mixed ethnic origin. The arab immigrants were the last significant ethnic group to arrive and did not come to the island in large numbers until after the First World War. Such leading figures in the Levantine community as Nagib Elias, Aziz Hadeed, Wadih Matouk and Anthony Abraham Laquis did not arrive in Trinidad until the twenties and thirties. The Sabga family had, it is true, established itself commercially by this time, but it was part of a very small community. With respect to the Lebanese population in Costa Rica, Mary Wilkie has observed that 'with each succeeding generation the tendency to marry outside the Lebanese group increases'.[42]

Figure 2 is the family tree of a fairly typical Trinidadian family of Syrian origin (the Sabgas). It is noticeable that there are more marriages among first and second cousins than there are marriages outside the ethnic group. Figure 1, showing a Dominican family of Lebanese origin (the Cury/Khouri family), manifests a strikingly different pattern. Marriages within the ethnic group are generally confined to the older generation or to those parts of the family which have remained in or returned to Lebanon. Some of the younger generation of Trinidadian arabs have, however, begun to marry outside the ethnic group and also look for employment beyond the commercial world.

It is often assumed that ethnic clubs and associations inhibit contact and co-operation between different ethnic groups and encourage 'divisiveness'. There is no evidence for this conclusion in the present study. In fact the country where the arabs have been the least ethnocentric in marital, social and political life – the Dominican Republic – is the one where they have been most highly organised into ethnic associations. I have suggested elsewhere that the attempt to impose or facilitate 'assimilation' of ethnic minorities by breaking down or undermining ethnic organisations and loyalties may well bring about the very situation of conflict which it is presumably designed to avert.[43]

With respect to the general welfare and prosperity of this entrepreneurial ethnic minority, it would seem to be the case that they thrive under dictatorship or at least under a strong government. Their worst time has been in the first decades of the present century in Haiti, where one weak government followed another in rapid succession and where an unpopular ethnic minority became a convenient whipping boy for aspiring politicians. Under the US occupation the arabs were protected, and they seem to have been one of the few groups to have benefited from the Duvalier dynasty. In Jamaica they were protected by the colonial government from popular hostility but during the late sixties and early seventies in the Commonwealth Caribbean they came under attack by some of the black power movements of the time. In the Dominican Republic under Trujillo they were generally left alone to make their money. As a result they tend to favour strong government.

Finally we might ask, what are the factors that determine entrepreneurial success in the case of such a small ethnic group? 'Throughout the history of economics', wrote Georg Simmel in a famous essay, 'the stranger everywhere appears as the trader, or the trader as the stranger.'[44] The jews, the Chinese, the Portuguese and the Indians in East Africa for example, and the arabs in Latin America or West Africa are the most obvious examples. None of these groups can plausibly be said to have arrived with a 'protestant ethic' in their carpet bags. Nor in the case of the majority did they have previous experience as traders.[45] As we have noted a large proportion of the Levantine migrants to the Caribbean came from a small farming background.

Rather it would seem that their mere position as an ethnic minority has stimulated entrepreneurial activity. As 'strangers' they are not readily welcomed by the natives and they come to terms with the fact by cheerfully exploiting the situation in a profitable, if unpopular, role. They drive hard bargains; they have no need to remain on good relations with their customers, except from a strictly commercial point of view; they can ignore the current mores which restrict the acquisitive propensities of indigenous tradesmen. Furthermore their minority status often leads to a solidarity among them on the assumption, in the early years, that they are likely to sink or swim together. Strong family traditions also help. Then again, it is usually the most adventurous and imaginative people who emigrate; having taken the initiative in leaving their homeland they are prepared to take risks and to work hard in their new environment.

As I have already noted, many of the arab businesses are still essentially family firms. In the smaller and medium sized stores the wife often sits at the cash desk, while her husband is not far from the scene. Sometimes he conducts his operations from an air-conditioned, glass-fronted office in the centre of the store, from which he is able to survey transactions. I met one owner, after speaking with his wife at the cash desk. He was in an air-conditioned office on the second floor of his ramshackle Port-au-Prince store. On his desk were five closed-circuit television sets trained on different parts of the store, with four telephones and two telex machines near by. *Lezarabs* have come a long way since the early days: here were no hawkers and pedlars!

Part IV
Domination and Revolt

Part Six

Domination and Revolt

9   Rural Protest and Peasant Revolt, 1804–1869

Perhaps the most notorious feature of Haiti under the Duvaliers has been the militia, popularly known as the *tontons macoutes* (after the figure in Haitian folklore who carries off wicked children in his bag). The organisation originated as a private paramilitary group during the election campaign of 1956–7, when its members were known as *cagoulards* (hooded men). After the victory of Duvalier in the election of September 1957, the *tontons macoutes* became a countrywide organisation of volunteers, under Clément Barbot, pledged to defend *la révolution duvaliériste* against its adversaries. The organisation was regularised in a decree of 7 November 1962 as *Volontaires de la Sécurité Nationale* (VSN). François Duvalier, who had studied the history of Haiti, was fully aware that many of his predecessors had fallen as a result of action by the army and that some counterforce was therefore necessary if he was to survive. He decided to revive an ancient tradition in the country by involving the masses in a paramilitary organisation. From the revolutionary period (1789–1803) to the US occupation (1915–34), large numbers of Haitians had been in possession of firearms, and it was only with the defeat of the *cacos* rebellion under Charlemagne Péralte in 1919 that the people were generally disarmed.

In this chapter I wish to discuss three rural protest movements in the period following the declaration of independence. Little has been written on this aspect of Haitian history[1] and most Haitian writers of the period treated these revolts as unfortunate disturbances to the normal course of events. As Louis Joseph Janvier remarked, 'up to now those who have written the history of the *piquets* were their enemies or their assassins'.[2] Rural movements of this period manifest a certain pattern which was to be repeated in the years immediately preceding the US invasion of 1915 and in the bold military resistance to the occupation led by Péralte and Benoît Batraville.[3] They were centred in the countryside and were, as Léon Laroche observed with respect to the *piquets*, directed largely against the towns.[4] The movements with which we are concerned in this chapter were usually led by black landowners with medium-sized properties, and it is likely that they were supported principally by small-holding peasants rather than by the landless and very poor.

Certain parts of Haiti were particularly prone to such risings. The region around Jérémie in the southern peninsular of Haiti, known as La Grand'Anse, has been the centre of two of the most important revolts. Owing to its physical characteristics the South was the last region to be colonised and developed by the French. Its mountainous terrain was less suitable for the establishment of large sugar plantations than were the plains of the North and West. La Grand'Anse was, then, a region of small coffee plantations, and by 1780 most of the properties were in the hands of the *affranchis*. During the coffee boom of the 1780s, however, they began to sell these properties as their value increased. The plantations were bought largely by *petits blancs*, who by the time of the British occupation of 1793 had become a formidable power in the region. Independent-minded and fiercely racialist, these white coffee farmers feared the return of the mulatto general Rigaud and were among the earliest French colonists to go over to the British. Another significant feature of the region was that among the slave population of La Grand'Anse was a high proportion of *bossals* (African-born slaves) who tended to predominate on the coffee farms of the colony.[5] During the revolutionary years and in the post-independence period large numbers of these blacks established themselves as independent small farmers in the interior. The city of Jérémie, where many of the mulattoes had settled, was known even in colonial times as a centre of the most bitter racial and colour prejudice.

While the rhetoric of the leaders of these movements was frequently revolutionary, the aim of the rank and file seems to have been reformist, to employ a distinction made by Eric Hobsbawm,[6] or even conservative. Their principal concerns were to maintain their property rights, to resist government taxation and to limit the power of urban money lenders and *spéculateurs*. The customary looting which took place does not imply a revolutionary determination to overthrow the economic and social system, but was rather a gesture of defiance towards the authorities. The colour issue was often raised, either by the rebels themselves or by their opponents. This is because of the fact that in Haiti, as in many other parts of the Carribean, dark colour is the *badge* of low economic status and the rhetoric of protest is commonly formulated in colour terms, though the real issues are economic and social. This was evidently so in the black power movement of 1968–70 in Trinidad.[7]

Finally, while many of these protest movements effected the overthrow of the government in Port-au-Prince their influence on the policy of the succeeding administration was minimal. Only in the revolt led by Goman was an independent state maintained for any length of time.

THE POLITICAL BACKGROUND

Haiti had become independent as a result of a bloody colonial war lasting many years and involving several European countries. It was a struggle in which large numbers of Haitians were involved and it might properly be called a war of national liberation. After independence had been declared the principal internal question which confronted the leaders of the country was that of land ownership. Jean-Jacques Dessalines, the first ruler (1804–6), was clearly unhappy about a situation in which a small proportion of the population, the class of predominantly mulatto *anciens libres*, owned large properties while the liberated slaves, *nouveaux libres*, were legally landless, though increasing numbers of them had begun squatting on vacant properties. He made it clear that he intended to rectify the situation, and this is undoubtedly one of the reasons for his assassination. Henry Christophe, ruler of the North, at first attempted to maintain a plantation system, producing crops for export and punishing workers who left their plantations without permission.[8] Later however, he followed Pétion's policy of land distribution. Pétion, who had become president of a republic in the South and West, had began to distribute and to sell state properties soon after his accession to power.[9] While it would be wrong to suggest that this land policy was a 'democratic' move, for the principal beneficiaries were the largely mulatto generals of his army, nevertheless it did lay the foundations for a landowning peasantry, which has been one of the features distinguishing Haiti from other principal islands of the Antilles.[10] The first protest movement we shall be considering occurred during the presidency of Pétion and continued into that of his successor.

Pétion's successor, Jean-Pierre Boyer, a spokesman of the mulatto elite, saw with distress the decline of plantation agriculture and endeavoured to check the trend towards a peasant economy by his rural code of 1826 and other legislation.[11] These efforts were generally unsuccessful. Boyer, who had invaded and occupied the eastern two-thirds of the island in 1822, ruled the whole of Hispaniola until his tenure of office came to an end in 1843. A period of instability followed in which four presidents succeeded each other in rapid succession. It was a time in which the rural black elite, with support from the black masses, particularly in the South, reasserted its position in reaction to the mulatto hegemony. Our second protest movement took place at this time. The shift in the balance of power towards the blacks was to some extent reinforced during the Soulouque era (1847–59) but the overthrow of the empire and the advent of Geffrard (1859–67) did something to re-establish the position of the mulatto elite.[12] This chapter ends with a consideration of the third rural protest movement which took place in the confused period of civil war during the presidency of Salnave (1867–9).

* * *　* * *

GOMAN'S PEASANT REPUBLIC

When a country has secured its liberation by armed struggle, a tradition of violence frequently persists into the period of independence. Haiti's sovereign status was not recognised by France until 1825 and in the two decades which preceded this there was a continual threat of French invasion. Also Napoleon's army remained on the island, at Santo Domingo, until 1809. Large standing armies were therefore maintained by all Haitian governments, in addition to which almost the whole male population over fifteen years of age was ready to take up arms at short notice.[13] Pétion and Christophe had issued fierce assertions of their determination to resist foreign invasions. The former warned that French troops would find nothing in Haiti but 'ashes mingled with dust', while Christophe declared: 'At my voice Hayti will be transformed into a vast camp of soldiers'. A war of ambush and guerrilla tactics would be pursued involving the whole population.[14] French observers who best knew the situation advised against any attempt to reconquer the country by arms.[15] The British consul, Charles Mackenzie, writing in 1826, concurred in this judgement, 'I am disposed to think that no invading European force can ever succeed in conquering Haiti unless through the treachery of the native chiefs'; this was due to the capacity of Haitian troops for what he called 'desultory warfare'.[16] In a situation of this kind, when a high proportion of the population is accustomed to carry weapons, it is not surprising that individual generals had considerable autonomy, and that disaffected groups should take up arms against the government from time to time.[17]

The insurrection of La Grand'Anse, which lasted from 1807 to 1819, is at once the most interesting and the least documented protest movement of nineteenth-century Haiti. It was led by a former slave, called Goman, who was a *bossal* from the Congo, well known as a maroon in colonial days. His full name was Jean-Baptiste Dupérier, or Perrier.[18] It is likely that he had been a slave on the Perrier plantation in La Plaine des Cayes. After the revolt on this plantation the mulatto general André Rigaud negotiated in 1792 with slaves and masters for a settlement which included 700 manumissions.[19] Goman, having returned to the plantation, was possibly one of these *affranchis* and was adopted by Rigaud as his 'godson'. Goman was among the considerable number of southern blacks who supported Rigaud against Toussaint in the war of the South (1799–1800). After Rigaud's defeat, Goman returned to work on the Perrier plantation, though during the struggle for independence he took up arms once more. His opposition to Toussaint and later to Dessalines was no doubt reinforced by the hostility which existed at this time between *créole* and *bossal* blacks.[20]

The assassination of Dessalines in October 1806 led to a period of confusion in Haiti. Christophe, heir-apparent, was unprepared to accept the restrictions which rival generals sought to impose upon the new head of state, and civil war broke out. It was at this time that an insurrection occurred in La Grand'Anse. The origins of this outbreak are unclear. It is possible, as Madiou maintained, that the revolt was started by Thomas

Durocher, a black officer who was inspector of agriculture for the region, and Bergerac Trichet, the brother of Théodat Trichet a supporter of Pétion. The reason for their discontent was said to be the appointment of General Francisque as commandant of La Grand'Anse. It is probable that they were encouraged in this revolt by Henry Christophe or at least by their belief that the black general would defeat Pétion and soon take control of the whole country.[21] The small black peasant farmers of the region, led by Jason Domingo, César Novelet and Bazile, took to arms, and on 8 January 1807 invaded the mulatto-dominated city of Jérémie. The residents of the city managed, however, to repel the attack. Goman, who was at this time leading the nineteenth batallion at L'Anse d'Hainault, was appointed head of the insurrection by a gathering of rebels held at L'Habitation Fiollé, near Dame Marie, in the following month. Durocher and Trichet (if indeed they had ever been involved in the insurrection, which Beaubrun Ardouin denied[22]) went over to the government side.

From 1807 until 1819, despite repeated attempts by the government to suppress the revolt, large inland areas in the southwest were controlled by Goman and his second in command, Saint Louis Boteau. A general amnesty was proclaimed in April 1807 and, on the advice of Durocher, the prisoners were released and organised into an army of 1500 men known as *éclaireurs*. It was hoped that this group, composed of men who knew the terrain, would lead the regular army in crushing the rebels. Goman successfully resisted, and organised a peasant republic in the area, maintaining close links with a number of collaborators in Jérémie and other coastal towns, from whom he secured supplies of arms and other necessities. He moved his headquarters from place to place, but eventually settled in the mountains about sixty-five kilometres from Jérémie at a village known as Grand-Doco, where he planted large areas in *vivres* (ground provision) and other food crops in order to support his army.

According to Madiou the perennial colour problem was raised by Boteau, who endeavoured to turn the struggle into a war of caste by stirring up the black peasants against the mulattoes on grounds of colour.[23] Swift action by black generals on the government side, including Durocher and Vaval, managed to prevent the struggle from becoming such a caste war and Boteau was obliged to abandon his black power propaganda.

Goman's ability to resist the assaults of the republican forces is partly explained by the fact that Pétion was fighting on two fronts. Most of his energy was taken up in a long war with Christophe's forces; also he was plagued by continual conspiracies from within. The presence of his former rival, General Gérin, in the South led to particular problems which were solved only by the suicide of Gérin in 1809 and by the arrest of Durocher and Trichet as alleged collaborators in an intended *coup*. Soon after these events, however, the tranquility of the republic was further disturbed in April 1810 by the arrival in Les Cayes of André Rigaud, the celebrated mulatto general, from exile in France. He was invited to Port-au-Prince by Pétion where he was received with honours and appointed commander of the forces in La Grand'Anse, charged with suppressing the revolt. Rigaud met his former disciple and godson Goman, who promised to submit to the government, a promise which the peasant leader failed to keep. Then Rigaud, encouraged by disaffected mulattoes including Bruno Blanchet, Guy-Joseph Bonnet and J.-M. Borgella, declared the independence of the South with its capital in Les Cayes. There were, then, four states in Haiti at this time, apart from the Spanish colony in the eastern part of the island. Whether Rigaud was sent by the French as an agent, as the British feared, or whether he remained a loyal Haitian patriot, as Pétion had maintained,[24] is not clear, but death soon removed him from the scene and in 1811 Borgella led the South back into Pétion's republic.

Goman maintained his independence and was created Comte de Jérémie by Christophe, who had become King Henry 1 in 1811. Goman evidently enjoyed popular support in the region and even Pétion recognised legitimate grounds for peasant discontent in La Grand'Anse. In a letter to General Bazelais, commandant of the region, the president wrote:

The cultivators, having never been considered as active citizens of the republic, have always been treated with rigour and with more or less injustice. This abject state, this stupid system, is one of the principal causes of the insurrection which is devouring this region.[25]

Goman remained in almost undisputed possession of his domains until after the death of Pétion in 1818. The new president,

Boyer, announced in January 1819 a campaign against the rebels. 'The time has come,' he declared, 'when the insurrection of La Grand'Anse must cease.'[26]

The attack on Goman was co-ordinated by Bazelais and included troops under the command of Borgella, Lys and Francisque, together with the national guard from a number of towns. The rebels retreated into the hills, where they were relentlessly pursued by government troops who destroyed the plantations of the rebels as they went. After several months government forces seized Grand-Doco, where Le Comte de Jérémie was living with his wives. He avoided capture but his headquarters were destroyed together with the plantations which had constituted his main source of food. With the exception of Goman himself and two of his officers most of the rebel leaders submitted and by the end of June 1819 the peasant republic had been conquered. The fate of Goman himself is unknown, although Beaubrun Ardouin suggested that he probably died of injuries received in the figthing.[27]

* * *   * * *

BOYER AND HIS LEGACY

After the death of Christophe in 1820, Haiti was reunited under Boyer, who occupied the former Spanish colony of Santo Domingo in 1822 and ruled the whole island until he was deposed in 1843. These years were marked by a concentration of power in the hands of a small group of mulatto families. It was a time of relative peace and stability, enlivened with only occasional plots and protests, led mostly by black generals. Rural discontent was, however, widespread owing to Boyer's attempt, enshrined in the rural code of 1826, to reimpose the plantation system and to his efforts to raise money from the peasants to cover the huge indemnity imposed by France as a condition for recognising Haitian independence.[28] Hostility towards France was almost universal and the government was unpopular for having accepted these conditions.[29] Boyer's fall in 1843 came as a result of divisions within the ranks of the mulatto elite rather than from a revolt among the black masses. The new president, Charles Hérard, was no less exclusivist in his policies, and black discontent exploded in the same year.

The most serious and prolonged insurrection was again in the region of La Grand'Anse, though there was also considerable resistance in parts of the North.[30] The southern revolt began under the leadership of the Salomon family, who were rich black landowners in the region of Les Cayes. The rising started in August 1843 and government forces under General Lazare were sent to put it down. It was estimated that Salomon's men were armed with roughly 300 rifles and 500 wooden pikes, from which they derived the name of *piquets*.[31] The revolt was temporarily suppressed and the Salomons were arrested. Leadership then passed into the hands of Louis Jean-Jacques Acaau. Born of a black small-holding family during the early years of the century in the commune of Torbeck, Acaau joined the army at an early age and soon became an officer. He was, in the words of the British consul, 'a man of some instruction for a negro'.[32] Nevertheless, promotion was difficult for blacks in the Boyer era and consequent discontent among black officers was one of the causes of the rising. The principal complaints of the small farmers of the region were about the penalty of imprisonment for debt and the power of bailiffs. According to Madiou though, the unacknowledged objects of the rising were to destroy mulatto dominance in general, to install a black president, and to confiscate land from the rich of all colours, distributing it among the poor.[33] It was Acaau who is said to have first enunciated the well-known *Kréyol* proverb *nèg rich sé mulât, mulât pov sé nèg*.

Acaau's opponents and many foreign observers portrayed the struggle in the South as one of colour,[34] and feeling in the South was indeed such that three black generals told the French foreign minister, in an extraordinary letter, that they would prefer a restoration of French control to a continued domination by *petits mulâtres*. Acaau himself, however, explicitly denied inaugurating a caste war, claiming to defend the interests of the poor of all colours.[35]

Dressed in straw hats, with ragged trousers and jackets, these *piquet* leaders carried large machetes and had pistols in their belts. Acaau's followers proclaimed him *chef des réclamations de ces concitoyens*. 'The population of the countryside,' he declared, 'awaking from the slumber into which it has been plunged, is murmuring in its poverty and is determined to work for the securing of its rights.'[36] Acaau undoubtedly enjoyed widespread popular support, particularly in La Grand'Anse, as Goman had before him. He reinforced his position with claims to supernatural powers. Whether he practiced voodoo or *obeah* is not clear, but Frère Joseph – probably a *prêt savan* (bush priest) rather than a *houngan* (voodoo priest) – marched, candle in hand, in the midst of the *piquets*, conducting novenas of prayer to the Blessed Virgin Mary.[37]

Despite being poorly armed, Acaau's men were able to occupy the cities of Jérémie and Les Cayes and to put considerable pressure on the government. The fall of Charles Hérard and the election of the black General Guerrier did something to pacify the *piquets* and Acaau submitted to the government, being later appointed commandant of L'Anse à Veau. By August 1845 Acaau was named by the British consul as one of the possible successors to President Pierrot. His lieutenants Dugué Zamor and Jean Claude had in the meanwhile also secured official positions. 'These two men', wrote the British consul Thomas Ussher, 'are the terror of the peaceably disposed inhabitants of Aux Cayes. . . . the Government dare not dismiss them'. Many of those involved in the southern revolt were hostile not only to the French but to all foreigners. Pointing to British warships off the coast, General Lazare said to his men, 'There are your real enemies, the white men, beware of them'.[38] Acaau, however, had approached Commodore Sharpe with a request for British protection.[39]

BLACK EMPIRE AND BOURGEOIS REPUBLIC

The period of acute governmental instability which began with the fall of Boyer came to an end with the election of the black general, Faustin Soulouque, in March 1847. The new president was generally believed to be weak and stupid; mulatto politicians, including the Ardouin brothers, had supported his election thinking that they would be able to manipulate him. These men soon learned that this was not to be so. Soulouque proved to be a canny, ruthless and unpredictable leader with a mind of his own. One of the first things he did after his election was to replace many mulatto officers by blacks and build up a paramilitary group called the *zinglins* under the command of Maximilien Augustin, popularly known as Similien.[40] Recruited from the urban sub-proletariat, the *zinglins* were generally feared by the bourgeoisie of all colours.[41]

Acaau, having become disillusioned with the situation, committed suicide, and leadership of the southern *piquets* passed into the hands of Pierre Noir, Jean Denis and Voltaire Castor, though it is likely that the Salomons continued to exercise an influence over them. In 1848 a detachment of *piquets* invaded Les Cayes. The rich blacks, who had collaborated with the mulatto establishment in the city, laid down their arms, confident that their colour would save them. They badly misjudged the situation, however, and eighty-nine of these blacks were put to death, Castor himself killing seventy of them with his own hands. Thus came to pass, in the words of the French consul, the saying of Acaau *nèg rich sé mulât*. A similar event had occurred in the city two years earlier when the *piquets* had put to death 'blacks and mulattoes whom they supposed to be proprietors of anything'.[42]

Soulouque clearly believed that the *piquets* were getting out of hand and he charged Dugué Zamor with the task of suppressing them; Zamor was soon replaced by General André Thélémaque, who was in turn removed by Jean Claude who proclaimed himself commandant of the South. The situation was however brought under control by the government and Pierre Noir was executed in November 1848. In the following year Soulouque felt confident enough to relieve Similien of his duties and have himself proclaimed Emperor Faustin 1. The inauguration of the empire began a period of relative stability which lasted until General Fabre Nicolas Geffrard's successful revolution of 1859. The emperor took refuge in Jamaica, returning to Haiti only with the fall of Geffrard in 1867; he died a short while after at Petit Goâve.

Geffrard was an elite *griffe*[43] and was generally identified with the interests of the mulatto bourgeoisie. Although a change in government certainly led to a shift in the balance of power away from the blacks, the contrast between the regimes of Soulouque and Geffrard has frequently been overstated. While many of the emperor's ministers had been mulattoes, a number of blacks retained their positions under Geffrard; most of the army commanders survived the change.[44] Geffrard suppressed attempted *coups* by black generals from the South in 1862 and 1865, the former being led by members of the Salomon family. More serious was the revolt in Cap Haïtien in 1865 led by General Silvain Salnave, with support from the black politician and writer Demesvar Delorme. This rising, which lasted for several months, had backing from the USA and from elements in the Dominican Republic, but was put down by Geffrard with help from a British gunboat which bombarded the city. Renewed attempts by Salnave, together with a revolt led by General Nissage Saget at St Marc, were successful, and in 1867 sections of Geffrard's crack brigade, *les tirailleurs*, mutinied. In March 1867 the president left for Jamaica, where he died eleven years later. An economic and financial crisis had weakened the government and important elements of the national bourgeoisie had become disaffected, claiming that Geffrard favoured foreign merchants. The charges brought against him by Saget included turning the girls' schools in the country into *'maisons de séduction à son profit'*.[45] The following section of this chapter will consider the armed conflicts of the two succeeding years.

***   ***

SALNAVE AND THE CACOS WAR

The period of Salnave's presidency was marked by almost continuous fighting, and according to F. D. Légitime constituted the worst conflagration in Haiti since the war of independence.[46] The president was combating not only the peasant irregulars, known as *cacos* in the northern part of the country, but also groups of *piquets* in the South, both of which were supported by dissident generals of the regular army with their men.

Salnave was himself a handsome, light-skinned mulatto who managed to secure the bulk of his support from the blacks of Cap Haïtien and Port-au-Prince. He was a powerful orator and a populist who had an easy manner with the ordinary Haitian and treated all men (and women) as equals. Even his most bitter critics witnessed to the president's popularity among the urban poor.[47] With the fall of Geffrard a provisional government was set up with Nissage Saget as president and including Victorin Chevalier, a reluctant supporter of Salnave, whose followers called him *chef d'éxecution de volontés du peuple*. A constituent assembly was called for 8 April 1867, but it was clear that Salnave's claim to the presidency would be accepted. Popular chants were sung in Salnave's favour and enthusiastic support for him spread throughout the countryside. 'The people', reported the French minister in Port-au-Prince, 'wish only for him and they rise up as one man whenever he appears, from the Cap to Port-au-Prince.'[48] He was, as Firmin observed, 'the idol of the masses'.[49]

Opposition to the new regime was, however, swift to manifest itself. The French minister, Comte Méjan, referred to a revolt of *'cocos'* which broke out in the north-east in May 1867; it was centred at Ouanaminthe near the Dominican border and involved many of the same local chiefs who had opposed Salnave in 1865. They saw his rise to power as constituting a threat to their own established positions. There was also fighting in the region of Jérémie. 'Never has a government,' Méjan reported, 'never has a head of state, lost his popularity more completely or more rapidly.'[50] General Léon Montas, the principal leader of anti-government forces in the north-east was captured and put in prison where, after some months, he was found dead in December 1867. This increased the bitterness of the struggle.

Salnave's government earned the hostility of traders and *spéculateurs* by instituting a state monopoly in coffee and ensured support from the urban masses by the etablishment of *magasins d'état* for the sale of necessities at low prices: two steps which Salomon had attempted as finance minister in Soulouque's government. Salnave thus retained his popularity among the urban proletariat and sub-proletariat, particularly with the women. Chevalier claimed that Salnave's government was 'the expression of the needs, the sentiments, the interests of the masses'.[51] In October 1867 demonstrations in favour of the government were held in the capital, with women marching through the commercial centre of the city crying: *'Vive Salnave; à bas les négotiants cacos'*. The violent rhetoric of Salnave's supporters increased. 'The government,' declared the British minister Sir Spenser St John, 'has taken into its pay bands of the lowest negresses to parade the town armed with butchers' knives and threatening with death and with plunder and fire all the respectable inhabitants'. St John, whose hostility to Salnave and support for Geffrard was well-known, denounced the president for having 'turned the Palace into a rendezvous where the scum of the negresses assembled to dance and drink'.[52]

Meanwhile, opposition to Salnave was growing throughout Haiti, and he took personal charge of the army in its campaign against the northern *cacos*. In the spring of 1868 a rising at

Gonaïves proclaimed as president General Philippeaux (a government minister under Geffrard). In Hinche a revolt forced the commandant to retreat to the fort. Nissage Saget, whose power base was St Marc, issued a proclamation on 26 April against the government. He was in turn denounced by the president for 'profiting from the brigandage of the *cacos*'.[53] May 1868 witnessed a further rising in the South, which began at Léogane and spread westwards. Three divisions, headed by the generals Domingue, Faubert and Dubois, declared against the government. Salnave was faced with yet another revolt at Dondon led by Nord Alexis. From May to September, Port-au-Prince was under siege with rebel troops occupying Carrefour, just five kilometres west from the city centre, and Croix-des-Bouquets somewhat further to the east. Salnave countered by encouraging *piquet* leaders in the South to rise up against his enemies. In the countryside around Jacmel, Léogane, Petit Goâve and in La Grand'Anse the *piquets* revolted, thus compelling the armies of Domingue which were besieging the capital to withdraw and defend the cities of the South. From this time on there were effectively three separate states in Haiti: the north with its capital at Saint Marc, under Nissage, the south under Domingue, centred at Les Cayes, and – between the two – the government of Salnave, controlling the capital, some northern cities and (through the *piquets*) considerable parts of the rural South. The civil war led to serious famine and to outbreaks of cholera and yellow fever in the cities of the South and West.

Who were the *cacos*? I have argued elsewhere that the *cacos* came from the middle class of peasants rather than from the very poor, as has been asserted by several writers.[54] The name is probably derived from the fierce little bird called the *taco* and was first used to designate the black guerrillas who harrassed the French in 1802. Government forces attacked by the *cacos* in the period prior to the United States invasion of 1915 were known as *zandolites*, after the large lizard which the *taco* finds tasty. Père Cabon, however, claimed that the term *cacos* derives from the *caraco*, a garment worn by peasants.[55] These peasant irregulars took up arms on the initiative of local chiefs, or of disaffected army officers, with the hope of payment or at least opportunities for pillage. When government forces advanced, the *cacos* bands would usually dissolve and the peasants would return to cultivate their land; they would then reassemble elsewhere when the troops had gone.[56] The same was generally true of the *piquets* in the South. One consequence of this mode of operation was that the area within which each band could act effectively was limited by the unwillingness of its members to move far from their properties.[57]

The colour question played a part in the struggles of these years. It was widely believed by peasants in the countryside that Salnave was black and he received considerable support from such *piquet* leaders as Siffra Fortuné, who controlled the region around Baradères in the South. In September 1868 an English observer recorded how Salnave's army which was surrounding the rebel city of Jacmel was mostly composed of 'country people (the true black)'.[58] When, according to Janvier, the *piquets* discovered that Salnave was a very clear-skinned mulatto many of them were less keen to support him. Sections of them went over to the black general Michel Domingue, who eagerly exploited his colour advantage, denouncing Salnave for not having a drop of African blood in his veins.[59]

Although, as I have pointed out, much of Salnave's support came from urban blacks, most mulattoes in the capital were also prepared to give him tacit support, owing to their fear of a black head of state taking his place. At least Salnave was the right colour![60] Whether the president practiced voodoo, as his opponents claimed, is not certain, but his policies were undoubtedly anti-clerical and erastian. The president attempted to reinstate some irregular clergy who had ministered in Haiti prior to the *Concordat* of 1860, but who had been deposed by the new hierarchy. Government troops imprisoned a number of priests and others were chased from their parishes by *piquet* leaders loyal to the government. From the days of the *Concordat* onwards the hierarchy of the Roman Catholic church had tended to side with the mulatto elite, while the *noiriste* elite, with which Salnave had associated himself, had frequently practised freemasonry and adopted an anti-clerical stance. Salnave's dispute with the hierarchy culminated in a decree of 28 June 1869 deposing the archbishop of Port-au-Prince, Mgr Testard du Cosquer. The vicar general, Mgr Guilloux, denounced the decree as null.[61]

With the raising of the siege of Port-au-Prince in September 1868 and the arrival of a new government warship from the USA the fortunes of Salnave seemed to be turning. Nevertheless fighting continued in various parts of the country throughout

1869; Gonaïves fell at the end of August, and a decisive development occurred at the beginning of December when the *cacos* seized Cap Haïtien. Then on the night of 18 December Generals Brice and Boisrond Canal invaded the capital from the sea. Salnave remained in the palace until the last moment when he fled to the hills hoping to reach the Dominican border. He was captured and brought back to the capital where he was shot in the following month. Thus came to an end the *cacos* war. Only the *piquets* of La Grand'Anse remained faithful, refusing to believe that Salnave had fallen.[62] As André Adam has convincingly shown, [63] Salnave's defeat was due to an alliance between the bourgeois classes in the towns and large sections of the *classe intermédiaire* in the countryside. These groups were encouraged by French and British consuls and by the Roman Catholic hierarchy. So exhausted was the country that the new president, Nissage Saget, an elite *griffe*, was able to rule in relative peace and was one of the few Haitian heads of state to remain in office for his constitutional term and then retire.

Owing to his populism and his anti-clericalism Salnave soon became a hero of the *noiriste* tradition in Haiti and is frequently said to have been the founder of the National Party. He is one of the few mulattoes to receive a favourable report in the writings of Duvalier and his followers.[64] Whether Salnave can truly be said to have founded the National Party is doubtful, though its members sought inspiration from the legend of his struggles and death. The actual founder of the Party was Septimus Rameau, the nephew of the same Michel Domingue who had fought against Salnave; in 1868 Rameau had told foreign consuls in Haiti that his southern army was marching against the government 'under the banner of civilisation'.[65] Delorme, who can be called a co-founder of the National Party was of course associated with Salnave for some years, but became alienated in 1868 and denounced him vigorously.[66]

* * *   * * *

CONCLUSION

Our study raises the complicated issue of the relationship between class and colour in rural Haiti and more generally throughout the Caribbean. Class loyalties often supersede colour loyalties, as when the invading *piquets* put to death their fellow blacks from the bourgeois class or when the black proletariat and sub-proletariat of the capital supported Salnave through the most harrowing months of the siege. As we have also seen, however, there are clearly situations when colour must be recognised as a significant and independent variable in explaining the course of events. The case of the rural blacks whose attitude to Salnave changed when they discovered his true colour is not an isolated incident. The black politician Anténor Firmin recorded how his National Party opponents spread the rumour that he was 'a mulatto as clear-skinned as a white', so that the blacks of the rural North would not vote for him.[67] Domingue's attempt to exploit the colour issue and to convince the poor blacks that their interests were the same as those of the black elite has been imitated by succeeding politicians of the black elite and middle class. Estimé and Duvalier were both denounced by their opponents for exploiting the colour issue in just this way.

It would be true to say though, that colour normally becomes significant in Caribbean politics only when it is reinforced by other factors, real or imagined. The change in attitude towards Salnave on the part of rural blacks who did not know him was due to the fact that in their experience mulatto leaders tended to act in the interests of the urban bourgeoisie, while the black leaders at least knew enough about the countryside to realise that they must take some account of peasant interests. Their belief that they should not support Salnave is therefore understandable in the light of the general coincidence between colour and class in Haiti. Colour prejudice, having come into being for whatever cause, develops a dynamic of its own and often leads men to act in ways which are in conflict with their material interests.

While the protest movements I have been considering have certain features in common there are clear differences between them. In its determination to maintain an independent peasant state, Goman's revolt stands out as peculiar. All three movements were in certain respects conservative. The first two were defending the interests of the small peasants against perceived threats from the urban bourgeoisie. The *cacos* revolt was a movement of peasants with small and medium-sized holdings, in alliance with the urban bourgeoisie against a government which was seen to be acting in the interests of the growing proletariat and sub-proletariat in the towns. In all three movements the principal leaders of the revolts had been regular army officers, but professional soldiers played a much larger part in the two later revolts than in the movement headed by Goman. The personal factor, depending on the charismatic leadership of local chiefs and on a patron–client relationship was a basic feature of all three movements. Local chiefs who had established such a dependency relationship with the poorer peasants in their region were able to call on their support in time of need. The power of these rural chiefs increased during the latter part of the nineteenth century and contributed in a major way to the political instability of the country in the period prior to the US invasion. Thanks to the work of Haitian historians Alain Turnier, Roger Gaillard and Kethly Millet, we know a good deal about these later peasant movements. The researches of these writers generally confirm the pattern which has emerged from our brief study of the three earlier revolts.

With the defeat of the *cacos* revolt of 1918–19, however, the balance of power shifted from the countryside to the capital. In the years following the withdrawal of the marines all important decisions were made in Port-au-Prince and successful protest movements were invariably centred there. The election of Dumarsais Estimé in 1946 and of François Duvalier in 1957 marked a reassertion of rural claims, though the subsequent policies of their governments have hardly done anything to disturb the hegemony of 'the republic of Port-au-Prince'. Despite the rhetoric, little consideration has been given to the interests of rural Haitians who, after all, still comprise about 90 per cent of the country's population.

One of the methods Duvalier used to recruit support in rural areas and to maintain control throughout the country was by developing the organisation of *tontons macoutes*. 'Excellency,' declared one *macoute* leader in 1960, addressing the president, 'the gun that Sonthonax gave us to defend our liberty and that the American occupation has taken away from us is the gun that, without fear, you have given back to us – be assured that this gun will not be used against you.'[68] Many *macoute* leaders come from that class of medium-sized land owners which provided leadership and much of the rank and file membership of the nineteenth-century movements, some like Zacharie Delva of

Gonaïves, were also *houngans*. The notorious slaughter of mulatto families in Jérémie in August 1964 also bears comparison with some of the deeds of the *piquets*. Nevertheless, the difference between the *macoutes* and the groups which we have been considering is clear. The former has become a movement dedicated to preserving a government, like the *zinglins* of Soulouque, rather than for defending the interests of the masses. Perhaps the true successors of the *cacos* and *piquets* of former days are the peasant bands which, following the death of François Duvalier in April 1971, stoned the houses of Delva and other unpopular *macoute* leaders, forcing them to take refuge in the capital.

10   Voting with their Feet: the Haitian Migration

It is a common misapprehension that Haiti was an 'isolated' country during the nineteenth century. There was in fact a constant movement of individuals and small groups from Haiti to Europe, to the USA and to other countries of the Caribbean, as well as the arrival in Haiti of numbers of temporary or permanent immigrants. It is true that in general these movements affected principally the capital and the coastal cities, but foreign influences were indirectly felt throughout much of the country. European and North American newspapers, journals and books circulated freely among the small literate groups in Haiti. Foreign businessmen – first British, French and American, then German – dominated the commerce of the country. The end of the nineteenth century saw the arrival of Italian, Cuban and Levantine migrants. Attempts to attract freed slaves from the USA, made principally by Boyer (1818–43) and by Geffrard (1859–67), were only partially successful. There had been a lively debate in the 1840s about the possibility of organising indentured labour from India or China on the lines of the system adopted in Trinidad and Demerara.[1] In the late nineteenth century many hundreds of Jamaicans, however, worked in the capital as coachmen or in other menial occupations. Haitians went abroad to study in France, or to seek refuge as exiles in Jamaica, the Dominican Republic, St Thomas, or further afield in the USA or in Europe. Large scale emigration from Haiti, however, was a feature of the twentieth century.

With respect to this twentieth-century migration of Haitians, a number of questions need to be answered. In the first place the facts must be established about the numbers involved. What kind of people left: what age, what class, what sex were they? Where did they go? Then there are questions of motivation: why did such large numbers leave Haiti? Why did they go to one country rather than another? Was the migration a seasonal phenomenon or did it have a more permanent character? Other questions concern the effects of the migration on Haiti itself and on the countries to which the migrants went.

In the following sections I shall try briefly to answer these questions, indicating some of the literature on the subject. The conclusion will outline the significance of the migration both for Haiti and for the countries to which the migrants have travelled.

CUBA AND THE DOMINICAN REPUBLIC

The phenomenon of empire facilitates migratory movements and neo-imperialism has had the same effect. The US investment in and occupation of Caribbean countries around the turn of the century had a major impact on the population pattern of the islands. In the last quarter of the nineteenth century the Dominican sugar industry had begun to expand, while in Cuba sugar production received a boost in 1903 due to the reciprocity treaty with the USA. The first decade of the century saw significant US investment in both these countries. Sugar was and still is one of the most labour-intensive industries. An acute labour shortage in Cuba led to a demand for *braceros* to cut cane, and in 1913 1200 Haitians migrated to Cuba under the auspices of the United Fruit Company. Further investment was stimulated by the 1914–18 War. Within a month of the outbreak of war the price of sugar doubled. Britain had, for example, depended for two-thirds of her sugar supplies on Germany and Austria-Hungary and now needed to look elsewhere.[2] The number of Haitian sugar workers in Cuba reached 5000 in 1916 and had rocketed to 36 000 by 1920. The expulsion of thousands of Haitian peasant farmers from land which their families had farmed for generations, which took place during the US occupation, and the related attempt to create a plantation economy led to rural dislocation, unemployment and a consequent willingness to emigrate.[3]

With the world depression of the twenties and thirties, however, Cuban sugar production declined and workers were laid off. Many Haitians in Cuba attempted to find other jobs in the years following 1921, and some were successful. Widespread unemployment in Cuba led to strong anti-Haitian feeling and

large numbers were repatriated. In one year alone (1936–7) it
has been estimated that about 30 000 Haitians were repatriated
either voluntarily or by deportation.[4] Nevertheless considerable
numbers remained in Cuba and can still be found today in small
communities in the Sierra Maestra and elsewhere.[5]

Returning migrants were known as *viejos*. During the boom
years some arrived home to Port de Paix, Les Cayes, Petit Goâve
and to other areas with relatively large sums of money and local
business picked up for a while. Many returned to Cuba, others
remained. Although some *viejos* had made their fortune the
majority returned to Haiti with little or nothing but a few gold
teeth and some flashy clothes. Manuel, the hero of Haiti's most
celebrated novel, *Gouverneurs de la rosée*, by Jacques Roumain, was
such a returned migrant. All he brought back was the memory of
fifteen hard years and a new vision of a brighter future for his
fatalistic compatriots.

The history of relations between Haiti and the Dominican
Republic has been marked by hostility, suspicion and prejudice.
Revolutionary leaders, Toussaint Louverture and Jean-Jacques
Dessalines made no secret of their belief that the Spanish colony
was a legitimate part of their realm and determined 'to recognise
as frontiers only those established by nature and the sea'.[6] These
early ambitions were later realised in 1822 when Haitian forces
occupied the eastern part of the island with encouragement from
a number of Dominicans who had recently expelled their Spanish colonial masters. President Boyer's rule of the Spanish
speaking part of the island, however, became increasingly unpopular, and soon after his fall in 1843, the Dominicans expelled the
occupying troops. Despite a number of attempts at reconquest,
notably under Soulouque (1847–59), Haiti was never able to
repossess her eastern department, as she regarded the Dominican Republic.

These events left a legacy of fear on the part of the less numerous Dominicans that the 'barbarous hordes' from the west
would overrun their country. The Dominicans saw themselves as
representing European, Catholic civilisation under threat from a
pagan and inferior race. Elsewhere I have illustrated the role
played by racial ideas in the early years of Dominican independence. These attitudes have been perpetuated into the twentieth
century.[7] Nevertheless small numbers of Haitians settled in the
Dominican Republic in the latter half of the nineteenth century,

and with the growth of the Dominican sugar industry in the 1870s more arrived. Some leading figures in Dominican public life were of Haitian origin, including President Ulises Heureaux. By 1884 there were over 500 foreign workers – many of them Haitians – in the Dominican *ingenios* (sugar mills).[8]

The US occupation of the Dominican Republic from 1916 to 1924 led to further growth in the sugar industry and the need for cheap labour, especially for cane cutting. Much of this labour came from Haiti and by 1930 there were almost 30 000 Haitians officially resident in the country. By 1935 the figure was 52 657.[9] The frontier regions had particularly high proportions of black Haitians and there was considerable hostility towards these migrants, a hostility which dictator Rafael Trujillo exploited in 1937 when as many as 12 000 Haitians were massacred by the Dominicans in a campaign to 'de-Africanise the frontier'.[10] Since that date the flow of migrants has continued. In 1960 there were still 30 000 official Haitian residents, with the number rising to 42 000 ten years later. More important was the fact of illegal migration to the Dominican Republic. By the very nature of this population flow it is difficult to estimate numbers, and judgments vary wildly from a total of 100 000 to 200 000 Haitian residents, legal and illegal.[11]

By 1976 the Dominican sugar industry, with its sixteen or so mills, accounted for 43 per cent of industrial capital in the country and employed 75 per cent of the industrial labour force. It occupies today a key role in the Dominican economy and depends largely on Haitian migrant labour for its operation.[12] Though the general standard of living in the Dominican Republic is significantly higher than in Haiti, the situation of the small farmer is not much better than that of his western counterpart, and unemployment is estimated at well over 20 per cent.

It is useful to distinguish three categories of Haitians in the Dominican Republic.

(1) In the first place, there are those officially resident in the country, who have perhaps been there for many years or who have been born there. Many of these still work in the sugar industry or have become unable to work through old age, accident or illness and do not have sufficient funds to return even if they wanted to. This group of official residents would also include those who have been relatively successful

and who have established themselves in small businesses, skilled trades and in coffee or rice cultivation.

(2) Secondly, there are a number of contracted labourers who are recruited each year in Haiti by government agents, being transported to the sugar fields and *ingenios* to work on the *zafra* (sugar crop). They are then transported back to Haiti. The men live in compounds known as *bateyes*, many of them in overcrowded and insanitary conditions. This system is the result of an intergovernmental agreement according to which the Haitian government receives a certain sum of money for each worker recruited, and part of the worker's wage is withheld until he has returned home. Needless to say there are numerous occasions when this money is seized by local *macoute* leaders or government officials involved in the business. Nevertheless these workers return to Haiti with a small sum of money, perhaps around $30–$60. In 1967 it was estimated that the 16 300 migrant workers returned after the *zafra* to Haiti with a total of about half a million dollars. [13] In recent years the numbers recruited have varied from 12 000 to 17 000 per year. An agreement signed in October 1978 fixed the number at 15 000. A representative of the Anti-Slavery Society of London recently attempted to obtain a copy of the contract for the 1981–2 *zafra* but without success. Despite the appalling conditions in which these men must work there is considerable competition for inclusion, which means that they must often pay recruiting agents a bribe in order to be chosen. [14]

(3) Finally, there is an indeterminate number of illegal residents, some of whom crossed the border clandestinely and others who, having entered the country as contract labourers, have stayed beyond their permitted time. These migrants are in a particularly weak position and can be compelled to work for very low wages and in inhuman conditions under the threat of imprisonment or of repatriation. Police and army officers have frequently captured these illegal immigrants and sold them to sugar factories or to other employers. There was a recent case of a Haitian boy of ten sold in this way. The anti-Slavery Society has documented such instances. [15] Migrants, working as small shopkeepers or street vendors, have on more than one occasion been rounded up by the police and transported against their will to the cane fields. [16]

Certain questions arise in connection with this migration. In the first place, which Haitians are involved? It is perhaps surprising to learn that most of the migrant workers do not come from the class of landless rural proletariat but they are small landowners, particularly from the regions around Léogane and Jacmel. The majority are males under thirty years of age.[17] The second question is why these young men are willing to give up their own plots of land to work in such conditions for quite low wages. They are mostly paid piece work at something over one dollar per ton, which is twice the rate paid in Haiti itself. Nevertheless the miserable barracks in which they live, apart from their families, often without sanitation, electricity or health services, must be a considerable disincentive. In Haiti however increasing soil erosion and the continual division of properties into smaller and smaller plots (due to the inheritance laws by which, at his or her death, a person's land is divided among all the children) has made it impossible for many to live from their land. There is the need to increase the size of one's holding, to consolidate a number of separate plots into a single unit or to make occasional capital investment in the form of buildings or animals. The acute shortage of cash in rural Haiti is one of the principal explanations for the migration.[18] Even the $30–$60, with which the migrant returns, can pay for one or two animals, together with such necessary consumer goods as clothes. While the man is away he will often leave his common law wife, or wives, to supervise his property.

It is possible to identify groups in both countries which profit from the migration business. In the Dominican Republic the owners of the sugar industry are clearly the principal beneficiaries of this supply of cheap and relatively docile labour. The industry is run by the government – taken over from the Trujillo family after the assassination of the dictator – by the Vicini family, or by the enormous US company Gulf & Western. The latter owns the huge sugar mill at La Romana which refines about one-third of all sugar produced in the country. While these employers clearly benefit from the contract labour arranged through official channels they have a particular interest in the illegal migration, for it is here that they are able to find the cheapest and most pliant workers. Local army and police officers on the Dominican side of the border are also able to profit, from bribes by clandestine migrants wishing to cross and to find employment. Thus there is considerable pressure on the government not to attempt to enforce too strictly the control of population movements across the border. A further effect in the Dominican Republic is to lower the general wage level and to prevent the effective unionisation of the sugar industry. Dominican workers are encouraged to think of cane cutting as inhuman and degrading work suitable only for an inferior race. Old racial prejudices are thus used to suggest a common interest between Dominican workers and bourgeoisie against the Haitian migrants.

In Haiti the main beneficiary of the system is the government which, as we have noted, receives a considerable sum for recruiting this labour force. The Dominicans also pay for supervisors and 'inspectors' to accompany the workers. Needless to say these men are usually *macoutes* whose job it is to keep the men in order. Presumably the migrant workers themselves must also be seen as beneficiaries – at least it would seem that this is how they see the situation, otherwise they would not be so eager to take part in the *zafra*. It should therefore be noted that any attempt simply to terminate the system of migrant labour would certainly be opposed by the Haitian workers themselves.

NORTH AMERICA

North America is today the principal target for Haitian migrants. In the late 1930s there was a small colony of about 500 Haitians in New York[19] but large-scale migration to North America began in the late 1950s. Today there are big, well-established Haitian communities in New York, Chicago, Boston and Montreal, including many who have adopted US or Canadian citizenship. The majority however have no permit to enter the country or have overstayed their visa limit and are thus 'undocumented' and capable of being exploited by unscrupulous employers due to their fear of deportation. A recent estimate suggests that there are almost half a million Haitian-born residents in the USA and Canada.[20] All classes are represented, and an enterprising migrant has even produced a 'Bottin' directory of Haitian commercial and professional agencies in the USA.[21] More than one weekly newspaper is published, together with numerous periodicals in French and *Kréyol*. Bilingual education programmes are sponsored by the US government[22] and a number of churches and community organisations are dominated by Haitians.[23]

It is likely that there are now over 250 000 Haitians resident in New York. They tend to be concentrated in the upper west side of Manhattan, in Brooklyn (particularly in the Bedford-Stuyvesant district) and in parts of Queens. In some districts of New York the principal language is *Kréyol*, while shops, restaurants, and other commercial enterprises are owned by Haitians. Their businesses are notably to be found in Linden Boulevard (Queens), Amsterdam Avenue (Manhattan) and Rogers or Flatbush Avenue (Brooklyn).[24]

Many Haitians in New York come from the middle and even upper social classes. An enquiry conducted in 1976–7 showed that among the fifty-four Haitian migrants interviewed, the average number of years of schooling is higher than in most other immigrant groups in the city, though somewhat lower than that of the labour force in general. Almost a quarter of them claimed over twelve years of education. Although none of them were in the first four categories of occupation (professional, technical, managerial and clerical) half of them had had jobs of this kind in Haiti, six of them in the top category. A further interesting fact which emerged from this enquiry was that 42.8 per cent of these migrants were supporting two or more persons in Haiti. One writer has estimated (on what evidence he does not say) that $80m was transferred to Haiti in 1977.[25] The sample of fifty-four contained a large number of unmarried women. Susan Buchanan has also observed how women, employed as domestics, factory workers or hospital orderlies have often been the first members of their family to arrive in New York. When they have become established they have then brought other members of the family to join them.[26]

Class and colour distinctions characteristic of the Caribbean are replicated in the larger Haitian colonies in North America, especially in New York. The poorer tend to live in Brooklyn and Manhattan and the more successful in Queens. I remember meeting a mulatto lady at an elite party in Haiti who told me that she lived in New York. 'There is a very large community of Haitians in New York, I believe', was my banal but wholly innocent response. 'Not', she replied firmly, 'in the part of New York where I live.' Even the division – found among the upper and middle classes in Haiti – between francophiles and those who look to North American culture is reproduced in the USA.[27]

Recent migrants to the USA include the so-called 'boat people', who landed in Florida. By 1979 it is estimated that there were about 9000 undocumented Haitians in South Florida. In 1980 alone, 12 400 Haitians arrived there, and in the same year 11 per cent of the births in Miami's county hospital were Haitians. The majority have probably settled in the state, which now has a Haitian population of around 40 000. Though most of the migrants live in the greater Miami district, over 5000 Haitians have joined Jamaicans and US blacks as cane cutters.[28] It has popularly been assumed that these Haitians come from the poorest sections of the population. Enquiries have shown that this is not normally so. Ship captains charge up to 2000 dollars for the trip, and many of the migrants sell property which has been in the family for generations in order to raise the money; others are able to borrow from neighbours and members of their family, while many receive financial assistance from those already resident in the USA.[29] A considerable number of Haitians, especially those who have been in North America for some time, have done fairly well and think of themselves as constituting something of an elite among the black and coloured population, looking down on the US blacks. Some even go so far as to deny the existence of racialism in the USA.[30]

As with the voyage to the Bahamas, the trip is perilous and some ships have failed to arrive. US naval vessels have on occasions intercepted these boats and turned them back to Haiti and the Immigration and Naturalization Service has often dealt with the Haitian boat people in a summary fashion which has contrasted with the generally favourable reception given to Cuban migrants. This differential treatment was sometimes justified by drawing a distinction between economic migrants and political refugees. Recently it would appear however that the efforts of various religious and civil rights groups who have campaigned on behalf of the Haitians, have borne fruit. Court cases sponsored by these groups have forced the INS to review its procedures and the migrants have been receiving somewhat fairer treatment from immigration officials of late. I shall comment further on this in the conclusion to this chapter.[31]

Many of the early migrants to Canada were professional people who left Haiti either because of political persecution or in search of higher salaries and better working conditions. Haiti in fact suffered from a serious 'brain-drain'. Of the 761 doctors who graduated from the medical school in Port-au-Prince from 1945 to 1968 only 242 were practising in Haiti by 1970.[32] A certain

feeling of unease or even guilt is evident among these professional people for having left their native land.[33] In Montreal to
the end of the sixties migrants were of this kind but in the 1970s
large numbers of unskilled or semi-skilled migrants reached
Canada. In the mid-sixties less than a hundred Haitian legal
immigrants arrived in Canada each year; in 1971 and 1972 the
figure was under a thousand. By 1974 however the number had
quadrupled, and lots of undocumented Haitians began
arriving.[34] In 1973 an amnesty was issued for illegal foreign immigrants in a campaign known as '*Opération mon pays*'; this, however, was followed almost immediately by a police drive against
those who did not come forward, including 800–1500 Haitians.
Many of these had been suspicious of '*Opération mon pays*' and had
decided to lie low.

Today of the 40 000 or so Haitians living in Canada at least 90
per cent are to be found in the area of greater Montreal. Large
numbers of them do low-paid work in factories making textiles,
shoes and similar goods. Taxi driving is a favourite occupation of
Haitians in Montreal. Recently they have been organising trade
unions, and now the union at Tex Bleach, situated in the
suburbs of Montreal has a majority of Haitian members. It is
doing something to improve the conditions of the workforce in
that company.[35] Montreal is still the home for a significant
number of medical doctors, nurses, university teachers and
students from Haiti. The problems faced by Haitian children in
the Montreal school system has been the subject of recent
concern.[36] The city has been the centre of some of the most
important exile publications such as *Nouvelle Optique* and more
recently *Collectif Paroles*.

BAHAMAS

It is estimated that there are today in the Bahamas between
20 000 and 40 000 Haitians, almost all of whom are illegal and
undocumented workers or dependants. The higher figure would
represent almost a quarter of the total population of the islands.
A few Haitians were to be found working in the Bahamas prior
to 1957, but in that year there was a significant growth in their
numbers. The sixties witnessed a rapid development in tourism,
with the number of hotel rooms rising from 2570 in 1960 to

10 522 in 1970.[37] Bahamians took the relatively well-paid jobs in the tourist industry, leaving a demand for workers to do types of manual work the locals now rejected.

Most of the Haitian migrants in the Bahamas come from the North West, where the standard of living is lower than in any other part of the country; there is little industry and the region suffers from frequent droughts. Nevertheless the migrants are not from the worst-off sections of the population. Of the 135 respondents to Dawn Marshall's enquiry conducted in 1971 at Carmichael (New Providence), 50 had enjoyed a better standard of living than the average in Haiti, which means a considerably better standard than that in the North West. Many of them had owned, or still owned, land; of these Marshall observes 'the resource base of the respondents was larger than the average for the Haitian farmer'.[38] This is not surprising when one considers that the cost of the passage by 1970 was about $200 and by 1980 had risen to over $600. Over 80 per cent of the male respondents were farmers, sailors or fishermen before leaving, while nearly half the women were *commerçantes*.

The journey to the Bahamas, which may take over a week, is often extremely hazardous and unpleasant. Some boats never arrive, and on other occasions captains fearing coastguard patrols have been known to drop their passengers several hundred yards from the shore. In general the Haitian migrants do work of a kind that the Bahamians reject. Many of them are casual labourers while others work in agriculture and forestry in Andros, Abacos and some of the smaller islands. There are no effective trade unions and being illegal immigrants the Haitians have little political influence. The problems they face on arrival are considerable. In the first place the vast majority of them are illegal entrants, which means that they can be compelled by employers to work for lower wages than the market rate, owing to the threat of deportation which can be held over them. Secondly, most of them have little training or experience except in farming and in petty commerce. Finally, there is a high rate of illiteracy and they have to communicate in a foreign language. Deportation is one of the chances which the illegal migrant takes. In the 1960s over 15 000 Haitians were deported from the Bahamas, many of them more than once; thousands of others were voluntarily repatriated. The deportations have continued and it has been estimated that in 1980 alone 3000 Haitians were returned to their homeland.[39]

The principal effects of the Bahamian migration in Haiti itself have been the easing of population pressure, the remittances sent to relatives and friends and the money brought back by returning migrants. Dawn Marshall states that in 1969 alone the bank at Port de Paix received $1 200 000 in remittances from abroad. Whether this includes only money received from the Bahamas is not clear, but as she points out, many migrants send back cash with returning friends rather than through bank transfers.[40] It is certainly the case that the majority of migrants have left dependants in Haiti, particularly children; half of Marshall's 135 respondents had left a total of 226 children in Haiti.[41] As with the *viejos* of former times, returning migrants from the Bahamas form a particular sub-class of the population in parts of the North West. They tend to build rather pretentious homes – 'Nassau houses' as they are called – in the hope of being able to let them, as happens in the Bahamas. Unfortunately they rarely find Haitians with enough money to pay the rents they demand. The returned migrant frequently cuts a somewhat sorry figure and becomes the laughing stock of his compatriots who remained at home.

OTHER COUNTRIES

Smaller numbers of Haitian migrants are to be found in many parts of the world. The communities in France and Belgium have a high proportion of students and intellectuals, though in recent years Haitians of all classes have been arriving. J. Allman estimates that there are about 5000 Haitians in France, most of them living in Paris.[42] A number of exile groups are organised from Europe. Many Haitians are to be found working in the francophone countries of Africa in various technical or professional posts with governments and with international agencies. French Guyane has received some 2000 Haitian immigrants in recent years and others are to be found in Martinique and Guadaloupe. Students, academics and professionals are also resident in Latin American countries including Mexico, Cuba, Puerto Rico, Venezuela and Brazil. Such prominent exiles as Gérard Pierre-Charles and his wife Suzy Castor have been active in Mexico, promoting interest in Haiti. René Depestre lived for many years in Havana and Leslie Manigat has made Caracas the headquarters of his political movement.

CONCLUSION

It is sometimes assumed that the Haitian migrants must have come from the poorest sections of the community. In the case of the Cuban migration of the post 1913 period a number of writers – most recently Mats Lundahl – have asserted this to be the case. Lundahl states that 'it appears as if most of the emigrants to Cuba were landless peasants'. On the subject of the more recent migration to the Dominican Republic he refers to 'the poorer sections' of the rural population of Haiti as those whom 'we would expect to emigrate'.[43] Economists, unlike other social scientists, are in the fortunate position of being able to deduce human behaviour from certain motives which they confidently assume to be paramount, without having to waste time on the tedious business of empirical investigation. As we have seen, the conclusions of those who have actually investigated the situation is that the migrants do not in fact come from the poorest class of the landless and that the majority are landowners. The sea voyage to Cuba, the Bahamas and the USA, of course, demands more expenditure than the overland journey to the Dominican Republic, but even in the latter case a high proportion of migrant cane cutters are proprietors of land in Haiti. The migrants, then, need money for the journey and for the bribes which may be necessary to ensure employment. The poorest would not be able to raise enough; the small landowner is able to secure a loan or to sell part of his property and so have sufficient money to migrate. While it is true that some migrants are subsidised by relatives or friends who are already abroad, and others can afford the journey because of revolving credit associations, often known in the Caribbean as *su-su banks*, the evidence we have suggests that most migrants are not from the poorest sectors of the Haitian community. Even to join one of the credit clubs it is necessary to have a little spare cash.[44]

While it is proper to draw a distinction between political exiles or refugees on the one hand and migrants in search of a better standard of life on the other, this distinction has been used in recent years in the USA in a manner which has led to great injustices to Haitian boat people. The general assumption has been that Cuban migrants are properly able to claim the status of political refugees, but that Haitians are mere economic migrants like the Mexicans who enter the USA seeking work. It is sometimes suggested that Cuba is a totalitarian state while Haiti is merely an authoritarian regime and that this enables immigration officials to distinguish between the two classes of migrant. The distinction between totalitarian and authoritarian regimes is, I believe, a valid one [45] but it is mistakenly applied to the issue of migration. In the first place, the way in which countries are categorised depends less upon the internal structure of the regime in question than upon the vagaries of United States foreign policy by which even Pol Pot can be regarded as an authoritarian member of the free world. More importantly an authoritarian regime may be quite as oppressive in certain fields as a totalitarian government. Many Haitian boat people claim for example that they have been the victims of injustice and oppression at the hands of local *macoute* leaders who are officials of an authoritarian regime. The Immigration and Naturalization Service has generally failed to pay attention to claims of this kind made by Haitian refugees. I am not asserting here that all Haitian migrants to the USA can properly claim political asylum but that immigration officials should be prepared to listen to them and make a judgment on the basis of each individual case, rather than making the blanket judgment that they are all economic migrants. Recently, as has already been observed, the treatment meted out to these migrants seems to have improved.

With respect to the Dominican migration there is a further theoretical, or rather terminological, issue which needs attention. While it is true that patterns of indentured labour clearly share important features with the institution of slavery, both being labour systems designed to maintain plantation agriculture, and both invoking the sanctions of criminal law to maintain labour relations, they ought not to be confounded. There are two significant differences between them. Slaves do not choose to leave their homeland but indentured labourers, for whatever reason, do. Secondly, slavery is usually for an indefinite duration, whereas indentureship is for a limited period. Thus to speak of indentureship as 'a new system of slavery'[46] obscures these differences. It is clearly the case that there are powerful factors such as acute poverty, unemployment, oppression and famine which lead some men and women to opt for migration, nevertheless the situation differs from that of slavery. It is an error to treat the distinction between human action (however circumscribed) and acts of coercion as trivial. No doubt the term 'slavery' has an emotive appeal which campaigners find useful and which may be justified in the context of their purpose, but clarity is important for social scientists who are trying to understand the migratory process. It is therefore misleading to speak of the Haitian migration to the Dominican Republic as a system of slavery, though certain incidents (such as the selling of detained Haitians to plantations from which they are not free to leave) would indeed qualify as slavery.

The effects of Haitian migration on the 'host' country has often been to lower the general wage level and to make more difficult the unionisation of the industries concerned; it has thus been generally encouraged by employers. Whole industries in the USA and Western Europe depend upon migrant labour. Also, many highly qualified and skilled migrants have contributed significantly to the economies of the countries to which they have migrated.

The effect of the migration on Haiti itself has been complex. On the one hand the country has lost many professional and technically qualified persons, particularly in the fields of medicine, agronomy, and education. With respect to the mass migration of rural Haitians the population pressures have to some degree been relieved, and considerable sums of money have been introduced into the country either by remittances or by returning migrants. Yet here again, many of these migrants are among the most enterprising and energetic groups in the population. They are normally men and women in their most productive stage of life and this represents a significant loss to the country. These emigrants are the people who might have constituted an effective alternative to the present ruling groups. Returning migrants, however, like Manuel in Jacques Roumain's celebrated novel, have brought back new ideas which might constitute the basis for development and progressive change in the future. Ironically, the relaxation of immigration and naturalisation procedures, advocated by liberals in the USA and Western Europe, may in certain respects damage the economies of the poorer countries from which the migrants come. While such open policies might solve some immediate problems in poorer countries and can often be justified on humanitarian grounds, the long-term effects may be harmful.

It is perhaps worth adding that the future of the sugar industry in the Caribbean, with which much of the migration we have been discussing is connected, is hardly secure. The US soft drinks industry in particular is turning more and more to the use of high fructose corn syrup. In past years this industry has devoured about two and a half million tons (roughly one-quarter) of the total US consumption of sugar but is quite rapidly cutting down its purchases. Over the past decade US consumption of high fructose corn syrup has increased from zero to four million tons per annum.[47] This trend is likely to have significant results in most of the Caribbean, with the exception of Cuba, whose crop is purchased by the Soviet Union and Eastern Europe where bureaucratic inertia will probably ensure that the people continue to consume sugar for the next half century.

11   Cultural Dualism and Political Domination

For William Wilberforce, Thomas Clarkson, and others who fought for the abolition of slavery, Haiti was seen as a test case; the story of her independence, of black self-government, would demonstrate conclusively the wisdom of their programme.[1] Opponents of emancipation, like James Franklin, also regarded Haiti as significant, providing an exemplification of the kind of situation that would exist if slavery were abolished in the British colonies.[2] The former group tended in consequence to paint a somewhat rosy picture of the situation in Haiti, while the latter exaggerated the undesirable features of life in the black republic. Throughout the nineteenth century and up to the present day, Haitians have seen their country as a symbol of black independence and dignity while, on the other hand, much of what is said and written about the country by foreigners contains a significant degree of racial prejudice. Most accounts of Haiti are therefore highly coloured by the preconceptions and commitments of the authors. Nevertheless it is, I think, possible to make a more or less disinterested, if provisional, assessment of the history and present condition of the country and of the French colonial legacy in Haiti.

'The power of the mighty,' observed Thomas Hobbes, 'hath no foundation but in the opinion and belief of the people.'[3] All political domination rests to a large extent upon a hoax – a confidence trick. No government could stand for long without a whole collection of myths, symbols and beliefs which – with their supporting institutional structures – reinforce its claims to obedience on the part of its subjects. Here I want to look at the role of two interconnected strands in this cultural complex: religion and language, seen as a consequence of colonialism and of the system of slavery which was integral to it. First, however, it is necessary to say a few words on the historical context.

French troops were finally expelled from the western third of the island of Hispaniola towards the end of 1803 and the independence of Haiti was proclaimed. Naturally in the early years there was a considerable degree of anti-French feeling among Haitians of all classes. A minority was in favour of reaching some kind of settlement which recognised French suzerainty, but the majority of both black and mulatto leaders insisted that full independence from the former metropolitan power was essential. Yet the legacy of French colonialism remained.

ECONOMY

In the first place, the colonial economy had been tied to that of France. It was centred on the large-scale production of a few crops: sugar, coffee, indigo and cotton for export to Europe. Agriculture was dominated by huge plantations, particularly in the North and Artibonite. After independence the former free coloureds or *affranchis* (known after emancipation as *anciens libres*) owned much of the property; some they had inherited, other plantations they seized when the white owners fled. Most of the former white-owned plantations were nationalised and in the early years, under Pétion (and later under Christophe), many of these estates were given to members of the army or sold in lots of various sizes. It is frequently suggested that by 1820 there were no large plantations left in Haiti. This is not so. Senior army officers and other members of the elite continued to own enormous tracts of land, which they attempted to cultivate with wage labour. Yet plantation agriculture ceased to dominate the economy. Large numbers of former slaves squatted on vacant, state-owned property and began to cultivate crops for local consumption. The export of sugar fell dramatically. In this respect Haiti has differed from the pattern which has predominated in other parts of the Caribbean. Even today in Haiti landless wage labourers make up a remarkably small percentage of the population, though the number of rural Haitians unable to support themselves from their own land is growing.[4]

In 1825 President Boyer accepted as a condition of the French recognition of Haitian independence an enormous indemnity of 150 million francs to be paid to the dispossessed French land owners. Haiti had to borrow large sums from Europe to pay the first installment of this debt and thus began significant foreign financial involvement in the Haitian economy. This was reinforced by the arrival of large numbers of foreign merchants who have dominated the commerce of the country throughout the nineteenth century and to the present day.

CLASS, COLOUR AND REGION

With respect to the class and colour situation in Haiti today, regarded as a legacy of French colonialism and slavery, I do not want to say much here.[5] Crudely the general (though not total) coincidence between colour and class can be said to date back to colonial times. As most of the slaves were black, so most of the poor are black today. As most of the *affranchis* were mulatto, so today most of the rich are light-skinned. This is a familiar feature of Caribbean social structures and its roots in the system of slavery and manumission are evident. It may also be worth mentioning that regional diffferences in the colour composition of the population, having significant political consequences, also date back to colonial times. The South was the last region to be developed, partly because of a terrain relatively unsuitable for large plantations; in this region the *affranchis* became strong in colonial times and here the mulatto leaders of the revolutionary and early independence periods had their power base. In the election of 1957 this was the region where Duvalier's principal opponent, the mulatto businessman Louis Déjoie received the bulk of his support.

POLITICAL AND MILITARY

Political and administrative aspects of the French colonial system have also been bequeathed to independent Haiti and persist into the present day. Colonial government was centralised, authoritarian and dominated by the military. The governor-general was invariably a military officer. This pattern persisted throughout the nineteenth century, though a degree of decentralisation occurred as a result of bureaucratic inefficiency and the inability of governments to control the activities of local army leaders. It was not until 1913, over a hundred years after independence, that Haiti had its first civilian head of state. Much of Haitian life manifests the influence of militarism. Many of the voodoo spirits, for example, are portrayed in military costume, and one of the principal figures in the voodoo liturgy is *la place* (from *Commandant de la Place*). The power of the local *chef de section* ensures a strong military element in rural administration. Efforts by the USA during the occupation of Haiti from 1915 to 1934 to secure a non-politicised military failed and the army emerged once more in 1946 as the arbiter of events. One of the achievements of François Duvalier has been to remove the army from its position as an independent and frequently determining variable in the political life of the country.[6] Since his death the military has continued to be controlled by the presidential palace. This is not, of course, to say that it will not once again play an active political role sometime in the future.

I wish now to turn to two aspects of Haitian life which have been powerfully influenced by its French colonial heritage. These are the connected phenomena of religion and language. In speaking of religion and language I do not simply refer to the fact that Roman Catholicism is the official religion of the country as French is its official language. The peculiar dualism, religious and linguistic, which is found in Haiti, predates independence and reflects the ambiguities of the colonial system of domination.

KRÉYOL AND FRENCH

French is and has always effectively been the official language of Haiti and no serious attempt has been made to challenge its status. Henry Christophe told Wilberforce that it was his hope and intention eventually to substitute English as the official language of Haiti but it is unlikely that he would have been able to do so. Despite being the official language, however, only about 5 per cent of the population speak and write French fluently, though somewhat more are able to understand spoken French. The true oral language of the country is *Kréyol*, which is spoken by all Haitians but is written and read by relatively few. The general level of illiteracy of about 85 per cent is the highest in Latin America. During the nineteenth century serious claims were made by Haitians to a literary tradition distinct from that of France; yet this literature was written almost entirely in French.[7] The linguistic dualism found among the elite in Haiti is technically called *diglossia*. All members of the Haitian elite, and also other professional people, speak both French and *Kréyol*. On formal and public occasions they will speak French and will normally speak with their children in French in order to help them to learn this indispensable means of social acceptance. Informally they will generally speak *Kréyol* or will move from one language to the other even within a single sentence. Jokes and stories are almost always told in *Kréyol*. The fact that elite groups are able to handle both languages gives them considerable power over the monolingual masses, a power not willingly to be relinquished.

It is a notable feature of the period of the US occupation that Haiti's French language and culture became a source of pride to nationalists who were resisting North American imperialism. In the 1918 constitution French was formally proclaimed the official language of the country, partly as a gesture of defiance to Haiti's uninvited guests. This is somewhat similar to the way in which Puerto Rican nationalists today revert to the culture and language of an older imperialism in reaction to the overwhelming presence of the USA in their country.

Kréyol is a French-based language, similar to that spoken in the French Antilles, in Dominica, St Lucia and parts of Trinidad. It has much in common with the *Kréyol* spoken in Louisiana and with the popular language of Mauritius. Much of the vocabulary is derived from French though sentence construction is radically different. Various theories have been suggested to explain the origin of creoles and pidgins:[8]

(1) Early theorists suggested that *Kréyol* was the product of attempts by African slaves to imitate the language of their masters, or that the white slave owner or seaman delib-

erately taught a simplified form of his language to a people he believed to be inferior.

(2) Another theory is that this patois developed in three stages: the slave attempted to copy the language of his master or foreman, the white man simplified his language in imitation of the slave and finally the slave imitated the French-speaker's own modification of his language.

(3) A third hypothesis rejects the idea that *Kréyol* was developed on the plantation, ascribing its origin to the lingua franca, spoken by seamen and traders of the seventeenth century, known as Afro-Portuguese pidgin. The French sailors later replaced Portuguese words with French words and it was then acquired by the slaves who further developed the language.

Most experts today agree that *Kréyol* developed as a result of attempts by African slaves to communicate with their masters and with each other. The role played by Afro-Portuguese, the influence of African languages and the mode of dispersion of the language among the islands remain matters of contention.

Although the *Kréyol* spoken in Haiti today manifests minor regional variations, it presents a high degree of standardisation. There is, however, a significant distinction between the *gros Kréyol* of the countryside and the somewhat more French-sounding *Kréyol* of Port-au-Prince. This raises the vexed question of the form in which the language should be written. There are two extreme positions. The first is that spelling of *Kréyol* words should be phonetic. The other view is that they should be spelled as nearly to the French as possible. This is not the occasion to enter into the technical aspects of this debate, but it is worth saying a word about some of the wider social implications.

Those who advocated French spelling saw *Kréyol* as a stepping stone to learning French and believed that if it was written in phonetic form it would be difficult to move on to French. Today, however, it is generally agreed that *Kréyol* is a distinct language and should be written phonetically, though there are some disagreements about the best system to use. Many advocates of the vernacular argue that *Kréyol* should be recognised as an official language of Haiti, together with French, and that it should be taught for its own sake rather than merely as a means to learning another language.

Naturally the French government is keen to maintain French

as an official language of Haiti and to ensure that *Kréyol* remains a subordinate means of communication. They have an active *Institut Français* in Port-au-Prince and have financed a large pedagogical centre to forward their interests and to form, in the words of a confidential memorandum to the French government, 'a sort of foreign legion of the French language, devoted to our cultural and political interests, within the Haitian administration itself'. An article in a prestigious French journal recently celebrated Haiti's alleged 'fidelity to France and her language' as more than mere sentiment. The author of this article – on Haiti as a part of *'la francophonie'* – does not so much as mention the fact that *Kréyol* is spoken in Haiti. No uninitiated reader would guess that a mere handful of the population is able to converse fluently in French.[9] Today, however, the French government appears to have accepted the need for literacy in *Kréyol* as part of a bilingual education programme. A former director of the *Institut Français* in Port-au-Prince has written that no one can contest the status of *Kréyol* as a distinct language and accepts that French has been an instrument of domination by a small elite.[10]

Most of the educated elite of Haiti also wish to maintain French as the official language of the country for obvious reasons. Speaking Haiti's official language puts them in a position of domination with respect to the mass of the population. It is one means of ensuring the continued hegemony of a small bilingual class.[11] Many of those involved in the early years of the Duvalier regime wrote about the importance of *Kréyol*, as followers of the so-called ethnological movement. Some small changes have been made, so that court cases at the lower levels are now conducted in a language which the participants can understand, and some primary school teaching is done in *Kréyol*.

A rather more serious attempt to challenge the predominance of French in the educational system of the country is being made at the moment. The proposal to establish *Kréyol* as the language of the early years of primary education was put forward by the government. This was greeted with fierce opposition from elements among the educated classes. The plan was to constitute *Kréyol* as the sole medium of teaching in the first years of education with a course of initiation into oral French and, at the end of the second year a course in written French. At the beginning of the sixth year French would become the principal medium of teaching, though *Kréyol* would continue to be taught up to the secondary stage of education.[12] The Department of Education had, however, failed to make adequate plans for the training of teachers who could operate the proposed scheme and for the provision of teaching materials, thus giving ammunition to opponents of the reform. The plans have since been suspended and the minister responsible, Joseph Bernard, has been replaced by Franck St Victor who, though favouring reform, is prepared to make compromises on the issue.

Despite his populist and anti-elite stance, François Duvalier almost invariably addressed mass rallies in French rather than in *Kréyol*, implicitly recognising the importance of maintaining this instrument of domination. Middle-class black Haitians who had in the past argued for a more extensive use of *Kréyol* have lately been among the most resolute defenders of the traditional role of French, since they have themselves secured a share in social and political power.

The linguistic problems of Haiti have been exported to those countries where Haitian migrants have settled. Susan Buchanan has recently shown how conflicts over whether to use French or *Kréyol* in the liturgy of a New York church reflect social tensions in a migrant community. The minority, led by a bookkeeper and a social worker, are portrayed as arguing for the retention of the French mass as part of an attempt to maintain their leadership position in the Haitian community. This group also saw a knowledge of French as a status symbol, distinguishing Haitians from other New York blacks, as belonging to a superior culture. The pro-*Kréyol* group, on the other hand, 'rejected the French identity and the idea of whiteness as superior to blackness', though they too wished to dissociate Haitians from US blacks.[13]

With respect to the political importance of *Kréyol* two other points should be made. First that in the late seventies when, under pressure from the USA, a limited degree of opposition was permitted, *Kréyol* was naturally the medium of the most effective criticisms of the government. *Kréyol* plays, such as *Pèlin Tèt* by Frank Etienne, containing thinly disguised attacks on the regime, were enormously popular, and the *Kréyol* broadcasts of Jean Dominique, Compère Filo and others contained hard-hitting and effective attacks on aspects of the administration.[14]

Secondly, it is noteworthy that one of the most powerful elements in the pro-*Kréyol* lobby, has been the protestant missionary movement. This movement, largely financed in recent years from the USA, has done most of its work in the countryside and has naturally worked almost exclusively in *Kréyol*. Though it would be wrong to suggest a conscious and concerted conspiracy between US business interests, the state department, and the protestant churches, these missions have indeed constituted an important arm of US penetration in Haiti. It is significant that much of the pressure for the educational reforms referred to above has come from the USA, with financial backing from the World Bank.

One of the most influential attempts to construct a *Kréyol* orthography was, however, the work of a Northern Ireland Methodist, O. H. McConnell who, in collaboration with Frank Laubach, produced in 1940 a phonetic orthography which has been widely used. The fact that this orthography took rural, or *gros Kréyol*, as the standard pronunciation has sometimes been resented by *Kréyol* speakers from the capital. The story is told of the maid who left her literacy class in Port-au-Prince because the word for 'egg' which she had pronounced '*zeu*' (nearer to the French) was spelled '*zé*'; she inferred that the purpose of the literacy classes was to impart a rural form of *Kréyol* which she regarded as inferior.[15] Today the vernacular is widely used in the liturgy of the Roman Catholic church and the *Kréyol* monthly *Bon Nouvel* with a circulation of some 30 000 is published by the church. *Kréyol* journals are also published by Catholic groups in New York, the Bahamas and elsewhere, perhaps the best known being *Sèl*.

As Albert Valdman has argued[16] there are two possible language strategies to be followed in Haiti. Either there must be a massive effort to transform French into the vernacular language by means of mass adult and child education programmes, or *Kréyol* must be accepted as the (or at least an) official language of the country. The enormous cost of the former, both financial and in terms of social resistance, makes it an unlikely option. Nevertheless the second possibility would also encounter opposition, not only from the bilingual elite, but also from the monolingual population, who might interpret the move as an attempt to keep them as second-class citizens by effectively closing one of the principal doors out of the rural maze. With the increased migration of rural Haitians to the USA and the Bahamas, however, English is coming to be seen as more useful than French as the linguistic pathway to salvation among the masses. It should be stressed, in conclusion, that compared with many countries in the world Haiti's linguistic problems are relatively simple and there is every reason to believe that a determined and consistent national programme over fifteen or twenty years could raise substantially the level of literacy and provide a solid basis for improved secondary education.

CHRISTIANITY AND VOODOO

The second form of cultural dualism I want to discuss is the phenomenon of christianity and voodoo. As in the case of language the dualism is not that of a simple either/or but rather a situation in which many people adhere to both.

Catholicism is the official religion of Haiti and has been recognised as having a privileged position in almost every Haitian constitution since 1806. The *Concordat* of 1860 formalised the relationship between the Haitian government and the Vatican and marked the beginning of a period in which foreign clergy and nuns came to dominate the educational system. By 1881 there were 74 priests and a considerable number of sisters working in the republic. Prior to the *Concordat* a few private and state schools existed, but these were soon overtaken in importance by the Catholic schools. Until recently little attempt has been made to incorporate local culture, such as the *Kréyol* language or the music of the tambour into christian liturgy. Latin and French were used in church and the music was European. The church hierarchy generally identified itself with the mulatto elite and was frequently in conflict with governments of a *noiriste* tendency, like those of Salnave and Salomon, which were dominated by freemasons who were sometimes also protestants.[17]

There is plenty of evidence to demonstrate that successive French governments have seen the activity of missionaries, most of whom were from France itself, as a crucial aspect of its policy of cultural imperialism. The French naval commander, Admiral Alphonse de Moges, wrote to Foreign Minister Guizot in 1843: 'we must retake Haiti, not by the force of our arms but by frankly aiding this new republic by our influence . . . by the sending of honourable and numerous clergy'.[18] During the period of the US occupation the French government looked to the Catholic priests and sisters to maintain French cultural influence in the country. The clergy, wrote the French minister in Port-au-Prince, are 'precious collaborators of our political propaganda'.[19]

Voodoo is an amalgam of various African religions which has also incorporated elements of christianity. It is concerned with the worship of God (*bondié* or *gran mèt*) and the spirits, (*lwas* or *mystères*, as they are called). The cult frequently involves an experience in which one of the *lwas* is said to 'ride' the devotee. The practice of voodoo also requires making certain sacrifices to the spirits. In Europe voodoo is frequently misunderstood and used as a term for black magic. This is not to deny that magic is involved in the practice of voodoo; it is often practised together with the religion and voodoo priests (*houngans*) may also act as magic-men (*bocors*).

This is not the place to enter into details on the esoteric aspects of the cult and in any case I am not competent to do so. I wish here merely to make some brief comments on the social and political importance of voodoo in the life of Haiti.[20] Whether the slave revolt of 1791 began with a voodoo ceremony, as tradition has it, is a vexed question among historians, but it does not seem to me unlikely that it did. The religion certainly provided a source of solidarity, by reminding slaves of their African past and by bringing them together for cultic ceremonies.

Throughout the nineteenth century voodoo remained the popular religion of the Haitian people, despite persecution of the cult by governments, black and mulatto, and in the face of aggressive missionary work by catholic and protestant churches. There was, for example, in the 1890s an active *Ligue Contre le Vaudou*. Not only were most Haitian governments keen to suppress the religion, but also intellectuals, whether from the mulatto liberal tradition or from the *noiriste* camp, were unanimous in their condemnation of voodoo. Some of them, in writings directed to a foreign audience, even denied the existence of voodoo, for it was seen as uncivilised and out of accord with the European model which all nineteenth-century Haitians accepted. (They did, however, remind their foreign readers that superstition was not a prerogative of African people and that some Haitian superstitions had European origins.)

It was only with the ethnological movement, beginning in the first decade of the present century, that Haitian intellectuals began to take voodoo seriously as a part of the national heritage. This theme was taken up by a number of young middle-class *noiristes* in the nineteen thirties, among whom was François Duvalier. These men emphasised the African roots of Haitian culture, and voodoo was seen as an integral part of this. This *noirisme* was fought by members of the mulatto elite and by the Roman Catholic hierarchy, who saw it as a challenge to the system of domination of which they were the representatives. This battle culminated in the so-called 'anti-superstition' campaign of 1941–2, in which the church, backed by the government of Elie Lescot, conducted a massive attack on the voodoo religion, involving not merely an oath against voodoo practices being administered to the faithful, but also the physical destruction of voodoo temples and sacred objects. Threats of violent resistance from devotees of the cult, however, led church and government to back down and terminate the campaign. This issue was by no means resolved, and emerged again during the government of Estimé (1946–50) who was thought by the church to be sympathetic to voodoo.

The Roman Catholic hierarchy generally backed Duvalier's principal opponent, the mulatto elite businessman, Louis Déjoie, in the election of 1957 and in the period from 1960 to 1966 the government of Papa Doc conducted a sort of *Kulturkampf* against the church, expelling bishops, priests and nuns and imprisoning many others. In 1966 agreement on a revised *Concordat* was reached with the Vatican and a new indigenous hierarchy was appointed. The new bishops were the result of a compromise between church and government but were generally prepared to back Duvalier's regime. When Duvalier came to power in 1957 ten of the eleven bishops were foreign, by the time of his death all but one were Haitians.[21]

It has been suggested that the backward state of the country is partly due to the fatalistic attitude cultivated by popular religion in Haiti, voodoo and catholic. One writer refers to 'a catholicism of resignation' which has been taught by the church and which is reflected in the popular *Kréyol* hymns published by the hierarchy.[22]

Since the death of Papa Doc in 1971, however, the bishops have on occasions cautiously raised objections against some of the more outrageous activities of government ministers, such as the export of blood to the United States by a company owned by

Luckner Cambronne. More recently the church has been vocal in the defence of human rights. In a more long-term perspective clergy have taken the lead in many parts of the country in projects for community development. These activities have been criticised by some opponents of the regime as reinforcing the status quo. Certainly many of the projects are administered in a somewhat paternalistic fashion, but it is likely that the long-term effects will be to raise the social and political consciousness of rural Haitians, leading them to question many institutions and practices hitherto taken for granted. Voodoo is still widely practised not only in remote country areas but in the capital and in other towns. It is therefore quite wrong to suggest that 'the antagonism town/country coincides with the antagonism catholicism/voodoo'.[23]

One important aspect of the religious scene is the greatly increased activity of protestant groups in the last decades. Some of these protestant sects are indigenous but, as already mentioned, many have their headquarters in the USA, from where they receive financial backing. While it is undoubtedly true that a number of these christian groups have improved the conditions of health, sanitation and agriculture in the countryside, others have been more concerned to forward US interests and to buy up tracts of land at low prices from peasants, for their own profit. One government minister referred to these protestant missions as a 'fifth column' inside the country and the Roman Catholic church has become alarmed at their proselytising activities.

The attitude of most protestants towards voodoo differs significantly from that generally adopted by catholics. The latter have tended to adopt a fairly lenient policy, encouraging their members to give up the practice of voodoo, but not insisting on a radical break with traditional ways. Priests have in the past pointed out that the *lwas* can be thought of as christian saints and there is even a sort of identification between voodoo spirits and particular christian saints: Erzulie Fréda with Our Lady, Damballah with St Patrick, Ogoun with St James the Great and so on. Even Bishop Paul Robert, an implacable opponent of voodoo who was one of the leaders of the 'anti-superstition' campaign, could write: 'There exist in voodoo, practices which are able to assist us wonderfully in understanding the sense of the christian calling and even of the priestly and religious vocation.'[24] The attitude of the Roman Catholic church in Haiti has thus been somewhat ambivalent with respect to voodoo, occasionally resorting in panic to repression and confrontation, but normally attempting gradually to wean its lay people from the cultic practices at the same time as infusing these practices with christian content.

Protestants, in contrast, have generally adopted a much more radical approach, insisting that converts make a complete break with all voodoo practices and beliefs, burning or otherwise destroying cultic objects in their possession. Many Haitians tend to identify catholicism and voodoo as part of a single religious system. Becoming a protestant means the renunciation of both. Alfred Métraux has suggested that one of the reasons for conversions to protestantism has been the desire to escape from the power of the *lwas*. Protestants do not in general deny the reality or the power of the voodoo spirits but insist that the spirit of God is more powerful and able to protect converts from the activity of the *lwas*.[25] Illustrative of the difference of approach is the debate about the best translation for the Greek word *kyrios*, or 'Lord'. The nearest equivalent in *Kréyol* is *granmèt*, but as we have already noted this is a term central to the voodoo liturgy and is derived from the system of domination in a slave-owning colony. Protestants have in general studiously avoided this term, preferring a word quite unfamiliar in *Kréyol*: *ségnè*, which is used, for example in the *Kréyol* translation of the Psalms in *Bon nouvèl pou tout moun*, published by the protestant *Alliance Biblique Universelle*. Roman Catholic and Episcopal (Anglican) churches have, however, used the term *granmèt* widely in *Kréyol* hymns and translations of the liturgy. Prayers frequently conclude with the words '*pa pouvoua Jezi-Kri, Granmèt nou-an. . .*'[26]

CONCLUSION

Haiti cannot, of course, be understood simply in terms of its colonial legacy and any attempt to do so, ignoring the deep and widespread African inheritance of the people, will come to grief. In this paper I have therefore been concerned with only part of the story, though one which is central to Haiti's history.

The linguistic and religious dualism found in Haiti is to be seen as a bequest of the colonial regime. Not only does this bequest involve those things brought from France and passed on to the colonial subjects: the French language and the christian religion. *Kréyol* and voodoo are also a part of the colonial legacy and furthermore the peculiar dualism in both language and religion is itself related to the ambiguities of colonial domination. The rejection of colonialism and slavery by a considerable number of the population was often combined with a recognition that preferment and even survival involved the adoption of certain aspects of the dominant culture. This is a familiar phenomenon in the anglophone Caribbean too, as C. L. R. James has pointed out and also, in certain respects, exemplifies. Yet the dualism both in religion and in language takes a somewhat different form in Haiti from that found in the Commonwealth Caribbean. This is due to a number of factors: the predominance of catholicism with its peculiar approach to the phenomenon of voodoo, the fact of 180 years of political independence and the less direct impact of European colonialism, and the relatively weak educational system which leaves large sections of the population untouched. While it is generally true to say that the *Kréyol* language and the voodoo religion are associated particularly with 'the masses', as French and Catholicism are with the elite, important reservations need to be made. As we have seen, members of the elite are fluent in *Kréyol* and it is also true that they are familiar with voodoo beliefs and practices. The role of the maid, and other domestic servants, is crucial here. The children of elite families spend much of the time in the company of black servants from whom they learn *Kréyol* and who pass on to them knowledge of the religion of their ancestors.

A vivid illustration of the linguistic ambiguity occurred in my house in Oxford, where we have a large and aggressive macaw sitting on a perch in the hall. The wife of a well-known Haitian playwright and poet came to see me some time ago. Her husband writes much of his work in *Kréyol*, but I noticed (though without great surprise) that she was talking to her children in French. As she was leaving, the bird said in a loud and clear voice: 'bye bye'. Now as anyone who knows Haiti will be aware, 'bye bye' is the *Kréyol* form of saying farewell. The lady looked at the bird, somewhat reproachfully as she might have done to one of her children and replied *'au revoir'*. I could not resist the remark: *'zwazo-a pa kapab palé Fransé, selman Kréyol'* (the bird does not speak French, only *Kréyol*).

12 Dynastic Despotism: From Father to Son

'Everyone was amazed,' writes an English journalist, 'when the succession passed smoothly . . . to Duvalier's teenage son.'[1] In this chapter I wish to examine the reasons for the amazement, to attempt an explanation for the smooth succession, and to consider some recent developments that have been taking place in the politics of Haiti. As archdeacon Paley[2] has suggested, the explanation for the amazement is to be found in a basic misunderstanding of the Duvalierist phenomenon and in a failure to see it in the context of Haitian history. There are certain enduring features of the Haitian past which must be taken into account in any attempt to explain the rise and progression of Duvalierism.

The first of these factors is the complex relationship between class and colour, the second is the importance of a *classe intermédiaire*, the third concerns the role of the state. They are, of course related, and together they provide a basis for understanding and explaining recent events in the black republic.

COLOUR AND CLASS

In Haiti, as in other parts of the Caribbean, there is a broad coincidence between class and colour, going back to the system of slavery in colonial days.[3] In general the blacks are poor and the lighter-skinned people are relatively rich. There are of course many exceptions, but the general assumption is that if you are poor you are likely to be black. Furthermore you are likely, not entirely without justification, to ascribe your poverty to your colour. Wealth is acquired by inheritance, by malversation and occasionally by enterprise or hard work. With respect to the first, mulatto children inherit from their mulatto fathers; the second

217

means of acquisition normally demands literacy combined with political or bureaucratic power; the third means is effective only when certain favourable conditions prevail, and these are set by individuals and groups who already possess economic or political power.

Throughout the nineteenth century literacy and wealth were largely the preserve of a small elite composed mostly of mulattoes, though it included a few black families. Beyond this elite there was however a considerable class of peasants with medium-sized holdings. When members of this class managed to achieve high rank in the army, at national or even local level, they were able to challenge the elite for political power. This brought with it the possibility of malversation or patronage and a consequent improvement in the long-term prospects for their families. Bitter divisions among the elite provided the opportunity for such moves, when rival members of the elite would recruit support among this *classe intermédiaire*.

From colonial times, however, the overwhelming majority of the blacks were poor. Attempts, by black politicians of the elite or of the *classe intermédiaire*, to secure their support were often made on the basis of colour. There was certainly among the masses a deeply felt antipathy towards the mulattoes, who were frequently identified *tout court* in the popular mind with the elite. Unscrupulous politicians, however, exacerbated the colour issue for their own ends and colour became one of the factors determining political alignments.

It is important to note that the explicit and public appeal to colour loyalties was generally resorted to only by blacks. Mulattoes, like the leaders of the nineteenth-century Liberal Party, tended to avoid an open discussion of colour, preferring to justify their discriminatory actions in terms of 'power to the most competent'; this, however, was little more than a thinly disguised appeal to colour prejudices. The 1946 election slogan which called for a president who was 'an authentic representative of the masses' was, to be sure, also a disguised appeal to black loyalties but *noiriste* politicians were less coy about explicit reference to the colour question than were their mulatto counterparts.

Although colour loyalties and antipathies have never been the sole factors in determining political alignments, they have rarely been absent from political conflict in Haiti, and have on occasions been predominant. The few situations when colour became the most important factor affecting the formation of contending parties have occurred in crises which followed long periods of mulatto dominance. One such crisis was in the years 1844–7, which succeeded twenty-four years of undisguised mulatto rule. The same may be said of the 1946 crisis, which followed a similar period of white (United States) and mulatto domination. No one who has read the political propaganda of the 1946 election campaign can fail to recognise the continued importance of colour in the political configurations of Haiti, and it is impossible to understand the Duvalierist phenomenon without reference to it. Nevertheless to ascribe all divisions in Haiti to colour factors would be an error only marginally less grave than to treat these factors as trivial. In most conflicts colour is one issue among many and frequently takes second place to economic class, regional loyalty or personal allegiance in determining the lines of battle.

THE MIDDLE CLASSES

In discussing the question of colour and class we have inevitably touched on the importance of the middle classes, though mostly in the rural context. The rural *classe intermédiaire* is, as we have noted, composed of peasants with medium-sized holdings; these men are in a position to offer occasional employment, to make loans and to give credit to their poorer neighbours, thereby building a whole structure of dependence and patronage. In addition to owning land, many of them also act as *spéculateurs* – agents of coffee exporters – who buy from peasant producers in their region. Each of them has built up a constituency, based on financial dependence and even on affective ties; the *spéculateur* may be godfather to one of the small proprietor's children, another of his children may be lodging at his house in the local town during school term. The small producer may thus have an obligation, customary as well as financial, to sell to a particular *spéculateur*. These middle classes, particularly in the countryside and in the small towns, formed the basis of *cacos* and *piquet* bands of irregulars, who played a vital role in political developments, particularly in the period leading up to the US invasion of 1915.[4]

The latter part of the nineteenth century saw the rise of an

urban middle class of some significance. This class was constituted mostly by members of black families who had managed –
by luck, hard work, corruption or by rising through the ranks of
the army – to achieve a level of literacy and education which
enabled them to become school teachers, clerks, and civil servants, or to save enough money to establish themselves in small
businesses. They sometimes joined together with rural blacks or
with the urban proletariat to remove an unpopular government,
replacing it with one thought to be more sympathetic to their
interests. One of the most profound and enduring consequences
of the nineteen years of US occupation was a decline in the
significance of the countryside and the provincial towns with the
centring of power in the capital. The rural *classe intermédiaire*
consequently suffered a loss of influence, while its counterpart in
the capital became a more crucial political force. With the
departure of the US marines in 1934, the stability of the government of Sténio Vincent depended upon support from some key
elements of this class and the collapse of the Lescot regime in
January 1946 is largely to be explained by the hostility of the
black urban middle class.

THE ROLE OF THE STATE

An acquaintance of mine once returned to his house on the
outskirts of Port-au-Prince, after a day in the countryside, and
could not find his servant. He called and eventually from behind
some bushes at the end of the garden the man appeared. On
being asked what he had been doing, the man replied '*létat té vini
è m'caché*' (literally: 'the state arrived and I hid'). An army officer
had arrived at the house, and the man's first thought was that
this meant trouble. When European or North American newspaper reports predicted the downfall of François Duvalier's
government on the ground that it had done nothing for the
people, they manifested a misunderstanding of Haitian history.
On the part of the mass of the people there has never been an
expectation that the state will do any good for them. The state
comes to confiscate, tax, prohibit or imprison; consequently the
less seen of it the better. When the Haitian proverb says '*Apré
bondié sé léta*' (after God comes the state), it is not the goodness or
the benevolence of God that people have in mind; it is rather his
remoteness, unpredictability and power.

Though the mass of the people have no expectations of welfare from the state, there is, however, a small class which lives from state patronage, or at least, whose standard of living depends upon the machinations of governments. Foreign aid, trade and investment are required to maintain its privileged position. The class I refer to is, of course, the urban and suburban bourgeoisie. In certain circumstances the fate of a government might depend upon this class – though this was not the case with the government of François Duvalier. I shall, however, return to this point when considering the position of Jean-Claude Duvalier.

The explanation for the fact that François Duvalier was able in 1971 to hand over power to his teenaged son is that by this time, having eliminated potential centres of opposition, his regime was fairly stable and was backed by key groups which had a vested interest in a continuance of Duvalierism in some form. Those who might have wished for a change were either without substantial political power or were so unsure of the outcome that they held on quietly, hoping for better days.

DUVALIERIST SUPPORT

François Duvalier had a profound knowledge of the expectations and fears of the Haitian masses. His study of Haitian history and social structure together with his ethnological research and practical experience as a country doctor combined with a shrewd and ruthless disposition to make him a formidable politician. He built up a system of support throughout the country, based on the key role which had traditionally been played by the *classe intermédiaire*. Many local leaders whose support he secured were *houngans* (voodoo priests), who had considerable influence in the communities where they operated. It is instructive to look at the photographs printed in Volume 2 of the *Œuvres essentielles* of Duvalier, to see the kind of people who were his promoters in the election campaign of 1956–7 and who continued to back the regime in the years that followed.

The countrywide organisation of the *Volontaires de la Sécurité Nationale*, the principal *tonton macoute* organisation, served not merely as an instrument of terror, but also as a means of recruiting support for the regime. The leaders of the movement came from just that class which had provided the backbone for the *cacos* and *piquet* bands of the pre-occupation period. The *noiriste* rhetoric of the Duvalierist regime appealed to this class rather than to the very poor, and it was through this middle class that the government was able to control the masses. Duvalier recognised their crucial importance and rarely tried to by-pass them; rather he used the structures of power which already existed to extend his control throughout the country.

Whereas in the period prior to 1915 successful revolutions frequently began in the countryside, after the US invasion it was events in the capital that were decisive. Only during the election campaigns of 1946 and of 1956–7 was there an apparent reversal of this trend. Once the election was over, however, power reverted to Port-au-Prince. Certain gestures were made by the governments of Estimé and François Duvalier in the direction of a rebirth of rural influence. The latter's electoral strength had been in the countryside and in the provincial towns, with powerful groups in the capital backing his opponents. The huge demonstrations which were organised in Port-au-Prince to support the regime on such anniversaries as 22 October and 1 January were largely composed of rural Haitians transported in trucks to the city by local *macoute* leaders. The significant thing to note here is that while Duvalier's basis of support might have been rural, it was essential to demonstrate this support in the capital where ultimate power lies. The growth of the *tontons macoutes*, many of whose leaders enjoyed a rural power base, has implications for the changing balance between capital and countryside. Although provincial *macoute* leaders enjoyed considerable local control, their activities were circumscribed by the president, and in order to exert influence at the national level it was necessary for them to have connections in the capital. François Duvalier's own rise to presidential office and his continued tenure depended to a great extent upon active endorsement by members of the *classe intermédiaire*. As we shall see, their changing role in the regime of Jean-Claude Duvalier is of considerable importance in understanding recent developments in the country.

The black middle classes, rural and urban, which formed the keystone of François Duvalier's power structure, were not accustomed to receiving many benefits from the state and their loyalty could therefore be purchased at a modest price; they knew that they were unlikely to improve their lot by switching support to opposition groups. Throughout the lean years of 1962–6 when foreign aid was practically cut off and determined attempts were made by the US government, together with the Dominicans, to remove Duvalier from office, these middle class leaders remained faithful to the regime; this was partly through fear and partly in the hope that things would improve. The class which suffered most from international pressure was the elite, which was – generally speaking – already hostile towards the government.

OPPOSITION FORCES

During the first years of his regime François Duvalier had reduced systematically the political power of all the major groups and institutions in the country. The army officers, the Roman Catholic hierarchy, the United States embassy, the business elite, the intellectuals, the trade union leadership, one by one had their wings clipped. By 1966 Duvalier was in a strong enough position to begin an accommodation with each of these former centres of power; it was, however, made quite clear that limited freedom to pursue their own ends did not include interference in politics. It was now evident that the president did not seriously intend to eliminate the economic power of the mulatto elite, to reduce the religious role of the Roman Catholic church, nor to move his country into the Soviet or into the non-aligned block, despite earlier hints to this effect. It appeared to be in the interests of these institutions – elite, army, church and US embassy – to reach an agreement with Duvalier on the terms which he offered. In the case of the church and the army this accommodation was facilitated by the changes in leadership which Duvalier had effected, replacing a determined and power-ful set of bishops and officers by more docile and compliant figures.

By 1971 the opposition had effectively been eliminated, through murder, imprisonment or exile and there remained no major group capable of constituting a centre of political resist-ance or revolution. The above-mentioned groups had decided that they could live with Duvalierism and that attempts to improve their position within the parameters of the system were preferable to the confusion which might result from revolution. Thus, when François Duvalier's death occurred in April 1971 they were prepared to support a smooth transfer of power to his son.

THE SMOOTH SUCCESSION

The generally held view, based upon newspaper accounts of Haiti, was that the regime of François Duvalier had no popular support and remained in office solely by a system of terror. This led to the confident prediction that the regime would fall on the death of 'Papa Doc'. In fact, although terror was widely used and was an indispensable requirement for survival, it was not the whole story; as I have indicated, Duvalier and his associates had carefully constructed a support structure throughout the country based on the *Parti Unité Nationale* and on the various *macoute* organisations. Although there was a considerable hostility on the part of the masses to the more ruthless *macoute* leaders, this hostility did not seem to be transferred to the president himself. There was the belief that if only he knew what was going on he would take steps to remedy the situation. Constant propaganda, particularly on the radio, led to a widespread acceptance of the government and even to a belief in its benevolence. The paternal image of 'Papa Doc' – a figure possessing fearful power yet having a deep love for his people – was developed. At Duvalier's funeral, which I attended, there were numerous scenes of sadness and distress. We may well think that this popular attitude was ill-founded and misplaced but it did exist, and is part of the explanation for the survival of the regime.

More important factors in accounting for the transition from father to son, were the disablement of the opposition and the belief among important groups that a major disruption of political life in Haiti would be against their interests. This certainly applies to the United States, to the army leadership, to the church hierarchy and to much of the business community. Jean-Claude succeeded his father, but how far has he managed to maintain the power structure so carefully and ruthlessly constructed throughout the 1960s? To this question I now turn.

THE TEENAGED PRESIDENT

The young Jean-Claude Duvalier faced a number of serious difficulties on assuming office. The system of support which had been built by his father was delicately balanced and needed continual adjustment. In particular there was a tension between *noiriste* politicians and *macoute* leaders on the one hand and younger technocrats recruited in more recent years, who were less committed to Duvalierist ideology, on the other. Also, there were the pretentions of ambitious businessmen and army officers to be watched. Relationships within the presidential family complicated the situation; François Duvalier's widow was associated with a number of the old guard of *noiristes*, while one of her daughters was married to a leading army officer.

To the surprise of foreign observers, the young president – under the tutelage of his mother – managed to hold the regime together and by astute moves to curb dangerous groups, in the army and elsewhere, he ensured his survival. Although he had obviously learned much from his father in this respect, he lacked that intimate knowledge of Haitian social structure and dynamics which had been acquired by Papa Doc over many years. After a few years the president began to take action independently of his mother and put into positions of power a number of individuals, mostly from sections of the elite whom he had met in school days. These moves were resented by the old guard of Duvalierists and Jean-Claude gradually lost touch with that important *classe intermédiaire* upon which his father had relied, especially those from the rural areas. More and more he has come to depend on the business community and on the younger technocrats, many of whom come from elite mulatto families. In order to secure foreign aid it is necessary to have people in government who are able to speak the right language. These men, like Marc Bazin and Henri Bayard, are prepared to cooperate with the president only if they think that it will pay them to do so.

Many younger technocrats were unwilling to collaborate with a government which included such notorious characters as Luckner Cambronne and other old guard Duvalierists. They realised that the presence of such figures in positions of power ruined the cosmetic operation designed to convince the international community that Haiti was a country deserving foreign aid and investment. The regime of President Carter in the USA was prepared to back the efforts of these technocrats. His interest in human rights, together with a desire to keep Haiti in the 'free world', led to considerable pressure being brought on Jean-Claude Duvalier to liberalise his regime.

THE 'LIBERALISATION' OF DUVALIERISM

Moderately independent journals, like *Petit Samedi Soir* and *Hebdo Jeune Presse*, began to appear and to make cautious criticisms of the administration, though carefully avoiding suggestions that the president himself was responsible for any of the problems of Haiti. Popular plays in *Kréyol* were performed in the capital, pouring scorn on the administration of the country. Radio commentators, including Jean Dominique and Compère Filo of Radio Haïti Inter, broadcasting in *Kréyol*, voiced outspoken attacks on the more scandalous aspects of government policy. By 1979 Sylvio Claude and Grégoire Eugène had formed their Christian Democrat parties and a non-Duvalierist had been elected to the legislative assembly. It was an extraordinary sight to behold newspapers and duplicated pamphlets, openly critical of the government, being sold on the street. The liberalisation of Duvalierism seemed to be in full swing and to be on a course which was irreversible.

The volume of opposition had clearly worried the presidential entourage and by a stroke of good fortune a change of administration in the United States coincided with a realisation that unless something was done to clamp down on the opposition the days of Jean-Claude were numbered. President Reagan's concern for human rights was somewhat less palpable than that of his predecessor and he was unprepared to risk good relations with a neighbour merely on the grounds that the courtesies which the US public had come to expect at home were sometimes dispensed with abroad. Towards the end of November 1980 the clamp-down occurred. Opposition leaders were arrested and others managed to flee to foreign embassies; Radio Haïti was destroyed; journals and news-sheets disappeared from the streets.

MIGRATION

Two aspects of the foreign affairs of Haiti are important in assessing prospects for the future. Both of them are the consequence of the economic misery of the mass of the Haitian people, exaccerbated by political oppression. The first is the migration of Haitian cane cutters to the Dominican Republic, the second is the relatively recent phenomenon of the 'boat people' arriving in the United States.[5] Rural Haitians have for many years migrated to other parts of the Caribbean to seek employment in the cane fields. In the last few years however this has become a major feature of the sugar industry in the Dominican Republic. Both the Dominican and the Haitian governments have a financial interest in the system. The Dominican government which owns much of the sugar industry is eager to maintain a supply of cheap labour, and pays the Haitian government a fee for each migrant. The cane cutters live in barrack-like buildings reminiscent of the Indian indentured labourers in Trinidad and Guyana up to 1917; church groups, together with humanitarian agencies, have recently protested against the system. Also the presence of these migrants is resented by Dominican workers who see it as undercutting wage rates. Both the Dominican and Haitian governments are thus likely to oppose any change in the system.

On the second issue, the USA appears anxious to reach agreement with the Haitian government to prevent this migration. The co-operation of the Duvalier regime has been sought and US vessels have been patrolling the northern waters off the island of Hispaniola to stop Haitians leaving. Both governments have been criticised for this policy. Liberals in the USA have attacked their government, while Haitian nationalists (some of whom had supported the Duvalier regime in the past) have been incensed by this humiliating situation. Although the 'boat people' crisis appears temporarily to have strengthened the hand of Duvalier in dealing with Washington, it may well be that a future administration in the White House will think that there is a more satisfactory way of coping with the phenomenon and cease supporting a corrupt and oppressive government.

One important consequence of the migration is the money being sent home by those who have worked abroad for some time (particularly in the USA) to relations all over Haiti. It is impossible to make an accurate assessment of the amount of money arriving in this way, but anyone familiar with the Haitian scene will be aware of its importance. These remittances have noticeably improved the situation of countless families throughout the country.

RECENT DEVELOPMENTS

Although, as I have already mentioned, François Duvalier had come to some kind of compromise with most of the business elite, the foundation of his power structure remained the black middle classes. In this matter there has been a major change in Duvalierism. The regime of Jean-Claude has come increasingly to depend upon elite support and his wooing of these groups has had the effect of alienating many of the *noiristes*. A number of *macoute* leaders in recent years have voiced disquiet with the way things have been going, and some of them no longer see any probability of future benefits; they are unwilling to stick out their necks very far to preserve a government from which they have little if anything to gain. The marriage of Jean-Claude to Michele Bennett, the daughter of a rich and ruthless mulatto businessman, set the seal on these developments. While it is unlikely that these erstwhile Duvalierist supporters will initiate a revolution, they can now no longer be depended upon to resist a serious attempt to overthrow the government, as they could in the past.[6]

The elite, upon which the regime now relies heavily, is very much less dependable than the black middle classes. This elite is composed of groups many of which live off the state and whose members expect the government to ensure that their standard of living is maintained. If it fails to do this, they are likely to look around for other presidential possibilities. Up to now the government, thanks largely to United States aid, has been able to satisfy the elite, but for how much longer?

François Duvalier used the black *classe intermédiaire* to control the rural masses. The present government, having lost influence among this group, has attempted to appeal over their heads to the people themselves. This has been done partly by means of such popular radio stations as Radio Nationale, which has encouraged ordinary Haitians to make known their grudges against the incompetence and corruption of local officials.[7] The move has met with a considerable response, but has had the side effect of further alienating local *macoute* leaders, *chefs de section* and other rural functionaries. The setting up of *conseils communautaires* and the activities of *Le Comité National d'Action Jeanclaudiste* (CONAJEC) have been further moves in the endeavour to re-establish grassroots support for the regime. These populist ploys are, however, likely in the long run to weaken rather than to strengthen the regime.

A key factor in the situation is, of course, the position of the armed forces. Haiti has a long tradition of militarism in politics. Independence was secured by military action and from 1804 to 1913 the head of state was invariably a military officer. One of the avowed objects of the US occupation was to remove the army from politics, but soon after the departure of the marines in 1934 the military began to reassert its traditional role. In 1946 a triumvirate of army officers took over the country and after just four years of civilian rule the same junta stepped in to ensure the termination of President Estimé's period in office. For the next six years the country was ruled by an army officer and in the disturbed period from the fall of Magloire in 1956 to the accession of François Duvalier the army's role was crucial. By a series of carefully designed moves, the new president dealt effectively with the danger of a military *coup*. Senior officers were changed frequently, new men – mostly blacks – were promoted to high positions and the various branches of the military and paramilitary apparatus were carefully balanced, with their hierarchies meeting only at presidential level. By 1964 Duvalier could claim, with some justification, 'I have removed from the army its role of arbiter . . . of national life.'

Today the armed forces number about 7000, with half of them composing the police. There are a few hundred in the navy and air force and the remaining men are divided between the *Casernes Dessalines*, the Presidential Guard (with roughly 800 each) and the *Léopards* – a more recently formed brigade, which is somewhat better trained and equipped than the rest of the armed forces – numbering about 600.[8] While it is always possible that army officers will in the future play an independent role in the political process there are certain institutional safeguards against their initiating a revolution at the present time.

Each branch keeps a check on the others and the *macoutes* in turn remain a considerable counter-force. Recent clashes between *macoutes* and members of the armed forces suggest that relations between them are frequently strained. Though it would be unwise to rule out the possibility of a military *coup*, it does not at the moment look likely. What is less clear is the role that various branches of the armed forces might play in the event of a serious invasion or a large-scale popular movement against the government. The performance of the armed forces in subduing the 1982 'invasion' of the island of La Tortue, by less than a dozen exiles, does not suggest that they are a particularly efficient and reliable butress!

By shifting the basis of his support, Jean-Claude Duvalier has placed himself in a vulnerable position, particularly with respect to the USA. While the father was able to resist enormous pressure from the Kennedy regime in the early 1960s, it is unlikely that the son could survive such pressure today. With President Reagan in the White House, he is perhaps safe from this quarter and even feels able to ignore US sensibilities, as he did recently in the sacking of Marc Bazin. Nevertheless with a US president less tolerant of dictatorship, corruption and torture, foreign aid might be withdrawn and the regime of Baby Doc, with its recently acquired feet of clay, would be likely to totter and fall.

Part V
Conclusion

Conclusion

'Dear Investor, There's a place close to the United States where the opportunities and profit potential are virtually unlimited. . . . It's the Caribbean, called "the new frontier" ', so begins an advertisement for *Caribbean Dateline*. It reflects an image of the region that is widespread in the USA and Europe, but one which many liberals will properly reject. In 1982 there was a conference on Haiti held in Wisconsin, composed almost entirely of North Atlantic academics and other experts. Few, if any of the participants would have adopted the position of *Caribbean Dateline*. In the discussion the puzzled question would frequently be asked, 'What ought we to do about the situation in Haiti?'. Towards the end someone raised the further questions, 'Who are we?' and 'Is it our job to do anything about Haiti?' Having suffered various forms of foreign intervention in the affairs of their country, most thinking Haitians would politely inform their country's foreign well-wishers that maybe the best thing they can do is to cease intervening. There is the danger of a kind of neo-neo-colonialism in the desire of North Atlantic radicals to run revolutionary movements in Latin America and the Caribbean.

Perhaps the most depressing aspect of the 1983 invasion of Grenada was the way in which most of the Commonwealth Caribbean governments and peoples instinctively looked to the USA to remove what appears to have been an unsavoury and brutal regime. In the old days London would have been expected to act. The colonial mentality is deeply rooted, and the absence of a sense of responsibility is one of the principal characteristics of post-colonial politics.[1] Almost the whole of the anglophone Caribbean supported the 'rescue', as it was seen. In Grenada itself the action was clearly popular, not only among the upper classes but much more generally. It may indeed be the case that the immediate consequences of the action, if taken in isolation, would justify the intervention, but it was interesting to contrast the attitudes of those countries in the region which have been victims of United States intervention. In the Dominican Republic and even in Haiti, among quite conservative groups, there was criticism of the action, which was seen as just one more instance of a general policy of domination going back to the late nineteenth century. The attitude of Commonwealth Caribbean people was thought of as somewhat naïve.

One of the most pervasive forms of foreign intervention in the affairs of Caribbean and other third world countries is by means of aid programmes financed by western governments and by various international agencies. Foreign aid, it has been said, is what poor people in rich countries give to rich people in poor countries. The modest programmes sponsored by such voluntary agencies as Oxfam and Christian Aid should, however, be distinguished from the huge amounts of money and soft loans given by official bodies. The former make a small but generally valuable contribution to improving the conditions of life for significant groups of poor people throughout the world. Although mistakes are sometimes made, the aid is carefully monitored and great care is usually taken to avoid some of the unfortunate consequences which this kind of aid can bring. There is usually an 'educational' aspect to the projects which these agencies support, designed to encourage poor people to discover the institutional and structural causes for their poverty and to take action to improve their conditions. Not all voluntary agencies, however, are equally careful in assessing the consequences of their gifts. Particularly in the matter of food aid whole areas have been reduced to a permanent state of dependence.[2] In the Ile de la Gonâve in Haiti, for example, not only has such a dependent community been created, but a whole system of patronage and power has been established by those who control the food supplies and whose interest is served by preventing constructive change.

OFFICIAL AID

Here I wish to deal with aid which is given by governments and by international agencies, which accounts for over 90 per cent of the total aid programme. Whether the money comes from the poor in rich countries is a question I will not attempt to answer now; though considering which social classes pay the bulk of direct and indirect taxes in donor countries we may recognise some plausibility in the assertion.

The effects of the kind of massive transfers of wealth, recommended by the Brandt Report, have often been to reinforce the power of corrupt and oppressive governments. For it is not to 'the people' but to *governments* that the aid goes in the first instance. The Duvalier family in Haiti receives many millions of dollars from the USA, France and Canada. General Idi Amin was collecting large sums in foreign aid up to the time of his political demise. In 1977 the British government gave $1.3 million to the Bangladesh government to provide telecommunications equipment for the police, while – according to Amnesty International – there were over 10 000 political prisoners languishing in the gaols of the country.[3] The increased power and patronage which such official aid gives to governments magnifies the importance of seizing or holding on to political power.

Official aid is often tied, so that the receiving government must buy particular sorts of product from the donor country, products which tend to benefit not the very poorest but the middle classes in the receiving country and act as a subsidy to inefficient firms in the donor country. All too often the aid pays for prestige national air lines and show-piece capital cities. President Reagan's Caribbean Basin Initiative clearly falls into this category, and it was astonishing to find the leading British voluntary aid agencies in 1983 pressurising the British government to support a 'massive Marshall aid' type of programme in the Caribbean, backed by the USA. It is difficult to conceive of anything which would do more damage, by making dependent countries more dependent and by exacerbating the internal political situation in Haiti and other countries of the region.

It might at first appear that the 'food for work' programmes, in which poor people get paid in food for working on such projects as canal digging or road building, would have more beneficial effects. Unfortunately those who benefit most from such schemes are the larger landowners who get free labour to improve facilities which only they are in a position to use. If the improvements affect rented land, the tenants have to pay higher rents and if the land of the small farmer is bettered, this has often, in Haiti, served to 'pave the way for land-grabbing by the relatively wealthy under a cloak of legality'.[4] The rich become richer and the poor become more dependent.

The much-celebrated Brandt report had a good deal to say on the subject of foreign aid.[5] The Commission, headed by a former West German chancellor was composed largely of unemployed politicians, a number of whom once enjoyed positions of power from which they might have done something effective. Mr Evan Luard (himself a former minister) tells us that the Commission 'had the benefit of high-powered economic advice'.[6] Undoubtedly the advice was favourable to the aid business, for economists, acting as highly paid 'consultants' and employed by institutes of development studies have been among the principal beneficiaries of the aid bonanza. The Brandt report advocated more aid being channelled through such international agencies as the World Bank or a proposed World Development Fund. This is not surprising when we remember that it was Mr Robert McNamara, president of the World Bank, who suggested the setting up of the commission. Such a step would effectively remove the aid business from the last vestiges of public accountability; a national government normally has to justify its aid programme before an elected legislature, but not so with international agencies, whose over-paid executives have enormous discretionary powers and a vested interest in the whole sordid business. They must keep the machine running or they will lose their lucrative jobs.

CHRISTIAN RESPONSES

The Brandt report was received among the churches and other establishment groups in Britain with considerable enthusiasm. Even those who could see the flaws in the proposals found themselves swept into supporting them. In a pamphlet published by the Scottish Churches Action for World Development, Danus Skane made some perceptive and devastating criticisms of the Brandt proposals.[7] They are elitist in their implications and they do not deal effectively with the rearrangements necessary for a just international order. Then suddenly on p. 13 the author's critical faculties are thrown to the wind when he talks of the 'contribution' which 'christian thought' can make, concluding that the churches should 'in the name of Christ try to press for changes in line with the Brandt proposals' – proposals which he has told us are likely to have the effect of strengthening an unjust and elitist world order!

Worshipping one who identified himself with the poor and denounced the hypocrisy and injustice of the ruling classes of his day, christians will undoubtedly be concerned about world poverty. If they are really serious about wanting a redistribution of wealth they will recognise that there are few cases indeed in the history of the world when a significant improvement has occurred in the conditions of a deprived social class by charitable action on the part of the better-off. Any real change will come not by rich countries giving to poor countries but by the latter becoming powerful enough to take what rich countries have wrongly assumed to be theirs. What will christians do when the mighty are being put down from their seat and the rich are being sent empty away? Will they support their governments in attempting to maintain the status quo by force. Because this is what governments will do in the name of the defence of the free world, democratic values or some other ideology. Or will christians in rich countries take the lead in subverting these attempts by their governments? This will be the real test of their seriousness.

PARTICIPATION

Two authors have defined political participation as 'activity by private citizens designed to influence governmental decision-making'.[8] The assumption is that political decision-making is the exclusive prerogative of governments and that the role of citizens, in groups and as individuals, is merely that of attempting to influence these decisions. Haiti inherited from its colonial past a centralised system of government. Governmental weakness and inefficiency in the nineteenth century led to the growth of a lively civic tradition in the provincial towns. Various clubs and other groups met; newspapers and reviews were published. Towns like Jérémie, Jacmel, Cap Haïtien and St Marc were regional centres of some importance, due largely to the fact that they were ports. With the US occupation power became centralised, land communications were improved and life was gradually drained from the provincial towns, with the possible exception of Cap Haïtien. The visitor to Jacmel, Gonaïves or Petit Goâve today, finds it hard to believe that they were once active centres of social and cultural life.

1946 saw a brief revival of provincial life. Newspapers like *Le Populaire*, *La Cité*, *L'Artibonite Journal* and *Lumière* came from

Gonaïves alone, *Liberté*, and *La Digue* from Petit Goâve, *L'Eclai-reur*, from Port-de-Paix, not to mention the journals published in Le Cap, Les Cayes and other provincial towns. Some of these papers continued into the 1950s, but by the end of the decade the dead hand of Duvalierism had killed most local enterprises of this kind. As in Britain today, empty rhetoric about local initiative is accompanied by a relentless centralisation of power in the capital. Nevertheless there remains among the population in Haiti and in some other parts of the Caribbean a valuable tradition of self-help, for the masses have no reason to expect help from governments. Even in the midst of appalling poverty there are encouraging signs of inventiveness, initiative and artistic talent. All too often these manifestations come to nought in the face of official interference and corruption. There is also a sense of freedom and independence born of a long tradition of peasant ownership. These are aspects of Haitian life which visiting academics and North Atlantic experts on United Nations 'missions' (the term, incidentally, is significant) frequently fail to appreciate. Any sort of 'modernisation' or 'development' which fails to build upon what is valuable in Haitian rural life would be a disaster for the country.

Undoubtedly great things have been achieved in Cuba since the revolution in the fields of public health, education and community development, and there is much that other countries can learn from the Cuban experience, but it has been at a considerable cost. It would be a mistake to see the bureaucratic and oppressive regime as a model for other Caribbean states to follow. The role of the state should be to encourage and enable rather than to manage. The departmental and other regional loyalties which certainly still exist in Haiti need to be strengthened, with an effective system of local government. The mass of the people in Haiti – as in Jamaica, Grenada and other parts of the Caribbean – are basically conservative; the poorer they are the less ready they are to risk losing what they have for the promise of better things. Political strategies which assume the existence of a revolutionary working class or peasantry in the Antilles are bound to come to grief. Only by recognising the force and indeed the value of tradition will constructive change occur.

Notes and References

Abbreviations

AAE		Archives du Ministère des Affaires Etrangères, Paris:
	CPH	Correspondance Politique, Haïti
	CCC	Correspondance Consular et Commerciale
PRO		Public Record Office, London:
	Adm	Admiralty
	FO	Foreign Office
USNA DS		United States National Archives, Department of State, Washington DC

INTRODUCTION

1. I am thinking of Gabriel Coulthard, whose book *Race and Colour in Caribbean Literature* contains excellent chapters on Haiti.
2. J. Michael Dash, *Literature and Ideology in Haiti, 1915–1961.*
3. Dawn Marshall, *'The Haitian Problem': Illegal Migration to the Bahamas*; Mirlande H. Manigat, *Haiti and Caricom.*
4. E. K. Brathwaite, *The Times Literary Supplement*, 23 December 1983, p. 1425.
5. Eric E. Williams, *From Columbus to Castro*, p. 503.
6. Kortright Davis, *Mission for Caribbean Change: Caribbean Development as Theological Enterprise*, p. 29.
7. See for example the articles of Bissainthe, Bajeux and Parisot in A. Abble *et al.*, *Les prêtres noirs s'interrogent*; Claude Souffrant, 'Catholicism et négritude à l'heure du black power', *Présence Africaine*, N.S. 75, 1970, 'Un catholicisme de résignation', *Social Compass*, 17, 1970, 'La foi en Haïti', *Parole et Mission*, 55, mars 1971 and *Une négritude socialiste*; L. Hurbon, *Dieu dans le vaudou haïtien* and *Culture et Dictature en Haïti.*
8. George L. Beckford (ed.), *Caribbean Economy*, p. v.
9. K. Davis, *Mission for Caribbean Change*, p. 27, (my italics).
10. See below p. 22.
11. Some of the problems are discussed in Vaughan A. Lewis (ed.), *Size, Self-Determination and International Relations: the Caribbean.*
12. Dana G. Munro, *Intervention and Dollar Diplomacy in the Caribbean: 1900–1921*, and *The United States and the Caribbean Republics, 1921–1933*; Dexter Perkins, *The United States and the Caribbean*; Tad Szulc (ed.), *The United States and the Caribbean*; Jenny Pearce, *Under the Eagle.*

13. 'A Work of Combat: Mulatto Historians and the Haitian Past', *Journal of Interamerican Studies*, 16:1, 1974, pp. 15ff.
14. Léopold de Saussure, *Psychologie de la colonisation française*.
15. Lilyan Kesteloot, *Les écrivains noirs de langue française: naissance d'une littérature*.
16. Hollis R. Lynch, *Edward Wilmot Blyden: Pan-Negro Patriot, 1832–1912*.
17. Edmund D. Cronin, *Black Moses: the Story of Marcus Garvey and the Universal Negro Improvement Association*.
18. See Rémy Bastien in H. Courlander and R. Bastien, *Religion and Politics in Haiti*, pp. 45ff. On Péralte and Batraville see Roger Gaillard, *Les blancs débarquent*, vols 6 and 7. I have described a prayer book which was discovered on the body of Batraville in *From Dessalines to Duvalier*, p. 297, n. 36.
19. L. Gouré and J. Weinkle, 'Cuba's New Dependency', *Problems of Communism*, March–April 1972; but see also F. Fitzgerald, 'The Direction of Cuban Socialism: a Critique of the Sovietization Thesis', in Susan Craig (ed.), *Contemporary Caribbean: a Sociological Reader*, 2, pp. 243ff.
20. Clive Thomas, 'State Capitalism in Guyana: an Assessment of Burnham's Co-operative Socialist Republic', in Fitzroy Ambursley and R. Cohen (eds) *Crisis in the Caribbean*, pp. 27ff.
21. On the Haitian Revolution see C. L. R. James, *Black Jacobins*; the writings of Gérard M. Laurent, especially *Quand les chaines volent en éclats . . .*; and David Geggus, *Slavery, War and Revolution: the British Occupation of Saint-Domingue, 1793–1798*. On the US occupation and the Haitian resistance, see Hans Schmidt, *The United States Occupation of Haiti, 1915–1934*, Kethly Millet, *Les paysans haïtiens et l'occupation américaine, 1915–1930*; and the series of volumes by Roger Gaillard, *Les blancs débarquent*.
22. Fitzroy Ambursley and Robin Cohen in *Crisis in the Caribbean*, p. 9. Though Ambursley fully recognises that the defeat of Michael Manley cannot be ascribed solely to the machinations of the CIA, ibid., p. 72.
23. Ibid., p. 204. Further evidence for the petty bourgeois nature of the regime was that Maurice Bishop allegedly owned an apartment block.

1 CASTE, CLASS AND COLOUR IN HAITI

1. Morille P. Figaro, 'Contrition', *Le Jour*, 19–29 mai 1967.
2. On Accau see below, pp 175f. On Price Mars see L. S. Senghor *et al.*, *Témoignages sur la vie et l'oeuvre du Docteur Jean Price Mars* also, in a critical vein, R. Depestre 'Jean Price-Mars et le mythe de l'orphée noir ou les aventures de la négritude', *L'Homme et la Société*, 7, 1968, pp. 171f, printed in revised form in Depestre *Bonjour et adieu à la négritude*, pp. 43f.
3. 'Bulletin 57', *L'Action Nationale*, 6 mai 1946; see David Nicholls, 'Idéologies et mouvements politiques en Haïti', *Annales, Economies, Sociétés, Civilisations*, 30:4, 1975, pp. 654f.
4. M. L. E. Moreau de Saint-Méry, *Description topographique, physique, civile, politique et historique de la partie française de l'île Saint-Domingue*, 1, pp. 86f.
5. Fouchard writes of the *affranchis* 'numériquement parlant. . . cette classe se trouvait composée d'une large majorité noire', *Les marrons de la liberté*, p. 333. Fouchard, who

is an apologist of the mulatto elite in Haiti, is keen to maintain this interpretation of the past in order to undermine the general association between class and colour. These assimilated maroons – *'reputés affranchis sans l'être'* as they were called – cannot legitimately be included with the *affranchis* proper in colonial Saint-Domingue, as their position was quite different and they had distinct interests. While the *affranchis* were keen that the *Code Noir* be strictly enforced, these maroons were of course against such a policy.

6. I have attempted to show this in *From Dessalines to Duvalier*.

7. It would, however, be a mistake to regard Haitian peasants as congenitally apathetic, as *'des résignés'*, as Roger Riou does in his book *Adieu La Tortue*. See chapter 9 below.

8. See chapter 2 below.

9. A. B. Ardouin, *Études sur l'histoire d'Haïti suivies de la vie du général J.-M. Borgella*, 6, pp. 45–6.

10. *The Haitian People*, ch. 3. Leyburn's book was an outstanding contribution to the understanding of Haiti and it was deservedly republished in 1966 with an excellent introduction by Sidney Mintz. Nevertheless many subsequent writers have rather uncritically adopted some of Leyburn's mistaken judgments.

11. H. Courlander and R. Bastien, *Religion and Politics in Haiti* and David Nicholls 'Politics and Religion in Haiti', *Canadian Journal of Political Science*, 3:3, 1970, pp. 400f. For a brief discussion of voodoo see below pp. 212f.

12. I have discussed this controversy in 'A Work of Combat, Mulatto Historians and the Haitian Past', *Journal of Interamerican Studies*, 16:1, 1974, pp. 15f.

13. J. Brown, *The History and Present Condition of St Domingo*, 2, p. 259; V. Schoelcher, *Colonies étrangères et Haïti*, 2, p. 348.

14. Lepelletier de Saint-Rémy, *Saint-Domingue*, 1, p. 274.

15. Leyburn, *The Haitian People* and J. Lobb 'Caste and Class in Haiti', *American Journal of Sociology*, 46:1, 1940, pp. 23f. This matter was discussed by Price Mars in *De la préhistoire d'Afrique à l'histoire d'Haïti*, pp. 139f. Christian Beaulieu made an illuminating contribution to the debate from a marxist standpoint in 'Caste et classe', *Le Nouvelliste*, 29 juillet 1942 where he wrote,

   Il est clair que ce pays n'est pas soumis à un rigid système de castes, puisqu'on peut y observer une certaine mobilité sociale; mais il est non moins évident qu'on n'y trouve pas la société à classes dans sa purité classique, des conditions particulières constituant encore des barrières que réduisent singulèrement la mobilité sociale de l'individu.

   This position was largely followed by Etienne Charlier in a number of his writings.

16. O. C. Cox, *Caste Class and Race*. This is an important and interesting study, but there is, I think, no need to adopt such a narrow definition of the term 'caste'. A similar position is maintained on this question by L. Dumont in 'Caste, racisme et "stratification" ', *Cahiers Internationaux de Sociologie*, no. 29, 1960, pp. 91f.

17. *Report of the President's Commission for the Study and Review of Conditions in the Republic of Haiti*, p. 19. On the middle class in Haiti see C. Pressoir 'Étude sur la classe moyenne à Port-au-Prince', *Revue de la Société d'Histoire et de Géographie d'Haïti*, 21, 1950 pp. 1f; S. and J. Comhaire Sylvain, 'Urban Stratification in Haiti', *Social and Economic Studies*, 8:2, 1959, pp. 179f.; M. de Young, 'Class Parameters in Haitian Society', *Journal of Interamerican Studies*, 1:4, 1959, pp. 449f.; L. Paret-Limardo 'Les Classes moyennes en Haïti', in *The Development of a Middle Class in Tropical and Sub-Tropical Countries*; M. Sylvain Bouchereau, 'La classe moyenne en Haïti' in T.

Crevenna, *Materiales para el estudio de la clase media en la América Latina'*, pp. 67f.; R. Wingfield and V. J. Parenton, 'Class Structure and Class Conflict in Haitian Society', *Social Forces*, 43:3, 1965, pp. 338f.

18. A. C. Millspaugh, *Haiti under American Control, 1915–30*, p. 163. The principal Haitian writers concerned with this question at the end of the nineteenth century were Sténio Vincent, Moravia Morpeau, J. B. and J. C. Dorsainvil.

19. See J. J. Doubout and U. Joly, *Notes sur le développement du movement syndical en Haïti*; also J. B. Brutus 'Aperçu historique du mouvement syndical en Haïti', *Rond Point*, 7, mai 1963, pp. 6f. and other articles in this number of *Rond Point*. On development of new industries see 'An Observer', 'Dynastic Republicanism in Haiti', *Political Quarterly*, 44:1, 1973, pp. 77f.; more recently, Anthony Barbier, 'État, classes sociales et industrialisation dépendante en Haïti, 1970–1980', *Collectif Paroles*, no. 23, mai/juin 1983, pp. 33f.

20. Maurice de Young is thus wrong when he asserts that the *cacos* were recruited from the lowest class of landless labourers, 'Class Parameters', p. 450. On the social composition of the *cacos* see F.D. Légitime, 'Souvenirs historiques 1867–70', *Revue de la Société de Législation*, 2 décembre 1907, p. 138. For general literature on peasant life in Haiti see Paul Moral *Le Paysan Haïtien*, M. A. Lubin 'Quelques aspects des communautés rurales d'Haïti', *América Latina*, 5:1, 1962, pp. 3f.; H. Courlander *The Drum and the Hoe*; R. Bastien 'Haitian Rural Family Organisation', *Social and Economic Studies*, 10:1961, pp. 478f.; M. J. Herskovits *Life in a Haitian Valley*; A. Métraux, 'Les Paysans haïtiens', *Présence Africaine*, no. 12, 1951, pp. 112f.; J. Price Mars, *Ainsi parla l'oncle*; Mats Lundahl, *Peasants and Poverty: a Study of Haiti*.

21. J. Casimir, 'Aperçu sur la structure sociale d'Haïti', *América Latina*, 8:3, 1965, pp. 40f.

22. 'The soldiers who belonged to our first peasant-type guerrilla armies,' wrote Che Guevara, 'came from the section of this social class which shows most strongly love for the land and the possession of it; that is to say, which shows most perfectly what we can define as the petty-bourgeois spirit.' *Che Guevara Speaks*, p. 29.

23. M. de Young 'Class Parameters', p. 454.

24. The criticism of Boyer came from a group of southern blacks in their open letter to General Lazare; there is a copy of this letter in 'Haitian Papers', in the New York Public Library (*KF+PV 97); C. Hérard to Lord Aberdeen, (n.d.), PRO FO 35/29; for Pierrot's law see Thomas Madiou, *Histoire d'Haïti: années 1843–1846*.

25. See Naomi Garret, *The Renaissance of Haitian Poetry*; J. M. Dash, *Literature and Ideology in Haiti, 1915–1961*. See also below pp. 48f.

26. Roger Dorsainville '1946 ou le délire opportuniste', *Nouvelle Optique*, nos. 6 and 7, 1972, pp. 117f.; David Nicholls, 'Ideology and Political Protest in Haiti, 1930–1946', *Journal of Contemporary History*, 9:4, 1974, pp. 3f.

27. David Nicholls, 'Embryo-Politics in Haiti', *Government and Opposition*, 6:1, 1971, pp. 75f. and *From Dessalines to Duvalier*, ch. 8.

28. Peter Worsley, *The Third World*, p. 193.

29. In Colin Clarke (ed.), *Caribbean Social Relations*, p. 11.

2 THE WISDOM OF SALOMON: MYTH OR REALITY?

1. George Orwell, 'As I please', in *Collected Essays, Journalism and Letters*, iii, p. 110.

2. Michael Oakeshott, *Rationalism in Politics*, pp. 137f.

3. David Nicholls, 'A Work of Combat: mulatto historians and the Haitian past', *Journal of Interamerican Studies*, 16:1, 1974, pp. 15f.; and *From Dessalines to Duvalier*, pp. 87f.

4. Salomon *jeune*, 'Discourse, 29 octobre 1845, Procès Verbal'.

5. Levasseur à Guizot, 19 septembre 1843, AAE, CPH, 11/75.

6. M. A. Antoine, *Salomon jeune, martyr volontaire de sa classe*, p. xxxiv.

7. U. Saint Louis, in République d'Haïti, *Ouverture solennelle de la 6ème et dernier session de la 39ème législature*, 18 avril 1966, p. 33; see also U. Pierre Louis, *La révolution duvaliériste*, p. 22; F. Duvalier, *Œuvres essentielles*, 1: p. 312; *see also* ibid., 2: p. 152; 3: p. 94.

8. On the events of 22–23 September 1883, the British minister in Port-au-Prince wrote, 'It was quite a war of colour, the blacks massacring the coloured people', Hunt to Granville, 26 September 1883, PRO FO 35/118.

9. L. F. Manigat, *Un fait historique*, p. 30.

10. R. A. Saint Louis, *La présociologie haïtienne*, p. 108.

11. This position was also maintained by Liberals like Firmin *(L'égalité des races humaines)* and Price *(De la réhabilitation de la race noire par la république d'Haïti)*.

12. L. Laroche, *Haïti: une page d'histoire*, p. 119; Nord Alexis, for example, was later denounced by the *noiriste* Alcius Charmant as *'ce grand pontife du Vaudoutisme'*, *Haïti: vivra-t-elle?*, p. 266.

13. Delorme à Salomon, 4 juillet 1867, PRO FO 35/71.

14. Delorme, *Adresse: au citoyens de la république d'Haïti*.

15. For a critique of Delorme see H. Trouillot, *Demesvar Delorme*, and J. Price Mars, *Ainsi parla l'oncle*, p. 190.

16. L. J. Janvier *L'égalité des races*, pp. 25–6; Janvier in J. Auguste, *et al.*, *Les détracteurs de la race noire*, p. 27.

17. Janvier, *La république d'Haïti et ses visiteurs, 1840–1882*, p. 94; Janvier, *Humble adresse aux electeurs de la commune de Port-au-Prince*, p. 54, and Janvier, 'Notre république', *Haïti Littéraire et Sociale*, 5 janvier 1907.

18. *L'Oeil*, 23 juillet 1881.

19. J. F. T. Manigat, *Conférence sur le vaudoux*, p. 1. See also 'Le diabolisme et le vaudoux', in the *noiriste* journal, *L'Impartiale*, 10 septembre 1896, and Charmant, *Haïti*, p. 266.

20. Burdel à Challemel-Lacour, 5 octobre 1883, AAE CPH 33/107. The instructions, in the hand of Fénélon Faubert, Salomon's secretary, that were sent to the Haitian minister in Paris, Stéphen Preston, read, *'que la nature, la communauté d'origine, de langue, de loi, nous destiner à servir de point d'appui à la politique française dans la Golfe de Mexique'*, in Wyndham to Granville, 22 April 1885, PRO FO 35/125.

21. L. F. Manigat, *Amérique latine au XXe siècle*, p. 147.

22. S. St John, *Hayti or the Black Republic*, p. 97; and Byron to Malmesbury, 26 February 1859, PRO FO 35/53.

23. M. Macleod, 'The Soulouque Regime in Haiti, 1847–1859: a Re-evaluation'. *Caribbean Studies*, 10:3, 1970.

24. See A. G. Adam, *Une crise haïtienne, 1867–1869: Sylvain Salnave*, p. 44.

25. This is one of the principal themes in David Nicholls, *From Dessalines to Duvalier*.

26. L. F. Manigat, *Le délicat problème de la critique historique*.

27. The Haitian government's position on this affair can be found in République d'Haïti, *Documents diplomatiques, relations extérieurs, l'affaire Maunder*; there is an account of the situation from the standpoint of the Maunder family in Maunder to Granville, 9 January 1885, PRO FO 35/125.

28. Fouchard à Villevaleix, 9 septembre 1883, PRO FO 35/120. For details on the invasion of Miragoâne, see E. Chancy, *Pour l'histoire*, and J. Price Mars, *Jean-Pierre Boyer Bazelais et le drame de Miragoâne*.

29. Langston to Frelinghuysen, 30 May 1883, quoted in R. Logan, *The Diplomatic Relations of the United States with Haiti, 1776–1891*, p. 374.

30. Burdel à Challemel-Lacour, 5 octobre 1883, AAE CPH 33/107.

31. Fouchard à Villevaliex, 3 novembre 1883, in Logan, *The Diplomatic Relations*, p. 375.

32. Ferry à Burdel, 15 novembre 1883, AAE CPH 33/198.

33. Langston to Frelinghuysen, 19 November 1883, in Logan, *The Diplomatic Relations*, p. 376.

34. Salomon à Manigat, 24 juin 1884, PRO FO 35/125.

35. Hunt to Granville, 24 December 1883, PRO FO 35/118.

36. L. F. Manigat, 'La substitution de la prépondérance américaine à la prépondérance française en Haïti au debut du XXe siècle: la conjoncture de 1910–11', *Revue d'Histoire Moderne et Contemporaine*, 14:4, 1967, pp. 321f. This is published in an English translation in L. F. Manigat (ed.), *The Caribbean Yearbook of International Relations, 1975*, pp. 188f.

37. Quoted in *L'Avant-Garde*, 12 avril 1883.

38. E. Paul, *Haiti au soleil de 1880*, p. 62. See p. 107 below.

39. A Millspaugh, *Haiti under American Control, 1915–1930*, p. 96.

40. See below pp. 111f. This prohibition of foreign ownership had, however, been omitted from Christophe's constitutions of 1807 and 1811.

41. A. Michel, *Salomon jeune et l'affaire Louis Tanis*, pp. 159–60.

42. Salomon à Manigat, 24 juin 1884, PRO FO 35/125; Delorme also viewed the prohibition as '*un mesure transitoire*', in E. Pinckombe, *L'article 7: lettre à D. Delorme*, p. 53. 'Pinckombe' is sometimes spelled 'Pinkcombe'; there is no consistency even in his own publications.

43. Hunt to Granville, 13 December 1882, PRO FO 35/115.

44. Burdel à Challemel-Lacour, 5 mars 1883, AAE CPH 33/54.

45. *Le Moniteur*, 1 mars 1883. L. F. Manigat refers to '*la loi agraire Manigat-Cameau*', but fails to note article 5, *L'Amérique latine au XXe siècle*, p. 147.

46. *Le Moniteur*, 8 mars and 29 mars 1883.

47. 'La république radicale', *L'Oeil*, 17 novembre 1883. See pp. 112f. below.

48. Janvier, *Les antinationaux*, p. 46.

49. Salomon, *Circulaire*, 18 février 1882.

50. *Discours de S. E. le Président de la République, session extraordinaire*, 1883.

3 BIOLOGY AND THE POLITICS OF FRANÇOIS DUVALIER

1. 'Préjugé de couleur et lutte de classes', *Analyse schématique 32–34*, p.v.

2. 'Jean Price Mars et le mythe de l'orphée noir ou les aventures de la négritude', *L'Homme et la Société*, 7, 1968, p. 176.

3. Interview with Piquion, quoted in *L'Assaut*, 11 septembre 1935. Piquion went on to insist that it was not a question of aggressive racialism, but of an intelligent appreciation of racial differences.

4. *The Inequality of the Human Races*, p. 48.

5. Cf. Michael Biddiss, *Father of Racist Ideology*.

6. Gobineau, *The Inequality*, p. 133.

7. Ibid., p. 205.

8. Ibid., p. 50.

9. *De l'égalité des races humaines*, p. 662.

10. *De la réhabilitation de la race noire par la république d'Haïti*, p. 531.

11. This mistake is made by D. Fardin, *Cours d'histoire de la littérature haïtienne*, p. 51; by G. Coulthard, 'Negritude – reality and mystification', *Caribbean Studies*, 10, 1970, p. 42, and by René Depestre, 'Les métamorphoses de la négritude en Amérique', *Présence Africaine*, 1970, p. 27. Gobineau is, of course, the true grandfather of *négritude!*

12. *Ainsi parla l'oncle*, p. 220.

13. *Rapport entre l'instruction, la psychologie et l'état social, p. 19.*

14. *Les daïmons du culte voudo*, p. 11.

15. Holly, *Rapport*, p. 20.

16. Cf. G. Coulthard's excellent discussion of this movement in *Race and Colour in Caribbean Literature*, and J. M. Dash, *Literature and Ideology in Haiti 1915–1961*.

17. 'Les sanglots d'un exile', reprinted in F. Duvalier, *Hommage au martyr de la non-violence*, pp. 76f.

18. 'Les civilisations négro-africaines et le problème haïtien' (1936), reprinted in F. Duvalier, *Œuvres essentielles*, 1 (3rd. edn), pp. 71–2.

19. *Essais de vulgarisation scientifique et questions haïtiennes*, p. 74. This appeared originally in *Les Griots*, octobre-décembre 1936.

20. *Incidences*, p. 22.

21. 'L'éthnologie et des cultures noires', *Présence Africaine*, juin-novembre 1956, p. 149.

22. *Le Nouvelliste*, 30 décembre 1935; reprinted in Duvalier, *Œuvres essentielles*, 1 (3rd edn), p. 50.

23. Ibid., p. 53.

24. Suzanne Césaire, 'Leo Frobénius et le problème des civilisations', *Tropiques*, 1, 1941.

25. *Contribution à l'étude de l'homme haïtien*, p. 15.

26. Ibid., p. 44.

27. *On African Socialism*, p. 72.

28. 'Negritude and African Socialism', in K. Kirkwood, (ed), *African Affairs* (St. Antony's Papers, 15) 2, p. 11.

29. Ibid., p. 16.

30. 'L'ésprit de la civilisation ou les lois de la culture négro-africaine', *Présence Africaine*, juin-novembre 1956, p. 53.

31. *Œuvres essentielles*, 1 (3rd edn), p. 50.

32. F. Duvalier and L. Denis, 'L'évolution stadiale du vodou', *Œuvres essentielles*, 1 (1st edn), pp. 163f. Cf. also Rémy Bastien, and H. Courlander, *Religion and Politics in Haiti*; C. Souffrant, 'Un catholicisme de résignation en Haïti', *Social Compass*, 17, 1970, pp. 425f; and above 1.

33. Gobineau, *The Inequality*, pp. 41–2.

34. Ibid., pp. 46f.

35. *Œuvres essentielles*, 1 (3rd edn), p. 53.

36. Duvalier and Denis, 'Tribus mandinque?', *Le Nouvelliste*, 26 octobre 1936.

37. *Œuvres essentielles*, 1 (3rd ed), p. 67f.

38. 'L'essentiel de la doctrine des griots', in *Œuvres essentielles*, 1 (1st edn), p. 40.

39. 'Considérations sur nos origines historiques', in ibid., p. 53.
40. Ibid., p. 54.
41. Introduction to the Hebrew translation of *Le problème des classes à travers l'histoire d'Haïti*, p. 65.
42. Cf. C. Wauthier, *The Literature and Thought of Modern Africa*, pp. 51f.
43. *Pages retrouvées*, p. 84.
44. *L'ethnie haïtienne*, p. 65.
45. 'L'art et la science au service de l'action', *L'Action Nationale*, 4 mai 1932.
46. 'La place au soleil', *L'Action Nationale*, 18 avril 1932.
47. 'Force ou dictature', *La Relève*, avril 1934, p. 13; cf. also Piquion, 'Le salut par la force', *La Relève*, mars 1934.
48. *Œuvres essentielles*, 4, p. 125.
49. Ibid., 1 (1st edn), p. 63 and 320, and 4, p. 149.
50. Ibid., 4, p. 173.
51. *Political Development in the New States*, p. 21.
52. Ibid., p. 68n.
53. U. Pierre Louis, *La révolution duvaliériste*, p. 34.
54. *Œuvres essentielles*, 4, p. 218.
55. *Africa: the Politics of Independence*, p. 98.
56. Article in *L' Unité Africaine*, 26 novembre 1964, quoted in I. L. Markovitz, *L. S. Senghor and the Politics of Negritude*, p. 204.
57. David Nicholls, *From Dessalines to Duvalier*, pp. 232f.
58. *Capital*, 1, p. 766.
59. Marx and Engels, *Selected Works*, 2, p. 490.

4 EAST INDIANS AND BLACK POWER IN TRINIDAD

1. Quoted in F. B. Barbour (ed.) *The Black Power Revolt*, p. 157.
2. *The Running Man* (vol. I, part I.)
3. *New York Post*, 19 August 1967.
4. Gordon Lewis, *The Growth of the Modern West Indies*, p. 403.
5. In the face of these figures, and despite the role which Indians have played in the history of Trinidad, we find a writer as well acquainted with the Caribbean as Gordon Lewis writing of the Indians as a 'marginal' group in Trinidad (ibid., p. 33). Lewis was closely associated with Dr. Williams and the PNM in its early years, and perhaps betrays some of the assumptions and prejudices of this movement.
6. Walter Rodney, *The Groundings with my Brothers*. 'The black people of whom I speak, therefore, are non-whites.' he declares, 'the hundreds of millions of people whose homelands are in Asia and Africa, with another few million in the Americas' (p. 16). Later, on p. 28, he explicitly includes Indians as 'black'. Yet elsewhere he maintains that 'blacks in the West Indies accept ourselves as African' (p. 37), and insists that 'the African past is one with which the black man in the Americas can identify with pride' (p. 52).
7. ASCRIA, *Teachings of the Cultural Revolution*, p. 7.
8. 'The Black Power Movement – What it Means', *Impact*, September 1968, p. 23.

9. From a typescript of the speech taken from tape recording.
10. From a paper by S. R. Ramessar on unemployment, issued by the Industrial Development Corporation.
11. Gordon Lewis, op. cit., p. 38.
12. *Trinidad Guardian*, 8 March 1970.
13. Ibid., 10 March 1970.
14. Ibid., 10 March 1970. Italics mine.
15. Ibid., 10 March 1970.
16. Ibid., 11 March 1970
17. Ibid., 18 March 1970. The basically conservative position of Primus is clear from an earlier statement of his: 'The Desired Black Vote at 18 Years', *Vanguard* 22 February 1969.
18. *Trinidad Guardian*, 25 March 1970.
19. 'What Independence', *Vanguard*, 23 August 1969.
20. V. S. Naipaul, *The Middle Passage* p. 48. Cf. D. Darbeau, 'Cultural Slavery', in *East Dry River Speaks*; there were a number of issues of this mimeographed review, but they are not dated or numbered.
21. Quoted in Naipaul, op. cit., p. 49.
22. *Black Sound*: this is another duplicated review produced by the black power movement.
23. 'This Republic Business', *East Dry River Speaks*; Princess Alice was Chancellor of the UWI.
24. Michael Als, 'A Change is Coming', *Vanguard*, 17 January 1970.
25. 'This Republic Business',
26. G. Granger, 'Corruption', *East Dry River Speaks*.
27. 'The English people believes itself to be free; it is gravely mistaken; it is free only during the election of Members of Parliament; as soon as the Members are elected, the people is enslaved; it is nothing.' Rousseau, *The Social Contract*, Book 3, ch. 15.
28. *Liberation*, June 1970.
29. Editorial, *Vanguard*, 21 March 1970.
30. D. Darbeau, 'The Chains are Bursting', *East Dry River Speaks*.
31. D. Darbeau, 'The Values and Social Responsibility in an ex-colonial Society'. *Vanguard*, 22 November 1969.
32. *Black Sound*.
33. *Trinidad Guardian*, 14 April 1970.
34. *Liberation*, June 1970.
35. 'The Chains are Bursting'.
36. *Vanguard*, 7 March 1970. Cf. Earl Lewis, An Open Letter to the Press', *Moko*, 31 January 1969.
37. G. Weekes, 'The Catalyst of Change', *Vanguard*, 22 March 1969.
38. *Liberation*, June 1970.
39. *Moko*, 11 April 1969.
40. *Black Sound*.
41. 'Right here in Trinidad we are going to confirm the power of our blackness/Africanism. . . . Ethiopia shall one day stretch forth her hands to claim her children'. In 'I'm Black and Proud', *Vanguard*, 22 March 1969.
42. D. Murray, L. Taylor, and S. McLear, 'Towards a Reassessment of the Relevance of Black Power to the West Indies', *Pivot*, December 1969.
43. Ibid.

44. D. Murray, 'Afro-Carib Consciousness', *Tapia*, 28 September 1969; cf. also Darbeau, 'Laventille', in *Moko*, 22 December 1969.
45. 'The New Movement', *Embryo*, 20 April 1970.
46. 'Mamaguy', in Trinidad slang, means 'to mock', or 'to make a fool of'.
47. Though in the case of the negro bourgeoisie, there was occasionally a certain emotional attraction to some of the ideals of the movement; many members of this group must have been reminded of the early radical days of the PNM. Nevertheless, this emotional attraction was more than compensated for by a sober realisation that their economic and social position would suffer if the black power movement were to become more powerful.
48. D. Ali, 'Black Power and the Indian', *Embryo*, 9 February 1970.
49. R. Jagessar 'Indian Iceberg', *Tapia*, 16 November 1969.
50. 'African-Indian Solidarity', *Vanguard*, 21 March 1970.
51. *Trinidad Guardian*, 7 March 1970.
52. 'Black Liberation Organisation', in *Trinidad Express*, 23 March 1970.
53. *Trinidad Guardian*, 10 March 1970.
54. Editorial, *Vanguard*, 21 March 1970.
55. V. S. Naipaul, *The Middle Passage*, p. 91.

5 ECONOMIC DEPENDENCE AND POLITICAL AUTONOMY, 1804–1915

1. The term 'autonomy' is used as a synonym for *effective* independence and the term 'independence' refers to the formal status of a so-called 'sovereign state'. The usage is thus significantly different from the French, particularly with respect to the term '*autonomie*' which refers to a situation of internal self government without legal independence as a sovereign state.
2. E. Barker (ed.), *The Politics of Aristotle*, pp. 4f. and 292; Thomas Aquinas *On Kingship: to the King of Cyprus*, pp. 75–6; G. W. F. Hegel, *The Philosophy of Right*, p. 213; H. S. Reiss, (ed.), *The Political Thought of the German Romantics*, p. 94.
3. Rex Nettleford, *Mirror, Mirror*, p. 147.
4. David Nicholls, *From Dessalines to Duvalier*.
5. A. O. Hirschman (ed.), *Latin American Issues*, p. 5.
6. See C. Frostin, *Les révoltes blanches à Saint-Domingue aux XVIIe et XVIIIe siècles*.
7. 'Report by James Walker and Hugh Cathcart', 7 August 1803, PRO Adm 1/253.
8. *Gazette Politique et Commercial d'Haïti*, 17 octobre 1805; A. Turnier, *Les États Unis et le marché haïtien*, p. 95.
9. B. Ardouin, *Études sur l'histoire d'Haïti suivies de la vie du général J.-M. Borgella*, 6, p. 26.
10. *Gazette Politique et Commerciale d'Haïti*, 19 décembre 1805.
11. S. Linstant (de Pradine), *Recueil général des lois et actes du gouvernement d'Haïti*, 1, pp. 32–3; Ardouin, *Études*, 6, p. 61.
12. Quoted in Ardouin, *Études*, 8, p. 57. J. S. Milscent, also defended the prohibition of foreign ownership ('Politique', *L'Abeille Haytienne*, 16 octobre 1817, p.5.)
13. E. Bonnet (ed.), *Souvenirs historiques de Guy-Joseph Bonnet*, pp. 334–5..
14. Linstant, *Recueil*, 1, pp. 156 and 201.
15. Linstant, *Recueil*, 1, p. 212.

16. Linstant, *Recueil*, 1, p. 340. See also J. S. Milscent, '*Le commerce forme donc la chaîne qui lie les peuples. C'est lui qui assoupit la grande querelle des hommes et les sollicite à la réconciliation*'. ('Politique', *L'Abeille Haytienne*, 16 août, 1817)

17. Ardouin, *Études*, 6, p. 94.

18. The decree was published in London under the title *Adresse du gouvernement d'Haïti au commerce des nations neutres*, but was mistakenly dated 24 October.

19. *Gazette Officielle de l'État d'Haïti*, 4, 28 janvier 1808, p. 16.

20. P. V. Vastey (Baron de Vastey), *An Essay on the Causes of the Revolution and Civil Wars in Hayti*, pp. 207–8.

21. E. L. Griggs and C. H. Prator (eds), *Henry Christophe and Thomas Clarkson*, p. 146. Clarkson was a leading advocate of the abolition of slavery.

22. Comte de Limonade, *Relation des glorieux événements qui ont porté leurs majestés royales sur le trône d'Hayti*, p. 203.

23. W. W. Harvey, *Sketches of Hayti*, p. 343.

24. Linstant, *Recueil*, 2, p. 275.

25. J. B. Inginac, *Mémoires*, p. 29.

26. *Gazette Politique et Commerciale d'Haïti*, 29 novembre 1804.

27. Ardouin, *Études*, 7, p. 14.

28. Ardouin, *Études*, 2, p. 48.

29. P. Moral, *Le paysan haïtien*, p. 3.

30. Bonnet, *Souvenirs*, p. 221.

31. Linstant, *Recueil*, 2, p. 245.

32. Lepelletier de Saint Rémy, *Saint-Domingue: étude et solution nouvelle de la question haïtienne*, 2, p. 169.

33. Jean Price Mars, *De la préhistoire d'Afrique à l'histoire d'Haïti*, pp. 170f. and L. F. Manigat, *La politique agraire du gouvernement d'Alexandre Pétion*. See also a more recent article by R. K. Lacerte, 'The First Land Reform in Latin America', *Interamerican Economic Affairs*, 28:4, 1975.

34. Ragueneau de la Chainaye au Baron le Damas, 26 avril 1826, AAE CCC, Les Cayes, f. 66. It is often repeated even today that as a result of the land reforms 'not a single plantation was left intact.' (Mats Lundahl, *The Haitian Economy*, p. 30; see also p. 55.)

35. Baron de Vastey, *Political Remarks on Some French Works and Newspapers Concerning Hayti*, p. 54.

36. De Vastey, *Le système colonial dévoilé*, p. 12.

37. Linstant, *Recueil*, 2, p. 245. The republican writer J. S. Milscent also emphasised the importance of a thriving agriculture. '*L' agriculture*', he wrote '*n'exclut ni les arts ni l'industrie; mais elle rend leur absence supportable dans les circonstances difficiles. Elle procure une existence plus indépendante que celle qui se lie simplement aux rapports extérieurs. C'est pour cette raison que des nations agricoles, assaillies de toutes parts, ont résisté longtems aux efforts de leurs adversaires et ont supporté patiemment la stagnation du commerce*' ('Politique', *L'Abeille Haytienne*, 1 septembre 1817.)

38. Linstant, *Recueil*, 3, p. 233.

39. Linstant, *Recueil*, 4, p. 54.

40. A. Rouzeau, *De la république d'Haïti, île de Saint-Domingue*, quoted in *Journal des voyages* (1821 edn). 1, p. 389.

41. Linstant, *Recueil*, 3, p. 474.

42. Boyer, quoted in Linstant, *Recueil*, 4, p. 3. I have dealt with this question in more detail in *From Dessalines to Duvalier*, ch. 3.

43. Turnier, *Les États Unis*, pp. 118 f.

44. Leslie Manigat in *Le délicat problème de la critique historique* has, however, suggested that Pétion and Boyer were privately prepared to accept some kind of French suzerainty, but that public opinion in Haiti prevented them from openly advocating this view. The case with respect to Boyer is stronger than with Pétion, where the evidence is far from conclusive. I have discussed this further in *From Dessalines to Duvalier*, pp. 49f. and 64f.

45. Pétion à Dauxion Lavaysse, 27 novembre 1814, in J.-B. Wallez, *Précis historique des négotiations entre la France et Saint-Domingue*, p. 169.

46. W. S. Robertson, *France and Latin American Independence*, p. 451.

47. *Le Moniteur*, 12 août 1825.

48. Ragueneau de la Chainaye à Damas, 7 juin 1826, AAE CCC, Les Cayes, f. 66. There is an excellent discussion of French attempts to establish a 'neo-colonial' domination of Haiti in Benoît Joachim, 'Le néo-colonialism à l'essai', *La Pensée*, no. 156, 1971, pp. 35f., in 'Commerce et décolonisation', *Annales: Economies, Sociétés, Civilisations*, 27, 1972, pp. 1497.f. and in 'Aux sources d'un blocage du développement', *Cahiers des Amériques Latines*, no. 17, 1978, pp. 5f.

49. Postscript of 3 mai in Ragueneau à Damas, 26 avril 1826, AAE CCC, Les Cayes, f. 51; and T. G. Swain to Forsyth, 25 January 1838, USNA DS, Despatches from US Consuls, Port-au-Prince, 1.

50. Ardouin, *Études*, 8, p. 93.

51. *La Concorde*, 14 octobre 1821, quoted in Ardouin, *Études*, 9, pp. 20-1. A chamber of commerce was officially set up by a senate decree of 23 April 1807, but appears to have been moribund for several years; see *L'Abeille Haytienne*, 16 janvier 1819. The renewed interest in the chamber of commerce was partly due to the demand by Félix Darfour that such a chamber be effectively established; see 'Commerce: de l'agriculture', *L'Eclaireur Haytien*, 23 octobre 1818. The writers of *l'Abeille Haytienne* agreed about the desirability of such a chamber but thought that Darfour wished to give it powers which ought to rest with the legislative assembly. See J. F. Lespinasse, 'A Monsieur Darfour', *L'Abeille Haytienne*, 16 janvier 1819.

52. The journal *L'Agriculture Haïtien*, edited by J. B. Leblond, was the mouthpiece of this group; see for example the edition of 10 janvier 1826.

53. *Circulaire du Président d'Haïti aux Commandans d'Arrondissement sur l'Agriculture*, p. 5.

54. J. Franklin, *The Present State of Hayti*, pp. 377 and 240.

55. *Feuille de Commerce*, 19 mars 1831.

56. 'Agriculture', *L'Union*, décembre 1837. Ardouin ascribed the shortage of agricultural labour to a dislike for this type of work due to the colonial system. *Réponse du Sénateur B. Ardouin à un ecrit anonyme intitulé: 'Apologie'*, p. 37.

57. *L'Union*, 25 août 1839.

58. 'Industrie nationale', *L'Union*, 18 octobre 1838.

59. *Le Manifeste*, 19 décembre 1841. Ardouin also vigorously defended the prohibition of foreign ownership in *Réponse du Sénateur B. Ardouin à une lettre de M. Isambert*, p. 16. With the advent of Soulouque and the assassination of his brother Céligny Ardouin, however, the historian changed his position radically and urged a policy of white immigration; the granting of citizenship and property rights to Europeans would, he maintained, encourage *'le développement de notre civilisation et de notre prosperité'*, A. B. Ardouin à T. N. Ussher, 17 septembre 1849, PRO FO 35/36.

60. *Le Manifeste*, 20 août 1843.

61. T. Madiou, *Histoire d'Haïti: années 1843–1846*, pp. 150–9. For more details on the revolt led by Acaau, *see below*, pp. 175f.

62. Turnier, *Les États Unis*, pp. 131f.

63. S. St John, *Hayti or the Black Republic*, p. 97.

64. R. S. E. Hepburn, *Haiti as it is*, p. 15.

65. *De la gérontocratie en Haïti*, pp. 87–8.

66. Placide David, 'Edmond Paul', *Cahiers d'Haïti*, mars 1945, p. 32.

67. E. Paul, *Questions politico-économiques: 2, Formation de la richesse nationale*, pp. 59 and 70. See also an article in *Feuille de Commerce*, 22 juin 1861, where an anonymous author linked the land-ownership issue to the racial question.

68. Paul, *Questions*, 2, p. 67.

69. President Geffrard created bureaux for immigration in the major ports of the country by a decree of 24 April 1860. Salomon *jeune*, however, accused the president of adopting a definite policy of importing mulattoes rather than blacks (Salomon, *Une défense*, p. 88). For the article by Monfleury see 'De l'immigration', *Feuille de Commerce*, 10 mars 1860. The author believed that Indian immigrants who would be prepared to work for some years as labourers on estates would be preferable to American negroes who would wish to set up as independent peasant farmers. Chinese, however, would be best of all: '*le chinois est plus robuste, plus alerte, plus éclairé que le coolie*'.

70. Paul, *Questions*, 2, pp. 56f.

71. Paul, *Questions*, 2, p. 51.

72. Paul, *Questions politico-économiques: 1, Instruction publique*, p. 37 and *Questions*, 2, p. 50.

73. *Questions*, 2, pp. 103–4 and *De l'impôt sur les cafés et lois du commerce intérieur*, p. 136.

74. *Questions*, 1, pp. 30–1.

75. *Questions*, 1, p. 30.

76. F. Marcelin, *Nos douanes*, p. 28.

77. Andrés Bello, *Obras completas*, 8, p. 220.

78. Discussing the situation in British India, Vera Anstey wrote, "Do we not find that, instead of teaching the people to understand the world about them, and how natural forces can best be utilized and controlled, they have been taught to write notes on archaic phrases in the works of sixteenth and seventeenth century Englishmen and to learn by rote the personal history of obscure rulers of a foreign land?', *The Economic Development of India*, p. 4. For a similar criticism with respect to French colonial practice in black Africa see C. A. Diop, *Nations nègres et cultures*, p. 10.

79. Paul, *Questions*, 2, p. 3 Leslie Manigat (*The Caribbean Yearbook of International Relations*, 1975, p. 522) takes me to task for suggesting a Saint-Simonian element in Paul's thinking, stating that he was in fact a disciple of the French economist Michel Chevalier. Manigat seems unaware that Chevalier was himself a Saint-Simonian. See Jean Walch, *Michel Chevalier: économiste Saint-Simonien*.

80. Paul, *Les causes de nos malheurs*, p. 238; this was the slogan which had been widely adopted by the Liberal Party.

81. Paul, *Les causes*, p. 225 and *Le Civilisateur*, 16 mars 1870.

82. Paul, *De l'impôt*, pp. 1 and 108n.

83. Paul, *Questions*, 2, p. 79.

84. Paul, *Haïti au soleil de 1880*, p. 62; and *L'Avant-Garde*, 12 avril 1883.

85. M. B. Bird, *The Black Man*, p. 349; see also B.J. Hunt, *Remarks on Hayti*, pp. 8–9.

86. J. M. Langston, 'Trade and Commerce of Haiti', in *Reports from the Consuls of the US on the Commerce, Manufactures etc. of their Consular Districts* (Washington 1885), no. 54, p. 361.

87. Salnave, quoted in J. Doazan au Comte Daru, 19 février 1870, AAE CPH, 29.

88. Quoted in Dantès Bellegarde, *Un Haïtien parle*, p. 9. See also F. Douglass to J. G.

Blaine, 9 November 1889, USNA DS, reprinted in N. Brown (ed.), *A Black Diplomat in Haiti*, p. 31.

89. L. Laroche, *Haïti: une page d'histoire*, p. 59.
90. Solon Menos, *L'affaire Lüders*.
91. Zohrab to Salisbury, 6 December 1889, PRO FO 420/110.
92. D. G. Munro, *Intervention and Dollar Diplomacy in the Caribbean, 1900–1921*, p. 326n.
93. L. L. Montague, *Haiti and the United States, 1714–1938*, p. 179.
94. W. F. Powell 'American Capital in Haiti', *Consular Reports* (Washington 1898), no. 220, pp. 147–8.
95. L. F. Manigat, 'Le substitution de la préponderance américaine à la préponderance française en Haïti au debut du XXe siècle: la conjoncture de 1910–1911', *Revue d'Histoire Moderne et Contemporaine*, 14:4 1967, pp. 321 f.
96. *La Discipline*, 25 janvier 1910.
97. D. Delorme, *La misère au sein des richesses: réflexions diverses sur Haïti*, pp. 123–4 and 22; see also Delorme, *La voie*, p. 5.
98. Alexandre Delva, *Considérations sur l'article 7 de la constitution d'Haïti*, and Edouard Pinckombe, *L'article 7: lettre à D. Delorme*; the latter pamphlet contains a response by Delorme
99. L. J. Janvier, *Les constitutions d'Haïti*, pp. 28–9.
100. Janvier, *Haïti aux haïtiens*, pp. 10–11. Janvier was not, however, entirely consistent in his economic nationalism and he praised Salomon for opening the country to French capital (see above p. 46). It is for this reason that I do not write of his position as 'coherent' as Leslie Manigat thinks I should (*Caribbean Yearbook of International Relations, 1975*, p. 523).
101. Janvier, *Haïti*, pp. 13–14 and Janvier, *L'égalité des races*, p. 11.
102. Janvier, *Le vieux piquet*.
103. Janvier *L'égalité*, p. 29 and Janvier *La république d'Haïti et ses visiteurs, 1840–1882*, pp. 374–5; Janvier, *Constitutions*, p. 286.
104. Janvier, *Haïti*, p. 36.
105. Janvier, *Les affaires d'Haïti, 1883–84*, p. 189. I say 'even Pétion' because of Janvier's general antipathy towards Haiti's mulatto presidents.
106. Janvier, *Les antinationaux*, p. 46.
107. Thus Gil Martinez is basically correct when he writes, '*Sur le champ des pratiques politique et surtout idéologique, libéraux et nationaux se rejoignent fondamentalement*', 'De l'ambiguité du nationalisme bourgeois en Haïti', *Nouvelle Optique*, no. 9, jan.–mars 1973, p. 32.
108. Laroche, *Haïti*, p. 30.
109. E. Edouard, *Solution de la crise industrielle française*, pp. 35 and 29–30.
110. H. Price, *Étude sur les finances et de l'économie des nations*, pp. 37f.
111. Roche Grellier, *Études économiques sur Haïti*, pp. 11–12.
112. Grellier, *Études*, p. 21.
113. J. Justin, *Étude sur les institutions haïtiennes*, 1, pp. 58–9.
114. J. Justin, *Les relations extérieures d'Haïti*, pp. 158–9 and 72.
115. J. Dévot, *Cours élémentaire d'instruction civique et d'éducation patriotique*, p. 177.
116. J. Dévot, *Considérations sur l'état mental de la société haïtienne*, pp. 48f.
117. L. J. Marcelin, *Haïti, ses guerres civiles*, p. v.
118. See *Le Travail*, 18 mars 1892 and 18 janvier 1893.
119. F. Marcelin, *Une évolution nécessaire*, p. 16; and *Haïti et l'indemnité française*, p. 43.

120. J. A. Firmin, *Lettres de Saint Thomas: études sociologiques, historiques et littéraires*, pp. 4–5.

121. See Roger Gaillard, *Les blancs débarquent: ii, 1914–1915: Les cent jours de Rosalvo Bobo*, pp. 24, 243 and 247. For an example of the campaign to allow foreign ownership see Antoine Laforest, in *Haïti Littéraire et Sociale*, 30 juillet 1905, 20 février 1906 etc.

122. Some of the arguments in this debate are considered in my book, *From Dessalines to Duvalier*, pp. 137f.

123. H. A. Wood, *Northern Haiti: Land Use and Settlement*, p. 146.

6 HOLDING THE PURSE STRINGS: WOMEN IN HAITI

1. See the classic work of James Leyburn, *The Haitian People*. Leyburn rather tends to over simplify the class situation and fails to take sufficient account of the middle sectors. See pp. 28f above.

2. Jean Fouchard, *Les marrons de la liberté*, p. 289.

3. M. Sylvain Bouchereau, *Haïti et ses femmes*, p. 63. Jean F. Brierre has written a play about these heroines, *Les Aïeulles*.

4. J. Brown, *The History and Present Condition of Saint Domingo*, 2, p. 281. See also the situation later in the century: 'Among the more numerous class, the work is done almost entirely by the women', US Consul J. S. Durham, 'Report on the Manufacture and Sale of Intoxicating Liquors in Port-au-Prince', in Durham to W. F. Wharton, 23 February 1893, USNA DS, microfilm T 346, roll 8.

5. H. Johnstone, *The Negro in the New World*, p. 196. J. P. Mars, *La vocation de l'élite*, p. 97.

6. A. de Laujon, *Souvenirs de trente années de voyages à Saint-Domingue*, pp. 53f.

7. B. S. Hunt, *Remarks on Hayti as a Place of Settlement for Afric-Americans*, p. 8. It should, however, be remembered that Hunt was trying to paint an attractive picture of Haiti.

8. St John to Stanley, PRO FO 35/74.

9. R. Gaillard, *Etzer Vilaire, témoin de nos malheurs*, p. 68.

10. J. P. Mars, *La vocation*, p. 104.

11. L. F. Hoffmann, 'The image of Woman in Haitian Poetry', *Présence Africaine*, numbers 34–35, octobre 1960, pp. 187f.

12. On educational facilities for women see M. Sylvain Bouchereau, *Éducation des femmes en Haïti* and D. Bellegarde, *La nation haïtienne*, ch. 23.

13. Leyburn, *The Haitian People*, p. 191.

14. Institut Haïtien de Statistique, *Résultats préliminaires de l'enquête démographique à passages répétés*, 2, 1975.

15. Dawn Marshall, *'The Haitian Problem': Illegal Migration to the Bahamas*, p. 25.

16. J. P. Mars, *Ainsi parla l'oncle*, pp. 199f.

17. S. Nedjati-Allman, *Rapport sur le questionnaire de l'enquête haïtienne sur la fécondité: étude linguistique*.

18. J. Allman and J. May, 'Fertility, Mortality, Migration and Family Planning in Haiti', *Population Studies*, 33:3, 1979, p. 512.

19. 'La Paysanne de la Region de Kenscoff', in R. Bastide (ed.), *La femme de couleur en Amérique Latine*, pp. 149f.

20. S. J. Williams *et al.*, 'Conjugal Unions among Rural Haitian Women', *Journal of Marriage and the Family*, 37:4, 1975, p. 1028. See similar findings by Judith Blake in 'Family Instability and Reproductive Behavior in Jamaica', *Milbank Memorial Annual Conference*, 1955, pp. 26f.

21. See E. Clarke, *My Mother who Fathered me*.

22. C. J. Legerman, 'Haitian Peasant, Plantation and Urban Lower Class Family and Kinship Organization: Observations and Comments', in R. Schaedel (ed.), *Papers of the Conference on Research and Resources of Haiti*, pp. 76f.

23. As Mats Lundahl points out, however, caution is needed in the interpretation of these figures. A lot depends on which season is being considered and whether unpaid family labour is taken into account. M. Lundahl, *Peasants and Poverty in Haiti*, p. 72.

24. S. Mintz, 'The Employment of Capital by Market Women in Haiti', in R. Firth and B. S. Yamey (eds), *Capital, Saving and Credit in Peasant Societies*, p. 270. On similar phenomena in other parts of the world, see M. J. Herskovits, *Economic Anthropology*, pp. 200f.; A. Nypan, *Market Trade: a Sample Survey of Market Traders in Accra*, p. 14; M. Katzin, 'The Jamaican Country Higgler', *Social and Economic Studies*, 8:4, 1959, pp. 421f.; Sol Tax, *Penny Capitalism*, pp. 122f.

25. Alfred Métraux *et al.*, *Making a Living in the Marbial Valley*, pp. 60f.

26. Lundahl, *Peasants and Poverty*, p. 147.

27. A. Métraux, *Making a Living*, p. 123; quoted in M. Lundahl, *Peasants and Poverty*, p. 148.

28. S. Comhaire Sylvain, in R. Bastide (ed.), *La femme de couleur en Amérique Latine*, p. 156.

29. S. Mintz, 'Men, Women and Trade', *Comparative Studies in History and Society*, 13:3, 1971, p. 259.

30. Erma, 'La lutte des femmes', *Présence Haïtienne*, no. 2, septembre 1975, p. 47.

31. Referring to Lorgina, a *mambo* of Port-au-Prince, to whom he dedicated his book, Métraux wrote, '*Bien qu'elle fut souvent emportée et prit, pendant ses transes, un air terrible c'était une excellente femme, bienveillante et hospitalière*', *Le vaudou haïtien*, p. 13. See also F. Huxley, *The Invisibles*, passim.

32. See, for example, the writings of Odette Mennesson-Rigaud; some of these are listed in Métraux, *Le vaudou haïtien*, p. 341.

33. See, for example, S. Comhaire Sylvain, 'La chanson haïtienne', in *Haïti: poètes noirs*, pp. 61f.

34. 'Evolution de la poésie féminine haïtienne, 1876–1976', *Le Nouveau Monde Supplément*, 22 octobre 1978 and following weeks.

35. On the Haitian feminist movement see W. A. Rochement, *Du féminisme national*; M. G. Sylvain, 'The Feminist Movement in Haiti', *Bulletin of the Pan American Union*, 73:6, June 1939; *La femme haïtienne repond aux attaques*. On the role of women in Haitian law, see Denyse Massena, *La femme dans le droit*.

36. '*L'Haïtienne d'aujourd'hui? Je la trouve terriblement apathique par rapport aux femmes de ma génération*', Lydia Jeanty, in *Le Nouveau Monde Supplément*, 29 octobre 1978.

37. M. Baptiste, 'Pour une approche de la question féminine', *Tèm*, 1:2, 1980, p. 11. This whole issue of *Tèm* is devoted to the role of women in Haiti.

38. F. Engels, *The Origin of the Family, Private Property and the State*, in Marx and Engels, *Selected Works*, 2, p. 240.

7 ECONOMIC PROBLEMS OF THE BLACK REPUBLIC: A CRITICAL BIBLIOGRAPHY

1. 'Décolonisation ou néocolonialisme?' University of Paris (Faculté des Lettres), 1969.
2. *La Pensée*, no. 156, 1971, pp. 35f.
3. 'La reconnaissance d'Haïti par la France (1825): naissance d'un nouveau type de rapports internationaux', *Revue d'Histoire Moderne et Contemporaine*, 22:1, 1975, pp. 24f. and 'L'indemnité coloniale de Saint-Domingue et la question des rapatriés', *Revue Historique*, no. 246, 1971, pp. 359f.
4. *Annales: Economies, Sociétés, Civilisations*, no. 27, 1972, pp. 1497f.
5. *Nouvelle Optique*, no. 4, 1971, pp. 50f. See also Joachim, 'La structure sociale en Haïti et le mouvement d'indépendance au dix-neuvième siècle', *Journal of World History*, 12:3, 1970, pp. 456f.
6. R. K. Lacerte, 'The First Land Reform in Latin America', *Interamerican Economic Affairs*, 28:4, 1975 and 'The Evolution of Land and Labor in the Haitian Revolution 1791–1820', *The Americas*, 34:4, 1978, pp. 449f.
7. *Conjonction*, no. 152, 1982, pp. 59f.
8. O. Ernest Moore, *Haiti: its Stagnant Society and Shackled Economy*, p. 263.
9. T. K. Morrison, 'Case Study of a "Least Developed Country" successfully exporting manufactures', *Interamerican Economic Affairs*, 29:1, 1975, pp. 21f.
10. *Collectif Paroles*, no. 23, 1983, pp. 33f.
11. *Collectif Paroles*, no. 24, 1983, pp. 5f.
12. *Cahiers des Amériques Latines*, no. 17, 1978, pp. 23f.

8 NO HAWKERS AND PEDLARS: ARABS OF THE ANTILLES

* Evidence, where not documented in these notes, is based on a series of unstructured interviews with people of Levantine origin in the four countries studied. They frequently use the term 'community' for the Levantine groups in the Caribbean and I have also used the term, but this should not be taken to imply the existence of a single community in the sense in which Tönnies used the term.

1. In the 600 pages of M. M. Horowitz (ed.), *Peoples and Cultures of the Caribbean*, for example, there are only two casual references to the arabs.
2. See H. Jalabert, *La vice-province du proche-orient de la Compagnie de Jésus*. On some of the effects of missionary education on village life in Lebanon see Afif I. Tannous, 'Missionary Education in Lebanon: a Study in Acculturation', *Social Forces*, 21:3, 1943, pp. 338f.
3. J. S. and L. D. Macdonald, 'Chain Migration, Ethnic Neighborhood Formation and Social Networks', *The Milbank Memorial Fund Quarterly*, 42:1, 1964, p. 82.
4. It is, of course, *possible* for indentured migrants to begin a chain migration, but this does not normally happen for a number of reasons.
5. Nellie Ammar recalls how her family returned from a visit to Lebanon in 1921 accompanied by a number of such new migrants. 'They Came from the Middle East', *Jamaica Journal*, March 1970, pp. 2f. On Levantine communities in the

Americas, see W. K. Crowley, 'The Levantine Arabs: Diaspora in the New World', *Proceedings of the Association of American Geographers*, 6, 1974, pp. 137f. For the situation in the USA see Philip Hitti, *The Syrians in America*. There is an interesting thesis by Mary Wilkie, 'The Lebanese in Montevideo, Uruguay', (Department of Sociology, University of Wisconsin, Madison, 1972) and an unpublished paper by the same author, 'The Lebanese in Costa Rica and Uruguay'. I am grateful to her for sending me this paper. Sélim Abou's *Liban déraciné* is a fascinating collection of biographical studies of Lebanese migrants to South America. There is an extensive literature on the migration of Levantines to West Africa.

6. Afif I. Tannous, 'Emigration: a Force of Social Change in an Arab Village', *Rural Sociology*, 7:1, 1942, pp. 63f and Tannous, 'Group Behavior in the Village Community of Lebanon', *American Journal of Sociology*, 48:2, 1942, pp. 231f.

7. It should be noted, however, that two of the most powerful families in Jamaica have Syrian connections. The wife of Elias Issa (mother of Abraham, Joseph and Bertha) was a Brimo from Damascus, also the birthplace of Joseph Matalon, father of the seven Matalon brothers who now run one of the largest businesses in Jamaica. The Issas, however, generally think of themselves as Palestinian, while the Matalons, who are of the jewish faith, identify themselves with the state of Israel. The only unequivocally Syrian families are the Hadeeds and the Ashkars, who arrived fairly recently from Trinidad.

8. A. H. Hourani, *Syria and Lebanon*, pp. 35f. Among Levantine migrants to Brazil there were 229 men to 100 women; 63 per cent of these migrants were unmarried. It is likely that the proportions were similar in the Caribbean. See C. S. Knowlton, 'Spacial and Social Mobility of the Syrians and Lebanese in the City of São Paulo, Brazil', PhD thesis (Vanderbilt University, 1955), pp. 77f.

9. H. Prichard, *Where Black Rules White*, p. 245.

10. Edmond Laforest, 'Ottomans et Haïtiens', *Haïti Littéraire et Scientifique*, 20 février 1912, p. 89.

11. *Le Petit Samedi Soir*, no. 465, 29 janvier 1983, p. 8.

12. G. Eisner, *Jamaica, 1830–1930: a Study in Economic Growth*, chapter 5.

13. Colonial Secretary to Sir W. Morrison, 5 January 1927, Jamaican Archives (Spanish Town), 1B/5/77/31 f. 8328.

14. *Minutes of the Legislative Council of Jamaica for the year 1935*, p. 319. The questioner was told that inquiries about the situation were being made.

15. *Minutes of the Legislative Council of Jamaica for the year 1935*, appendix 58.

16. Census of British West Indies, Jamaica, 1943 and 1960.

17. C. S. Holzberg, 'Social Stratification, Cultural Nationalism and Political Economy in Jamaica: the Myths of Development and the Anti-White Bias', *Canadian Review of Sociology and Anthropology*, 14:4, 1977, p. 371. See also Holzberg, 'The Social Organization of Jamaican Political Economy: Ethnicity and the Jewish Segment', *Ethnic Groups*, 1:4, 1977.

18. Wardrop to Lansdowne, 26 June 1903, PRO FO 35/179; Vansittart to Lansdowne, 12 May 1905, PRO FO 35/182.

19. Powell to Hay, 10 June 1903, USNA DS Consular Despatches, Haiti.

20. Arsène Chévry, in *Le Devoir*, 2 février 1903; 'La situation' and 'Chronique', *Le Commerce*, 18 novembre 1905; 'L'extirpation des Syriens', *Le Commerce*, 11 novembre 1905. Some politicians defended them, however, see 'La question syrienne', *L'Impartial*, 26 juin 1909 and 'La question syrienne', *La Voix du Peuple*, 25 mai 1909.

21. Vansittart to Lansdowne, 12 May 1905, PRO FO 35/182.

22. B. G. Plummer, 'Race, Nationality, and Trade in the Caribbean: the Syrians in Haiti, 1903–1934', *International History Review*, 3:4, 1981, pp. 517f. See also A. Poujol, in *Revue Général de Droit Public*, 12, 1905, pp. 441f.

23. J. N. Léger in *Exposé général de la situation de la République d'Haïti, 1912*, pp. 9–10. Vincent and Laforest in *Haïti Littéraire et Scientifique*, 20 février and 5 mars 1912.

24. Percival Thoby, 'Notes confidentielles sur l'explosion du palais national' (1912) printed in *Nouveau Monde: Supplément*, 17 septembre 1978. On anti-Syrian riots see Report by H. W. Furniss in USNA DS 838.001/14, quoted by Roger Gaillard in 'L'explosion du palais de Leconte', *Nouveau Monde Supplément*, 17 septembre 1978.

25. E. Aubin, *En Haïti*, p. 154n.

26. J. M. Simpson, *Six Months in Port-au-Prince*, pp. 32-3.

27. *Le Nouvelliste*, 6 janvier 1925.

28. *Le Matin*, 6 février 1925; A. Faubert replied on his behalf, pointing out that his acquisition of Cuban nationality was in order to be able to criticise French policy in the Middle East more freely; *Le Matin*, 7 février 1925. A memorial brochure was produced to commemorate this visit of Dr Estefano.

29. H. Hoetink, *El pueblo dominicano*, pp. 67–8 and 39.

30. *Le Nouvelliste*, 11 mars 1936.

31. C. Ramón Gervacio de Léon and J. Leonidas Sanchez, 'Los "Turcos" en la República Dominicana' (Thesis, Facultad de Humanidades, Universidad Autonoma de Santo Domingo, 1978–9) chs 9 and 11; see also an interesting series of articles by Eunice Lluberes in *Listín Diario*, beginning 19 julio 1983.

32. On the social composition of the colony at the time see the excellent book by Bridget Brereton, *Race Relations in Colonial Trinidad 1870–1900*.

33. Vice consul au Ministre, 19 septembre 1921, AAE, Levant: Syrie, Liban, Cilicie, 132.

34. '*Bon kalité, mon cher*'(good value, my friend) and the term '*pratik*' (meaning good customer) were quoted from memory by these Trinidadians.

35. C. S. Smith (ed.) *Trinidad, Who, What, Why*, p. 66.

36. Both quoted by Angela Laquis, 'The Syrian Lebanese Community in Trinidad', (Undergraduate thesis in Caribbean Studies, University of the West Indies, St Augustine, Trinidad, 1980), pp. 12 and 26. This brief study, by a member of the Levantine community in Trinidad, contains much useful information.

37. See David Nicholls, *Three Varieties of Pluralism*, p. 45.

38. E. C. Hughes, *et al.*, (eds.), *The Collected Papers of Robert Ezra Park*, 1, pp. 353–4.

39. Lloyd Braithwaite, 'Social Stratification in Trinidad', *Social and Economic Studies*, 2:2–3, 1953, p. 49. In a recent review article Roger Daniels is critical of writers on the subject of ethnic minorities for not defining the term 'assimilation', but he continues to use the term in a somewhat uncritical manner. Again he is hard on writers like S. Thompson and B. Wong for regarding immigrant communities as static and homogeneous, but he himself assumes the existence of a static 'society' into which they are (or are not) assimilated. E. Bonacich also writes of migrants' 'conflict with the host society' as though there is such a monolithic entity into which they come. ('A Theory of Middleman Minorities', *American Sociological Review*, 38:5, 1973, p. 593.)

40. Gordon Lewis, *The Growth of the Modern West Indies*, p. 33 and M. G. Smith, *The Plural Society in the British West Indies*, p. 4.

41. See above pp. 61f. and generally on the ethnic factor in contemporary Trinidadian politics, Selwyn Ryan, *Race and Nationalism in Trinidad and Tobago*.

42. M. Wilkie, The Lebanese in Costa Rica and Uruguay', p. 37; see also G. A. de Bruijne, 'The Lebanese in Suriname', *Boletin de Estudios Latinamericanos y del Caribe,* no. 26, 1979, p. 34.
43. David Nicholls, *The Pluralist State,* pp. 120f.
44. K. H. Wolff, (ed.), *The Sociology of Georg Simmel,* p. 403.
45. Peter Bauer has noted how many skilled traders come from a farming background, *Economic Analysis and Policy in Underdeveloped Countries,* p. 71.

9   RURAL PROTEST AND PEASANT REVOLT 1804–1869

1. Apart from the classical nineteenth-century Haitian historians, Thomas Madiou *fils* and Alexis Beaubrun Ardouin, few writers have dealt with these protest movements; most of those who have are heavily dependent on these two historians. Worthy of mention, however, are Camille Large ('Goman et l'insurrection de la Grande Anse', *Revue de la Société Haïtienne d'Histoire et de Géographie,* 12, 1940), Paul Moral (*Le paysan haïtien*), H. Pauléus Sannon, (*Essai historique sur la révolution de 1843*) and F. E. Dubois (*Précis historique de la révolution haïtienne de 1843*) in addition to the works cited in this chapter. Particularly interesting is the series of articles by F. D. Légitime, a former president of Haiti, on the *cacos* war of 1867–69, in which he took an active part; these appeared in *La Revue de la Société de Législation* in many instalments, beginning in 1907. Also reference should be made to a recent book by André Georges Adam, *Une crise haïtienne, 1867–1869: Sylvain Salnave.*
2. L. J. Janvier, *Le vieux piquet,* p. 4.
3. R. Gaillard, *Les cent jours de Rosalvo Bobo*; H. Schmidt, *The United States Occupation of Haiti, 1915–1934,* ch. 5; and S. Castor, *La ocupación norte-americana de Haití, 1915-1934,* ch. 7.
4. L. Laroche, *Haïti: une page d'histoire,* p. 85n.
5. M. L. E. Moreau de St Méry, *Description topographique, physique civil, politique et historique de la partie française de l'île Saint-Domingue,* 3, p. 1400.
6. E. Hobsbawm, *Primitive Rebels,* pp. 10f.
7. See above, pp. 61f.
8. 'Memorandum on Northern Haiti', in H. Popham to Lord Melville, 13 June 1819, Melville Papers (Rhodes House, Oxford), 2/323. The owners of estates were in turn obliged to support the old, injured and infirm. (ibid., 2/322).
9. L. F. Manigat, *La politique agraire du gouvernement d'Alexandre Pétion*; S. Thébaud, *L'évolution de la structure agraire en Haïti de 1804 a nos jours*; and R. K. Lacerte, 'The first land reforms in Latin America', *Interamerican Economic Affairs,* 28:4, 1975, pp. 77f.
10. On the wealth of some generals see above p. 94.
11. There was an English translation of the *Code Rurale* published in 1827 with a prefatory letter to Earl Bathurst stating that it would be of concern to those 'most deeply interested in ascertaining the possibility of obtaining regular and steady labour in tropical climates without compulsion' (*The Rural Code of Haiti,* p. iii). By 'peasant economy', in the text, I mean simply a situation in which the emphasis is upon growing crops for local consumption by persons owning their land, in contrast to a plantation economy geared to the cultivation on large estates of one or a few crops for export. This is not, of course, to deny that many large estates continued to exist in nineteenth century Haiti, (see Richard Hill, letters published in Z. Macaulay, *Haïti,* pp. 75f.)

12. See David Nicholls, *From Dessalines to Duvalier*, pp. 76f.

13. Estimates of the size of the armies at this time vary considerably. A French visitor gave the figure, for the republican army, of over 30 000, excluding the militia (A. Rouzeau, *De la république d'Haïti*, quoted in *Journal des voyages*, 1821 edn p. 385.) The northern army was thought by Vice Admiral B. S. Rowley to contain nearly 15 000 men together with a national guard of 10 000 (Rowley to J. W. Croker, 12 October 1810, PRO Adm 1/261). The figure for the kingdom of 18 000 was mentioned in the memorandum referred to in n. 8 above.

14. P. V. Vastey (Baron de Vastey), *An Essay on the Causes of the Revolution and Civil Wars of Haiti*, p. lxxxiv; King Henry, 'Discours', *Gazette Royale d'Hayti*, 19 juillet 1815. See also pamphlets published in the kingdom such as *Plan général du défense du royaume*, p. 2 and *Liberté et indépendance: royaume d'Hayti*, p. 16.

15. *'Reprendre St. Domingue de vive force est impossible'*, 'Mémoire sur Haïti', 9 février 1820, AAE CPH, 2/19 and A. Rouzeau, *De la république*, p. 385.

16. C. Mackenzie to G. Canning, 9 September 1826, PRO FO 35/4. Marcus Rainsford (*An Historical Account of the Black Empire of Hayty*, p. 360) had come to the same conclusion some years earlier.

17. T. Madiou, *Histoire d'Haïti*, 3, p. 228.

18. See de Vastey, *An Essay*, p. 76 and C. Mackenzie, *Notes on Haiti*, 2, p. 77.

19. De Vastey, *An Essay*, p. 86. I am grateful to David Geggus of the University of Florida, for some of these details.

20. C. Ardouin, *Essais sur l'histoire d'Haïti*, pp. 106f.

21. Madiou, *Histoire*, 3, p. 363 and F. Dalencour in A. B. Ardouin, *Études sur l'histoire d'Haïti*, 6, p. 111n.

22. A. B. Ardouin, *Études*, 6, p. 111.

23. Madiou, *Histoire*, 3, p. 437.

24. A. Pétion à B. S. Rowley, 23 mai 1810, PRO Adm 1/261.

25. S. Linstant (de Pradine), *Recueil général des lois et actes du gouvernement d'Haïti*, 2, p. 245.

26. A. B. Ardouin, *Études*, 8, p. 36.

27. Ibid., 8, p. 92.

28. G. T. Mollière au Baron le Damas, 8 juillet 1827, AAE CCC, Le Cap (Haïti); and R. M. Dimond to J. Forsyth, 2 February 1837, USNA DS, Despatches from US Consuls, Port-au-Prince 1; and Ragueneau de la Chainaye à Damas, 15 septembre 1827, AAE CPH 2/343.

29. Postscript of 3 mai in Ragueneau à Damas, 26 avril 1826, AAE CCC, Les Cayes, f. 51. The US consul also noted hostility between blacks and mulattoes on the one hand and a general antagonism towards France on the other; T. G. Swain to Forsyth, 25 January 1838, USNA DS, Despatches, Port-au-Prince 1.

30. Early in 1844 General Thomas Héctor and Deputé Bazin led a black revolt in the North and in May 1844 the black general Pierrot declared the independence of the North, *'pour la restitution de la suprematie de sa race'* (Madiou, *Histoire d'Haïti: années 1843–46*, p. 167.)

31. *Le Manifeste*, 3 septembre 1843. Leslie Manigat (*La révolution de 1843*, p. 25) writes *'Le piquétisme était né fruit de la conjonction d'intérêts entre grands et moyens propriétaires noirs et petits paysans parcellaires également noirs. Le revendication axée sur la couleur servait de liason organique.'* His further assertion that this movement had a basically *'progressiste'* tendency is more contestable and would certainly be disputed by the protagonists of what I have called the mulatto legend of the Haitian past.

32. T. N. Ussher to Lord Aberdeen, 24 May 1844, PRO FO 35/28.

33. Madiou, *Histoire. . . 1843–46*, pp. 66, 152 and 148.
34. Ussher to Aberdeen, 7 April 1844, PRO FO 35/28, and P. Bridgeman to Sir C. Adams, 23 April 1844, PRO FO 35/29.
35. P. Guerrier *et al.* à F. P. G. Guizot, 2 juillet 1843, AAE CPH 11/14; L.J.-J. Acaau, *Proclamation*, 6 mai 1844.
36. *Le Manifeste*, 26 mai 1844. Acaau's critics denounced him as a communist; see A. B. Ardouin, *Études*, 1, p. 24n. and G. d'Alaux, 'L'empereur Soulouque et son empire, 3', *Revue des Deux Mondes*, 9, 1851, p. 322.
37. G. d'Alaux, ibid., p. 322.
38. Ussher to Aberdeen, 18 August 1845 and 17 September 1845, both in PRO FO 35/30; Ussher to Aberdeen, 7 April 1844, PRO FO 35/28; see also Levasseur à Guizot, 14 janvier 1843, AAE CPH 10/190.
39. '*Fort de la loyauté de la Puissance Britannique, je viens avec confiance me mettre sous sa protection en la priant de me procurer mille fusils et autant de gibernes. . .*', Acaau au Commodore R. Sharpe, 4 mai 1844, PRO FO 35/29. Elsewhere I have written of Acaau 'it appears that he was prepared to accept some form of British protection or suzerainty for Haiti' (*From Dessalines to Duvalier*, p. 78.) Alain Turnier criticises me for having confused protection with protectorate (a term which I do not use) and dogmatically asserts '*Dans ce lettre, nulle part il n'est question de protectorat*' (*Avec Mérisier Jeannis*, p. 113). It is not clear exactly what Acaau had in mind by 'protection', but whatever it was, it involved just that kind of foreign intervention in the affairs of Haiti which has continually undermined the effective independence of the country.
40. M. J. MacLeod, 'The Soulouque regime in Haiti, 1847–1859: a re-evaluation', *Caribbean Studies*, 10:3, 1970; G. F. Usher to J. Buchanan, 23 September 1847, USNA DS, Despatches, Port-au-Prince 2; and J. Bouzon, *Études historiques sur la présidence de Faustin Soulouque*, p. 13.
41. Bouzon, *Études*, p. 56; '*La populace de Port-au-Prince insultait et menaçait non plus seulement les mulâtres, mais encore la bourgeoisie noire*' (d'Alaux, 'L'empereur Soulouque. . ., 3', p. 348.)
42. G. d'Alaux, op. cit., p. 336; and Lartigue au Ministre de la Marine, 23 avril 1846, AAE CPH 14/244.
43. The term *griffe* has two connotations in Haiti. It was the name given in colonial times to a person with one black and one mulatto parent (see Moreau de St Méry, *Description*, 1, pp. 96f.) The term is also used more popularly to describe a person with dark skin but with European features.
44. J. A. Firmin, *Monsieur Roosevelt, président des États Unis et la république d'Haïti*, p. 372.
45. 'Manifeste', quoted in Comte Méjan au Marquis de Moustier, 16 mars 1867, AAE CPH 26/23.
46. F. D. Légitime, 'Souvenirs historiques: la présidence de Salnave', *Revue de la Société de Législation*, 18:9, p. 149.
47. A. Thoby, 'Nos constitutions républicaines', *Revue de la Société de Législation*, 6:12, 1899, p. 8.
48. Méjan à Moustier, 4 avril 1867, AAE CPH 26/60; recording Salnave's arrival at Cap Haïtien in April 1867, Méjan wrote, '*il a été acclamé avec une unanimité et une energie vraiment incroyable*', Méjan à Moustier, 14 avril 1867, AAE CPH 26/64.
49. Firmin, *Monsieur Roosevelt*, p. 388.
50. Méjan à Moustier, 23 juillet 1867, AAE CPH 26/100.
51. F. D. Légitime, 'Souvenirs historiques, 1867–1870', *Revue de la Société de Législation*, 16:7, 1907, p. 103.

52. S. St John to Lord Stanley, 7 June 1868, PRO FO 35/74; S. St John, *Hayti or the Black Republic*, p. 119.
53. 'Adresse', *Le Moniteur*, 29 avril 1868.
54. See below, p. 242n.20.
55. J. Price Mars, 'Les cacos', *L'Essor*, 25 mai 1921; Gaillard, *Les cents jours*, p. 58n.; A. Cabon, *Mgr Guilloux*, p. 122n.
56. Méjan à Moustier, 23 mars 1868, AAE CPH 26/168.
57. E. de Courthial à Moustier, 4 novembre 1869, AAE CPH 27/35.
58. T. F. Jones to A. Phillimore, 23 September 1868, PRO FO 35/76.
59. L. J. Janvier, *Les constitutions d'Haïti*, 2, p. 345; de Courthial à Moustier, 4 novembre 1868, AAE CPH 27/36; M. Domingue, 'Aux citoyens trompés par Salnave', *La Voix du Peuple*, 6 octobre 1868.
60. St John to Stanley, 7 June 1868, PRO FO 35/74.
61. Cabon, *Mgr Guilloux*, p. 158.
62. Doazan à Daru, 8 février 1870, AAE CPH 29.
63. A. G. Adam, *Une crise haïtienne*.
64. David Nicholls, *From Dessalines to Duvalier*, pp. 195f.
65. S. Rameau *aux consuls étrangers*, 6 octobre 1868, in AAE CPH 27/24. The phrase he used has a particular connotation in Haiti of combating the *barbarisme* of Salnave, particularly his alleged practice of the voodoo religion.
66. D. Delorme, *La reconnaissance du général Salnave*.
67. J. A. Firmin, *Monsieur Roosevelt*, p. 426.
68. B. Diederich and A. Burt, *Papa Doc, Haiti and its Dictator*, p. 156.

10 VOTING WITH THEIR FEET: THE HAITIAN MIGRATION

1. See above pp. 99f.
2. Hugh Thomas, *Cuba: or the Pursuit of Freedom*, pp 536f.
3. Union Nationaliste, *Dépossessions*, p. v. The precise amount of land which was alienated in this way is difficult to estimate. Perhaps a total of about 43 000 acres had been leased to foreign companies by 1927, further concessions were made in the following years. Suzy Castor certainly exaggerates the figures. See *La ocupación norteamericana de Haití y sus consecuencias, 1915–1934*, p. 78. For example Castor gives the figure of 15 000 acres for the 'Haytian Corporation of America' (quoting as her authority R. Dunn, *American Foreign Investment*, pp 135–6); she gives the figure of 24 000 acres for the 'Haytian American Sugar Corporation' (quoting A. C. Millspaugh, *Haiti under American Control*, p. 152); she also gives the figure of 20 000 acres for the 'Haytian American Co.' (quoting the authority of E. G. Balch, *Occupied Haiti*, p. 74). In fact, as Montague makes clear (p. 252), the Haitian American Corporation was reorganised as the Haitian Corporation of America, of which the Haytian American Sugar Corporation was a subsidiary. The total for this whole company should therefore be 24 000. Also Balch does not list the 'Haytian American Co.' at all, and cannot therefore properly be quoted as an authority. Furthermore, Castor lists the *Société Commercial d'Haïti* as holding 9000 acres (giving as her authority Balch, p. 74). The figure actually given by Balch is 8000 acres. Castor gives

Millspaugh (p. 152) as her authority for stating that the 'Haytian American Development Co.' held 24 000 acres. In fact the figure given is 14 000 acres. These are not the only errors in the figures given by Castor.

4. Robert C. West and J. P. Augelli, *Middle America*, p. 161. On the Haitian migration to Cuba see a recent article by Mats Lundahl, 'A Note on Haitian Migration to Cuba. 1890–1934', *Cuban Studies*, 12:2, 1982, pp. 23f; reprinted in *The Haitian Economy: Man, Land and Markets*, pp. 94f.

5. J. Perez de la Riva, 'Haití: las consecuencias de una independencia frustrada', *Anuario de Estudios Cubanos*, 2, 1979, p. 21. There is a similar Haitian community surviving in Brazil. See Alberto Pedro Díaz, 'Guanamaca, una comunidad haitiana (central Brasil)', *Etnologia y Folklore*, 1966, pp. 25f.

6. J.-J. Dessalines, *Gazette Politique et Commerciale d'Haïti*, 30 mai 1805.

7. David Nicholls, *From Dessalines to Duvalier*, pp 79f.

8. H. Hoetink, *El pueblo dominicano, 1850–1900*, p. 31.

9. Frank Marino Hernández, 'La inmigración haitiana en la República Dominicana', *Eme Eme: Estudios Dominicanos*, 1:5, 1973, p. 34.

10. Estimates of the numbers slaughtered vary considerably. See R. W. Logan *Haiti and the Dominican Republic*, pp. 145f. and J. Price Mars, *La république d'Haïti et la République Dominicaine*, 2, pp. 309f.

11. André Corten, 'Migraciones e intereses de clases', in G. Pierre-Charles (ed.), *Política y sociologia en Haití y la República Dominicana*, p. 68.

12. A. Díaz Santana, 'The Role of Haitian Braceros in Dominican Sugar Production', *Latin American Perspectives*, 3:1 (number 8) 1976, p. 121. See also A. Corten *et al.*, *Azucar y política en la República Dominicana*.

13. André Corten, 'La migration des travailleurs haïtiens vers les centrales sucrières dominicaines', *Cultures et Développement*, 2:3–4, 1970, p. 726.

14. There is a copy of the 1978 contract in Maurice Lemoine, *Azucar Amargo*, pp. 379f.

15. The Anti-Slavery Society documents have contained a number of errors, however. There is a collection of documents published by the World Council of Churches, *Sold like Cattle: Haitian Workers in the Dominican Republic. La Voz*, published in Puerto Rico by the *Centro Ecumenico de los Derechos Humanos*, contains much material on the subject. See also Ramón Antonio Veras, *Inmigración, Haitianos, Esclavitud*.

16. *El Nacional de Ahora*, 14 abril 1980, reprinted in *Sold like Cattle*, pp. 48–9.

17. Corten, 'Migraciones e intereses de clases', pp. 68f.

18. This argument is stated by André Corten in a number of his writings, including 'La migration des travailleurs. . . .'. His position is disputed by Mats Lundahl in *The Haitian Economy*, pp. 135f. The latter is, of course, right in maintaining that the Haitian rural economy is in general a cash economy, though he underestimates the way in which rural Haitians are caught up in a system of debts and mortgages.

19. I. de Augustine Reid, *The Negro Immigrant: his Background, Characteristics and Social Adjustment, 1899–1937*, p. 97.

20. 'Guesses' would be more appropriate than 'estimates'. The US Immigration and Naturalization Service gives the total of legal and illegal Haitian immigrants as under 100 000 in 1981 (see Alex Stepick, *Haitian Refugees in the US*, p. 17.) James Allman gives the more likely figure of 450 000 for the USA and 40 000 for Haitian residents in Canada ('L'émigration haïtienne vers l'étranger de 1950 à 1980', *Conjonction*, no. 157, mars 1983, pp. 72 and 76).

21. H. de Delva, *Bottin professionel et commercial haïtiano-américain*.

22. Charles R. Foster, 'Creole in Conflict', *Migration Today* (Center for Migration

Studies, New York), 8:5, 1980, pp. 8f. There are other relevant articles in this no. of *Migration Today*. See also the popular review *Lyazon*, published by HAPTT (Haitian Parent-Teacher Training) in New York.

23. See for example, G. Sansaricq, 'The Haitian Apostolate in Brooklyn', *Migration Today*, 7:1, 1979, pp. 22f. also below pp. 209.
24. Michel LaGuerre, 'The Haitian Niche in New York City', *Migration Today*, 7:4, 1979, pp. 12f.
25. Franck Laraque, 'Haitian Emigration to New York', *Migration Today*, 7:4, 1979, pp 28f.
26. Susan Buchanan, 'Haitian Women in New York City', *Migration Today*, 7:4, 1979, pp. 19f.
27. Pierre-Michel Fontaine, 'Haitian Immigrants in Boston: a Commentary', in R. S. Bryce-Laporte and D. M. Mortimer (eds), *Caribbean Immigration to the United States* (Smithsonian Institution, Occasional Papers, 1), p. 119. See also S. H. Buchanan, 'Language and Identity: Haitians in New York City', *International Migration Review*, 13:2, 1979, pp. 298f.
28. Alex Stepick, *Haitian Refugees in the US*, p. 11. On anglophone West Indians in Florida see J. de Wint *et al.*, 'Contract Labour in US Agriculture: West Indian Cane Cutters in Florida,' in R. Cohen *et al.* (eds), *Peasants and Proletarians*.
29. Michael Browning in *Miami Herald*, 23 March 1981; see also Bryan O. Walsh, 'Haitians in Miami', *Migration Today*, 7:4, 1979, pp. 42f.
30. P.-M. Fontaine, 'Haitian Immigrants in Boston', pp. 111f; a similar phenomenon has been noted among Haitians in Paris, Bastide *et al.*, *Les Haïtiens en France*, p. 202.
31. See below p. 198f.
32. Institut Haïtien de Statistique, *Guide économique de la République d'Haïti*, décembre 1971.
33. Emerson Douyon, 'Sondage d'opinion sur la fuite des cerveaux', in Douyon (ed.), *Culture et développement en Haïti*, pp. 187f.
34. P. Rousseau, quoted by James Allman in 'L'émigration haïtienne' pp. 75f.; Emerson Douyon, 'Les immigrants haïtiens à Montréal', in H. E. Lamur and J. D. Speckmann (eds) *Adaptation of Migrants from the Caribbean in the European and American Metropolis*, pp. 144f. See also P. Déjean, *Les Haïtiens au Quebec*.
35. A. Dumas-Pierre, 'Les difficultés des chauffeurs haïtiens', *Collectif Paroles*, number 19, septembre/octobre 1982, pp. 12f. and L. Daumec and J. Dubois, 'Tex Bleach, le premier syndicat à majorité haïtienne à Montréal', *Collectif Paroles*, no. 10, février/mars 1981, pp. 8f.
36. Centre de Recherches Caraïbes, Montréal, *Enfant de migrants haïtiens en Amérique du Nord* and Gérard Baptiste, 'Un an après le colloque sur l'enfant haïtien', *Collectif Paroles*, no. 19, septembre/octobre 1982, pp. 15f.
37. Dawn I. Marshall, *'The Haitian Problem': Illegal Migration to the Bahamas*, pp 92–3.
38. Ibid., p. 33.
39. Ibid., p. 103 and Micheline Labelle, 'Le dossier des Haïtiens aux Bahamas: une Interview avec Jean-Claude Icart', *Collectif Paroles*, number 10, février/mars 1981, p. 26.
40. Marshall, *'The Haitian Problem'*, p. 117.
41. Ibid., pp. 47f.
42. J. Allman, 'L'émigration haïtienne', p. 77. See also R. Bastide *et al.*, *Les Haïtiens en France*; also Joseph Roney 'Dans la diaspora haïtienne de Bruxelles', *Collectif Paroles*, pp. 11f.

43. Mats Lundahl, *The Haitian Economy*, p. 138.
44. André Corten, 'La migration des travailleurs', pp 720f. Sassen Koob discusses the role of credit association in the Dominican migration to the USA in *International Migration Review*, 13:2, 1979, pp. 314f.
45. See David Nicholls, 'Embryo-Politics in Haiti', *Government and Opposition*, 6:1, 1971, pp. 75f.
46. Hugh Tinker has written an excellent book on Indian indentureship with the title *A New System of Slavery*. Haitian workers in the Dominican Republic are legally free to terminate their contracts and return home.
47. See *International Report*, 1:3, November 1983.

11 CULTURAL DUALISM AND POLITICAL DOMINATION

1. See W. W. Harvey, *Sketches of Hayti from the Expulsion of the French to the Death of Christophe*, and Z. Macaulay, *Haïti ou renseignements authentiques sur l'abolition de l'esclavage*.
2. See J. Franklin, *The Present State of Hayti*.
3. T. Hobbes, *Behemoth*, p. 16.
4. See above, pp. 191f.
5. See above, pp. 21f.
6. See Kern Delince, *Armée et politique en Haïti* and J. H. McCrocklin, *Garde d'Haïti, 1915–1934*; also David Nicholls, 'On Controlling the Colonels', *Hemisphere Report* (Trinidad) July 1970.
7. R. Berrou and P. Pompilus, *Histoire de la littérature haïtienne*. I discuss some of this literature in *From Dessalines to Duvalier*, ch. 3.
8. See Albert Valdman, 'The Language Situation in Haiti', in R. P. Schaedel, (ed.), *Research and Resources of Haiti*, pp. 155f; more recently Valdman in Jean Perrot, (ed.), *Les langues dans le monde ancien et moderne*; also L. Todd, *Pidgins and Creoles*, chs 3 and 4.
9. Paul Dumont, 'De la colonie à la francophonie', *La Nouvelle Revue des Deux Mondes*, mai 1973, pp. 352f.
10. Jacques Barros, 'Quel destin linguistique pour Haïti?', *Anthropologie et Sociologie*, 6:2, 1982, pp 49–50.
11. See L. Hurbon, *Culture et dictature en Haïti*, also D. Bébel Gisler and L. Hurbon, *Cultures et pouvoir dans la Caraïbe*.
12. Joseph Bernard, 'La réforme scolaire à Haïti', *Agecop Liason*, no. 66, 1982, pp. 36f.
13. S. H. Buchanan, 'Language and Identity: Haitians in New York City', *International Migration Review*, 13:2, 1979, pp. 298f.
14. See a brief article by Félix Morisseau Leroy, 'The Awakening of Creole Consciousness', *Unesco Courier*, 36:4, 1983.
15. A. Valdman 'The Language Situation in Haiti', p. 175. It should, however, be noted that McConnell himself saw his phonetic orthography as facilitating an ultimate transition to French. The rural pronunciation is today generally accepted as the norm for written *Kréyol*.
16. A. Valdman, 'The Linguistic Situation of Haiti', unpublished paper to conference on *Haiti: Present State and Future Prospects*, pp 20f; to be published in proceedings of the conference by The University Press of America.
17. See David Nicholls, *From Dessalines to Duvalier*, pp. 117f.
18. A. de Moges à Guizot, 3 juin 1843, AAE CPH 10/390.

19. L. Agel au Ministre, 2 juin 1921, AAE Amérique 1918–1940, Haïti 15. Also '*Le clergé français, soit séculier, soit régulier, propage ici notre langue et nos idées; de plus, il jouit d'une grande influence dans tout le pays.*' Agel au Ministre, 8 juin 1920, AAE Amérique 1918–1940, Haïti 15.

20. For more details on the social role of voodoo see L. Hurbon, *Dieu dans le vaudou haïtien*; H. Courlander and R. Bastien, *Religion and Politics in Haiti*; A Métraux, *Le vaudou haïtien*.

21. See David Nicholls 'Politics and Religion in Haiti', *Canadian Journal of Political Science*, 3:3, 1970, pp. 400f. François Duvalier tells his version of these events in *Mémoires d'un leader du tiers monde*.

22. Claude Souffrant, 'Un catholicisme de résignation en Haïti', *Social Compass*, 17:3, 1970, p. 428.

23. Ibid., p. 428.

24. Paul Robert, *Difficultés et ressources*, p. 20.

25. Alfred Métraux, 'Vodou et protestantisme', *Revue de l'Histoire des Religions*, 1953, 144:2, pp. 198f.

26. See, for example, the popular *Kréyol* song book of the Roman Catholic church in Haiti, *N-ap réglé tout bagay an chantan*, published with the *imprimatur* of the Archbishop of Port-au-Prince.

12 DYNASTIC DESPOTISM: FROM FATHER TO SON

1. N. Stone, 'The Many Tragedies of Haiti', *The Times Literary Supplement*, 15 February 1980.

2. William Paley, 'Haiti', *The Times Literary Supplement*, 29 February 1980.

3. David Nicholls, *From Dessalines to Duvalier: Race, Colour and National Independence in Haiti*; and ch. 1 above.

4. See the important works recently published by Alain Turnier, *Avec Mérisier Jeannis* and Roger Gaillard, *Les blancs débarquent* (six volumes have been published to date). For the role of these groups during the occupation see Kethly Millet, *Les paysans haïtiens et l'occupation américaine d'Haïti*.

5. See pp.189f above.

6. William Paley, 'Power Shift Imperils Haiti's Frail Stability', *The Guardian*, 13 January 1982.

7. I am indebted to Ira Lowenthal for drawing my attention to the significance of this development.

8. These figures are based on those given in Kern Delince, *Armée et politique en Haïti*.

CONCLUSION

1. David Nicholls, *From Dessalines to Duvalier*, pp. 245f.

2. Tony Jackson, *Against the Grain*; Christopher Stephens, *Food Aid and the Developing World*.

3. B. Hartmann and J. Boyce, *Needless Hunger*; Michael Scott (ed), *Aid to Bangladesh: for Better or Worse?*.

4. Clarence Zuvekas, *Agricultural Development in Haiti*, p. 260; Robert Maguire, *Bottom-up Development in Haiti*.
5. *North-South: a Programme for Survival*.
6. In Oxfam's study pack on the Brandt Report.
7. Danus Skane, *Brandt, Politics and the Church*.
8. S. P. Huntington and J. M. Nelson, *No Easy Choice*, p. 4.

Bibliography

Abou, Selim, *Liban déraciné*, Paris, 1978.

Adam, André G., *Une crise haïtienne, 1867–1869: Sylvain Salnave*, Port-au-Prince, 1982.

Alaux, G. d', *L'empereur Soulouque et son empire*, Paris, 1856.

Ambursley, Fitzroy and Cohen, R. (eds) *Crisis in the Caribbean*, London, 1983.

Anstey, Vera, *The Economic Development of India*, London, 1929.

Antoine, Max A., *Lysius Salomon jeune: martyr volontaire de sa classe*, Port-au-Prince, 1968.

Ardouin, A. Beaubrun, *Études sur l'histoire d'Haïti suivis de la vie du général J.-M. Borgella* (11 volumes), Port-au-Prince, 1958. (First published Paris, 1853–60.)

———, *Réponse du Sénateur B. Ardouin à un écrit anonyme intitulé: Apologie*, Port-au Prince, 1840.

———, *Réponse du Sénateur B. Ardouin à une lettre de M. Isambert*, Port-au-Prince, 1842.

Ardouin, C. N. Céligny, *Essais sur l'histoire d'Haïti*, Port-au-Prince, 1865.

ASCRIA, *Teachings of the Cultural Revolution*, Georgetown (Guyana), 1968.

Auguste, Jules *et al.*, *Les détracteurs de la race noire et de la République d'Haïti*, Paris, 1882.

Balch, Emily G. *et al.*, *Occupied Haiti*, New York, 1927.

Barbour, F. B. (ed.), *The Black Power Revolt*, New York, 1968.

Bastide, Roger (ed.), *La femme de couleur en Amérique Latine*, Paris, 1974.

Bastide, Roger, Morin, F., and Raveau, F., *Les Haïtiens en France*, The Hague, 1974.

Bébel-Gisler, Dany, and Hurbon, Laënec, *Culture et pouvoir dans la Caraïbe*, Paris, 1975.

Beckford, George L. (ed.), *Caribbean Economy*, Kingston (Jamaica), 1975.

Bellegarde, Dantès, *Un Haïtien parle*, Port-au-Prince, 1934.

Bello, Andrés, *Obras completas* (15 vols), Santiago (Chile), 1881–93.

Berrou, R. and Pompilus, P., *Histoire de la littérature haïtienne*, Port-au-Prince, 1977.

Biddiss, Michael, *Father of Racist Ideology*, London, 1970.

Bird, Mark B., *The Black Man, or Haytian Independence Deduced from Historical Notes*, New York, 1869.

Bonnet, Edmond, *Souvenirs historiques de G.-J. Bonnet*, Paris, 1864.

Bosch, Juan, *De Cristóbal Colón a Fidel Castro*, Madrid, 1970.

Bouzon, Justin, *Études historiques sur la présidence de Faustin Soulouque*, Port-au-Prince and Paris, 1894.

Brereton, Bridget, *Race Relations in Colonial Trinidad*, Cambridge, 1979.

Brierre, Jean F., *Les aïeulles*, Port-au-Prince, 1950.

Brouard, Carl, *Pages retrouvées*, Port-au-Prince, 1963.

Brown, N. (ed.), *A Black Diplomat in Haiti: the Diplomatic Correspondence of Frederick Douglass from Haiti, 1889–1891* (2 vols), Salisbury (N.C.) 1977.

Brown, Jonathan, *The History and Present condition of St Domingo*, Philadelphia, 1837.

Bryce-Laporte, R. S. and Mortimer, D. M. (eds), *Caribbean Immigration to the United States*, Washington, 1976.

Cabon, A., *Mgr Alexis-Jean-Marie Guilloux*, Port-au-Prince, 1929.

Candler, J., *Brief Notices of Hayti*, London, 1842.

Caprio, Giovanni, *Haiti: wirtschaftsliche Entwicklung und periphere Gesellschaftsformation*, Frankfurt, 1979.

Castor, Suzy, *La ocupación norteamericana de Haití y sus consecuencias, 1915–1934*, Madrid and Buenos Aires, 1971.

Chancy, Emmanuel, *Pour l'histoire*, Port-au-Prince, 1890.

Charmant, Alcius, *Haïti: vivra-t-elle?*, Le Havre, 1905.

Clarke, Colin G. (ed.), *Caribbean Social Relations*, Liverpool, 1978.

Clarke, E., *My Mother Who Fathered Me*, London, 1957.

Cohen, Robin *et al.*, (eds), *Peasants and Proletarians: the Struggles of Third World Workers*, New York, 1979.

Cole, Hubert, *Christophe, King of Haiti*, London, 1967.

Corten, André *et al.*, *Azucar y política en la República Dominicana*, Santo Domingo, 1976.

Coulthard, Gabriel, *Race and Colour in Caribbean Literature*, London, 1962.

Courlander, Harold, *The Drum and the Hoe*, Berkeley and Los Angeles, 1960.

Courlander, Harold and Bastien, R., *Religion and Politics in Haiti*, Washington, 1966.

Cox, Oliver C., *Caste, Class and Race*, New York and London, 1970. (1st edn 1948)

Craig, Susan (ed.), *Contemporary Caribbean: a Sociological Reader*, St Augustine (Trinidad), 1982.

Crevenna, T. R. (ed.), *Materiales para el estudio de la clase media en la América Latina*, Washington, 1950.

Cronin, Edmund D., *Black Moses: the Story of Marcus Garvey and the Universal Negro Improvement Association*, Madison (Wisconsin), 1968.

Dash, J. Michael, *Literature and Ideology in Haiti, 1915–1961*, London, 1981.

David, Placide, *L'héritage colonial en Haïti*, Madrid, 1959.

Davis, Kortright, *Mission for Caribbean Change: Caribbean Development as Theological Enterpise*, Frankfurt, 1982.

De Delva, H. (ed.), *Bottin professionel et commercial haïtiano-américaine*.

Déjean, P., *Les Haïtiens au Québec*, Montreal, 1978.

De la gérontocratie en Haïti, Paris, 1860.

Delatour, L. and Voltaire, K., *International Sub-contracting Activities in Haiti*, Chicago, 1980.

Delince, Kern, *Armée et politique en Haïti*, Paris, 1979.

Delorme, Demesvar, *Adresse: au citoyens de la République d'Haïti*, Paris, 1874.

———, *La reconnaissance du général Salnave*, Paris, 1868.

Delva, Alexandre, *Considérations sur l'article 7 de la constitution d'Haïti*, Paris, 1873.

Depestre, René, *Bonjour et adieu à la négritude*, Paris, 1980.

Dépossessions, Port-au-Prince, 1930.

The Development of a Middle Class in Tropical and Sub-Tropical Countries, Record of 29th session of the Institute of Differing Civilisations, Brussels, 1955.

Dévot, Justin, *Considérations sur l'état mentale de la société haïtienne*, Paris, 1901.

———, *Cours élémentaire d'instruction civique et d'éducation patriotique*, Paris, 1894.

Diederich, Bernard, and Burt, A., *Papa Doc: Haiti and its Dictator*, London, 1969.

Diop, Cheik Anta, *Nations nègres et cultures*, Paris, 1955.

Donner, Wolf, *Ayiti-potansyèl natirèl é dévelopman*, Fribourg, 1982.

———, *Haiti: Naturraumpotential und Entwicklung*, Tübingen, 1980.

Doubout, J. J. and Joly, U., *Notes sur le développement du mouvement syndical en Haïti*, n.p. n.d.

Douyon, Emerson (ed.), *Culture et développement en Haïti*, Ottawa, 1972.

Dubois, F. E., *Précis historique de la révolution de 1843*, Paris, 1866.

Duarte, Isis, *et al.*, *Inmigración haitiana y producción azucarera en la República Dominicana*, Santo Domingo, 1976.

Dunn, Robert W., *American Foreign Investments*, New York, 1926.

Duvalier, François, *Hommage au martyr de la non-violence*, Port-au-Prince, 1968.

——, *Œuvres essentielles*, Port-au-Prince, vol. 1 1966 (3rd edition 1968), vol. 2 1966, vol. 3 1967, vol. 4 1967.

Edouard, Emmanuel, *Solution de la crise industrielle française: la république d'Haïti*, Paris, 1884.

Eisner, Gisela, *Jamaica, 1830–1930: a Study in Economic Growth*, Manchester, 1961.

Exposé général de la situation de la république d'Haïti, Port-au-Prince, 1912.

Fardin, Dieudonné, *Cours de l'histoire de la littérature haïtienne*, Port-de-Paix, 1967.

Firmin, J. Anténor, *De l'égalité des races humaines*, Paris, 1885.

——, *Lettres de Saint Thomas: études sociologiques, historiques et littéraires*, Paris, 1910.

——, *Monsieur Roosevelt, président des États Unis et la République d'Haïti*, New York and Paris, 1905.

Firth, Raymond and Yamey, B. S. (eds), *Capital Saving and Credit in Peasant Societies*, Chicago, 1964.

Fouchard, Jean, *Les marrons de la liberté*, Paris, 1972.

Franco, José L., *Historia de la revolución de Haití*, Havana, 1966.

Franklin, James, *The Present State of Haiti*, London, 1828.

Frostin, Charles, *Les révoltes blanches à Saint-Domingue aux XVIIe et XVIIIe siècles*, Paris, 1975.

Gaillard, Roger, *Etzer Vilaire: témoin de nos malheurs*, Port-au-Prince, 1972.

——, *Les blancs débarquent, 2: les cents jours de Rosalvo Bobo*, Port-au-Prince, 1973.

——, *Les blancs débarquent, 3: premier écrasement du cacoïsm*, Port-au-Prince, 1981.

——, *Les blancs débarquent, 4: La république authoritaire*, Port-au-Prince, 1981.

——, *Les blancs débarquent, 5: Hinche mise en croix*, Port-au-Prince, 1982.

——, *Les blancs débarquent, 6: Charlemagne Péralte, le cacos*, Port-au-Prince, 1982.

——, *Les blancs débarquent, 7: La guérilla de Batraville*, Port-au-Prince, 1983.

Garret, Naomi M., *The Renaissance of Haitian Poetry*, Paris, 1963.

Geggus, David, *Slavery, War and Revolution: The British Occupation of Saint-Domingue, 1793–1798*, Oxford, 1982.

Georges Jacob, Kléber, *Contribution à l'étude de l'homme haïtien*, Port-au-Prince, 1946.

——, *L'éthnie haïtienne*, Port-au-Prince, 1941.

Girault, Christian A., *Le commerce du café en Haïti: habitants, spéculateurs et exportateurs*, Paris, 1981.

Gobineau, Arthur, *The Inequality of the Human Races*, London, 1915. (1st edn 1853–55)

Grellier, Roche, *Études économiques sur Haïti*, Paris, 1891.

Griggs, E. L. and Prator, C. H. (eds), *Henry Christophe and Thomas Clarkson: a Correspondence*, New York, 1968.

Guerra y Sanchez, Ramiro, *Sugar and Society in the Caribbean*, New Haven, 1964.

Haïti: poètes noirs, Paris, 1951.

Hartmann Betsy and Boyce, J., *Needless Hunger: Voices from a Bangladesh Village*, San Francisco, 1979.

Harvey, William W., *Sketches of Hayti, from the Expulsion of the French to the Death of Christophe*, London, 1827.

Hepburn, R. S. E., *Haiti as it is*, Kingston (Jamaica), 1861.

Heraux, Edouard, *Mélanges politiques et littéraires*, Corbeil, 1897.

Herskovits, Melville J., *Life in a Haitian Valley*, Garden City (New York) 1971. (1st ed. 1937)

Hirschman, A. O. (ed.), *Latin American Issues*, New York, 1961.

Hitti, Philip, *The Syrians in America*, New York, 1924.

Hobbes, Thomas, *Behemoth*, in *English Works*, London, 1839.

Hobsbawm, Eric J., *Primitive Rebels*, New York, 1965.

Hoetink, H. *El pueblo dominicano*, Santiago (Dominican Republic), 1972.

Holly, Arthur, *Les daïmons du culte voudo*, Port-au-Prince, 1918–19.

——, *Rapport entre l'instruction, la psychologie et l'état social*, Port-au-Prince, 1921.

Honorat, Jean-Jacques, *Enquête sur le développement*, Port-au-Prince, 1974.

——, *Le manifeste du dernier monde*, Port-au-Prince, 1980.

Horowitz, Michael M. (ed.), *Peoples and Cultures of the Caribbean*, Garden City (New York) 1971.

Hourani, Albert H., *Syria and Lebanon*, London, 1946.

Hughes, E. C. *et al.*, *The Collected Papers of Rober Ezra Park*, New York, 1974.

Hunt, B. S., *Remarks on Hayti as a Place of Settlement for Afric-Americans*, Philadelphia, 1860.

Huntington, Samuel P. and Nelson, J. M., *No Easy Choice*, Cambridge (Mass.), 1976.

Hurbon, Laënec, *Culture et dictature en Haïti*, Paris, 1979.

——, *Dieu dans le vaudou haïtien*, Paris, 1972.

Huxley, Francis, *The Invisibles*, London, 1966.

Inginac, J. B., *Mémoires de Joseph Balthazar Inginac*, Kingston (Jamaica), 1843.

Jackson, Tony, *Against the Grain*, Oxford, 1983.

Jalabert, H., *La vice-province du proche orient de la compagnie de Jésus*, Beirut, 1960.

James, Cyril, L. R., *Black Jacobins*, New York, 1963. (1st edn 1938)

Janvier, Louis Joseph, *Les affaires d'Haïti, 1883–84*, Paris, 1885.

——, *Les antinationaux*, Paris, 1884.

——, *Les constitutions d'Haïti*, Paris, 1886.

——, *L'égalité des races*, Paris, 1884.

——, *Haïti aux Haïtiens*, Paris, 1884.

——, *La république d'Haïti et ses visiteurs, 1840–1882*, Paris, 1883.

——, *Le vieux piquet*, Paris, 1884.

Joachim, Benoît, *Les racines de sous-développement en Haïti*, Port-au-Prince, 1979.

Johnson, John J., *Political Change in Latin America*, Stanford, 1958.

Johnstone, Harry, *The Negro in the New World*, New York, 1910.

Justin, Joseph, *Étude sur les institutions haïtiennes*, Paris, 1894–5.

——, *Les relations extérieures d'Haïti: études historiques et diplomatiques*, Paris, 1895.

Kesteloot, Lilyan, *Les écrivains noirs de langue française: naissance d'une littérature*, Brussels, 1965.

Lamothe, Camille *Contribution à la vulgarisation de la pensée coopérative*, Port-au-Prince, 1958.

——, *Le mouvement coopératif et la question sociale*, Port-au-Prince, 1954.

Lamur, Humphrey E. and Speckmann, J. D. (eds), *Adaptation of Migrants from the Carribean in the European and American Metropolis*, Leiden, 1979.

Laroche, Léon, *Haïti: une page d'histoire*, Paris, 1885.

Larose, Serge, *L'exploitation agricole en Haïti: guide d'études*, Montreal, 1976.

Laujon, A. de, *Souvenirs de trente années de voyages à Saint-Domingue*, Paris, 1835.

Laville, Lélio, *La traite des nègres au XXe siècle, ou les dessous de l'émigration haïtienne à Cuba*, Port-au-Prince, 1933.

Laurent, Gérard M., *Quand les chaines volent en éclats. . .: un moment de réflexion*, Port-au-Prince (n.d.).

Lemoine, Maurice, *Azucar Amargo*, Santo Domingo, 1983.

Lepelletier de Saint Remy, M. R., *Saint Domingue*, Paris, 1846.

Lewis, Gordon K., *The Growth of the Modern West Indies*, New York, 1969.

Bibliography
271

Lewis, Vaughan A. (ed.), *Size, Self-Determination and International Relations: the Carribean*, Kingston (Jamaica) 1976.

Leyburn, James, *The Haitian People*, New Haven, 1966. (1st edn 1941)

Liberté et indépendance: royaume d'Hayti, Cap-Henry, 1810.

Limonade, Comte de, (Julien Prévost), *Relation des glorieux événements qui ont porté leurs majestés royales sur le trône d'Hayti*, Cap Henry, 1811.

Linstant (de Pradine), S., *Recueil général des lois et actes du gouvernement d'Haïti*, (5 vols), Paris 1851–65.

Logan, Rayford, W., *The Diplomatic Relations of the United States with Haiti, 1776–1891*, Chapel Hill (N.C.) 1941.

——, *Haiti and the Dominican Republic*, London, 1968.

Luc, Jean (Yves Montas), *Structures économiques et lutte nationale populaire en Haïti*, Montreal, 1976.

Lundahl, Mats, *The Haitian Economy: Man, Land and Markets*, London and Canberra, 1983.

——, *Peasants and Poverty: a Study of Haiti*, London, 1979.

Lynch, Hollis R., *Edward Wilmot Blyden: Pan-Negro Patriot, 1832–1912*, London, 1967.

Macaulay, Zacharie, *Haïti ou renseignements authentiques sur l'abolition de l'esclavage*, Paris, 1835.

McCrocklin, James H. (ed.), *Garde d'Haïti*, Annapolis, 1956.

Mackenzie, Charles, *Notes on Haiti, Made during a Residence in that Republic*, London, 1830.

Madiou, Thomas, *Histoire d'Haïti* (3 vols), Port-au-Prince, 1847–48.

——, *Histoire d'Haïti: années 1843–1846*, Port-au-Prince, 1904.

Manigat, Charles, *et al.*, *Haïti: quel développement?*, Lasalle (Quebec), 1975.

Manigat, J. F. Thalès, *Conférence sur le vaudoux*, Cap Haïtien, 1897.

Manigat, Leslie F., *Le délicat problème de la critique historique*, Port-au-Prince, 1954.

——, *Un fait historique: l'avènement à la présidence d'Haïti du général Salomon*, Port-au-Prince, 1957.

——, *La politique agraire du gouvernement d'Alexandre Pétion*, Port-au-Prince, 1962.

——, *La révolution de 1843*, Port-au-Prince (n.d.).

——, *L'Amérique latine au XXe siècle, 1889–1929*, Paris, 1973.

Manigat, Mirlande H., *Haiti and Caricom*, Kingston (Jamaica) 1979.

Marcelin, Frédéric, *Haïti et l'indemnité française*, Paris, 1897.

——, *Nos douanes*, Paris, 1897.

——, *Une évolution nécessaire*, Paris, 1898.

Marcelin, L. J., *Haïti, ses guerres civiles, leurs causes, leurs conséquences présentes, leurs conséquences futures et finales, moyens d'y mettre fin et de placer la nation dans la voie du progrès et de la civilisation: études économiques*, Paris, 1892.

Markovitz, I. L., *L. S. Senghor and the Politics of Negritude*, London, 1969.

Mars, Jean Price, *Ainsi parla l'oncle*, New York, 1954. (1st edn Port-au-Prince 1928)

——, *Jean-Pierre Boyer-Bazelais et le drame de Miragoâne*, Port-au-Prince, 1948.

——, *Lettre ouverte au Dr. René Piquion: Le préjugé de couleur est-il la question sociale?* Port-au-Prince, 1967.

——, *De la préhistoire d'Afrique à l'histoire d'Haïti*, Port-au-Prince, 1962.

——, *La république d'Haïti et la République Dominicaine*, Port-au-Prince, 1953.

——, *La vocation de l'élite*, Port-au-Prince, 1918.

Marshall, Dawn, *'The Haitian Problem': Illegal Migration to the Bahamas*, Kingston (Jamaica) 1979.

Marx, Karl, *Capital*, Moscow, 1961. (1st edn 1886)

Marx, Karl and Engels, F., *Selected Works*, Moscow, 1958.

Massena, Denyse, *La femme dans le droit haïtien*, Port-au-Prince, 1975.

Menos, Solon, *L'affaire Lüders*, Port-au-Prince, 1898.

Métraux, Alfred *et al.*, *Making a Living in the Marbial Valley*, Paris, 1951.

Métraux, Alfred, *Le vaudou haïtien*, Paris, 1958.

Michel, Antoine, *Salomon* jeune *et l'affaire Louis Tanis*, Port-au-Prince, 1913.

Millet, Kethly, *Les paysans haïtiens et l'occupation américaine d'Haïti, 1915–1930*, La Salle (Quebec) 1978.

Millspaugh, A. C., *Haiti under American Control, 1915–30*, Boston, 1931.

Montague, Ludwell L., *Haiti and the United States, 1714–1938*, Durham (N.C.) 1940.

Moore, O. Ernest, *Haiti: its Stagnant Society and Shackled Economy*, New York, 1972.

Moral, Paul, *L'économie haïtienne*, Port-au-Prince, 1959.

———, *Le paysan haïtien*, Paris, 1961.

Moreau de Saint-Méry, M. L. E., *Description topographique, physique, civile, politique et historique de la partie française de l'île Saint Domingue*, Paris, 1958 (1st edn 1798).

Munro, Dana G., *Intervention and Dollar Diplomacy in the Carribean, 1900–1921*, Princeton (N.J.) 1964.

———, *The United States and the Caribbean Republics, 1921–1933*, Princeton (N.J.) 1974.

Naipaul, V. S., *The Middle Passage*, Harmondsworth, 1969.

Nejati-Allman, S., *Rapport sur le questionnaire de l'enquête haïtienne sur la fécondité: étude linguistique*, London, 1978.

Nettleford, Rex, *Mirror, Mirror*, Kingston (Jamaica) 1970.

Nicholls, David, *From Dessalines to Duvalier: Race, Colour and National Independence in Haiti*, Cambridge, 1979.

———, *The Pluralist State*, London, 1975.

———, *Three Varieties of Pluralism*, London, 1974.

North-South: a Programme for Survival, London, 1980.

Oakeshott, Michael, *Rationalism in Politics*, London, 1962.

Orwell, George, *Collected Essays, Journalism and Letters of George Orwell*, Harmondsworth, 1970.

Paul, Edmond, *Les causes de nos malheurs*, Kingston (Jamaica) 1882.

———, *De l'impôt sur les cafés et lois du commerce intérieur*, Kingston (Jamaica) 1876.

———, *Haïti au soleil de 1880*, Kingston (Jamaica) 1880.

———, *Questions politico-économiques: 1, instruction publique*, Paris, 1861.

———, *Questions politico-économiques: 2, formation de la richesse nationale*, Paris, 1863.

Pearce, Jenny, *Under the Eagle: US Intervention in Central America and the Caribbean*, London, 1981.

Perkins, Dexter, *The United States and the Caribbean*, Cambridge (Mass.) 1966 (1st edn 1947).

Perrot, Jean (ed.), *Les langues dans le monde ancien et moderne*, Paris, 1981.

Pierre-Charles, Gérard, *L'économie haïtienne et sa voie de développement*, Paris, 1967.

———, *Radiografía de una dictadura*, Mexico, 1969.

———, (ed.), *Política y sociología en Haití y la República Dominicana*, Mexico, 1974.

Pierre-Louis, Ulrich, *La révolution duvaliériste*, Port-au-Prince, 1965.

Pinckombe, Edouard, *L'article 7: lettre à D. Delorme*, Paris, 1874.

Piquion, René, *Manuel de négritude*, Port-au-Prince (n.d.).

Plan général de défense du royaume, Cap-Henry, 1814.

Price, Hannibal, *De la réhabilitation de la race noire par la république d'Haïti*, Port-au-Prince, 1900–01.

——, *Étude sur les finances et l'économie des nations*, Paris, 1876.

Prichard, Hesketh, *Where Black Rules White*, London, 1900.

Rainsford, Marcus, *An Historical Account of the Black Empire of Hayti*, London, 1805.

Reid, I. De A., *The Negro Immigrant: his Background, Characteristics and Social Adjustment, 1899–1937*, New York, 1939.

Riou, Roger, *Adieu la Tortue*, Paris, 1974.

Robert, Paul, *Difficultés et resources*, Gonaïves, 1952.

Robertson, W. S., *France and Latin American Independence*, Baltimore, 1939.

Rochement, A., *Du féminisme national*, Port-au-Prince, 1950.

Rodney, Walter, *The Groundings with my Brothers*, London, 1969.

Rotberg, Robert, *Haiti: the Politics of Squalor*, Boston, 1971.

Roumain, Jaques, *Analyse schématique, 32–34*, Port-au-Prince, 1934.

——, *Gouverneurs de la rosée*, Paris, 1968. (1st edn 1944)

Rouzeau, A. *De la république d'Haïti, île de Saint-Domingue*, Paris, 1818.

The Rural Code of Haiti, London, 1827.

Ryan, Selwyn, *Race and Nationalism in Trinidad and Tobago*, Toronto, 1972.

Safa, Elie, *l'émigration libanés*, Beirut, 1960.

St John, Spenser, *Hayti or the Black Republic*, London, 1889. (1st edn 1884)

Saint-Louis, R. A., *La présociologie haïtienne*, Ottowa, 1970.

Salomon, Lysius E. F. L., *Circulaire, 18 février*, Port-au-Prince, 1882.

——, *Une défense*, Brussels, 1861.

——, *Discours: 29 octobre, Procès verbal*, Les Cayes, 1845.

——, *Discours de S. E. le Président de la République*, Port-au-Prince, 1883.

Sannon, H. Pauléus, *Essai historique sur la révolution haïtienne de 1843*, Les Cayes, 1905.

Saussure, Léopold de, *Psychologie de la colonisation française*, Paris, 1899.

Schaedel, Richard (ed.), *Papers of the Conference on Research and Resources of Haiti*, New York, 1969.

Schmidt, Hans, *The United States Occupation of Haiti, 1915–1934*, New Brunswick (N.J.) 1971.

Schoelcher, Victor, *Colonies étrangères et Haïti*, Paris, 1843.

Scott, Michael, (ed.), *Aid to Bangladesh: for Better or Worse?*, Boston, 1979.

Senghor, Léopold, S., *On African Socialism*, New York, 1964.

Senghor, Léopold S. *et al.*, *Témoignages sur la vie et l'oeuvre du Docteur Jean Price Mars*, Port-au-Prince, 1956.

Shils, Edward, *Political Development in the New States*, The Hague, 1962.

Skane, Danus, *Brandt, Politics and the Church*, Edinburgh, 1980.

Smith C. S. (ed), *Trinidad, Who, What, Why*, Port of Spain, 1950.

Smith, Michael G., *The Plural Society of the British West Indies*, Berkeley and Los Angeles, 1974.

Sold Like Cattle: Haitian Workers in the Dominican Republic, Geneva, 1980.

Souffrant, Claude, *Une négritude socialiste*, Paris, 1978.

Stephens, Christopher, *Food Aid and the Developing World*, London, 1979.

Stepick, Alex, *Haitian Refugees in the US*, London, 1982.

Sylvain Bouchereau, Madelaine, *Éducation des femmes en Haïti*, Port-au-Prince, 1944.

——, *Haïti et ses femmes*, Port-au-Prince, 1957.

Thébaud, Schiller, *L'évolution de la structure agraire en Haïti de 1804 à nos jours*, University of Paris thesis, Faculté de Droit, 1967.

Thomas, Hugh, *Cuba: or the Pursuit of Freedom*, London, 1971.

Tinker, Hugh, *A New System of Slavery*, London, 1974.

Todd, L. *Pidgins and Creoles*, London and Boston, 1974.

Turnier, Alaın, *Avec Mérisier Jeannis: une tranche de vie jacmélienne et nationale*, Port-au-Prince, 1982.

———, *Les États Unis et le marché haïtien*, Washington, 1955.

Trouillot, Hénock, *Demesvar Delorme: ou introduction à une sociologie de la littérature haïtienne*, Port-au-Prince, 1968.

———, *Les origines sociales de la littérature haïtienne*, Port-au-Prince, 1962.

Vallés, Marie-Thérèse, *Les idéologies coopératives et leur applicabilité en Haïti*, Paris, 1967.

Vastey, Baron de (Pompée Valentin), *An Essay on the Causes of the Revolution and Civil Wars in Hayti*, Exeter, 1823.

———, *Political Remarks on Some French Works and Newspapers Concerning Hayti*, London, 1818.

———, *Le système colonial dévoilé*, Cap Henry, 1814.

Veras, Ramon A., *Inmigración, Haitianos, Esclavitud*, Santo Domingo, 1983.

Walch, Jean, *Michel Chevalier: économiste saint-simonien*, Lille, 1974.

Wallerstein, Immanuel, *Africa: the Politics of Independence*, New York, 1961.

Wallez, J.-B. W., *Précis historique des négotiations entre la France et Saint-Domingue*, Paris, 1826.

Wauthier, C., *The Literature and Thought of Modern Africa*, London, 1966.

West, Robert C. and Augelli, J. P., *Middle America: its Lands and Peoples*, Englewood Cliffs, 1966.

Wood, Harold, A., *Northern Haiti*, Toronto, 1963.

World Bank, *Haiti: Urban Sector Survey*, Washington, 1979.

Williams, Eric E., *From Columbus to Castro*, London, 1970.

Wolff, K. H. (ed.), *The Sociology of Georg Simmel*, New York, 1950.

Worsley, Peter, *The Third World*, London, 1967.

Zuvekas, Clarence, *Agricultural Development in Haiti: an Assessment of Sector Problems, Policies and Prospects under Conditions of Severe Soil Erosion*, Washington, 1978.

Index